Discover Combination
MICROWAVE RANGE
COOKING

From LITTON

Contents

*Pictured on cover: Rhubarb Custard Pie, **page 174**, Sirloin Tip Roast, **page 64**, Quick Casserole Bread, **page 130**, and Butter-Glazed Asparagus, **page 101**.*

The photographs in this book illustrate the recipes as prepared using the Litton combination microwave range.

LITTON
Microwave Cooking

GREETINGS FROM LITTON . . .

We are very pleased and excited about presenting to you our newest form of cooking — the COMBINATION MICROWAVE RANGE WAY.

During the development of this book, our staff of home economists became increasingly enthusiastic as the dramatic capabilities of this appliance became more and more apparent.

Although this range has some similarities to the range you are familiar with, it presents many new features for your convenience. The microwave and combination cooking possibilities open the door for unequalled flexibility and, of course, high quality food preparation.

Because microwave and combination cooking are new experiences and will take some time to master, we ask that you read the instructions carefully before you begin using your range. Just as you developed your cooking skills over a period of time, you will become accustomed to these new concepts gradually. As you prepare more and more foods with the microwave or combination methods, they will become as comfortable and automatic as your conventional ways. And until you feel thoroughly comfortable with these techniques, you can always rely on the familiar methods you used with your previous range.

For your enjoyment and convenience, we have presented a wide variety of thoroughly tested recipe ideas to meet your daily and special occasion menu planning. We do find that consumers occasionally wonder if their oven is working correctly when their timing is not precisely the same as the book's. Usually, your timing will be very similar. But, keep in mind that a number of factors, totally unrelated to the range, can cause variations. Therefore, it is best to refer to our timings as guides, but rely on the doneness descriptions for the most reliable doneness tests.

We at Litton are confident that your new range will be an attractive, productive asset to your kitchen and will provide many satisfying cooking experiences. And, we hope that this book enhances your learning experiences so you will enjoy cooking the Litton way.

Verna Ludvigson

Verna Ludvigson
Director Consumer Affairs
Litton Microwave Cooking
400 Shelard Plaza So.
Minneapolis, Minnesota 55426

About This Book

This book is designed to help you understand and enjoy combination microwave range cooking. There are several cooking options available with combination cooking, but they soon fit into easily identifiable cooking patterns. As your knowledge of the combination range increases, a new dimension of cooking flexibility will become available to you.

All the recipes in this book are directed toward the use of microwave or combination cooking. For recipes that use only bake, broil, or top-of-the-range techniques, use your other cook books and favorite recipes.

INTRODUCTION: The first section of this book gives an overview of microwave cooking and its effect when combined with baking or broiling. It is important to read through this section carefully before using your oven for either microwave or combination cooking.

RECIPES: This book features a large selection of recipes for cooking various foods appropriate for day-to-day and special occasion meals. The recipe sections begin on page 16 with Appetizers and Beverages and continue through Meats, Meal Accompaniments and Desserts.

OVEN MEALS: Following the recipe section is a chapter on Oven Meals. This section describes cooking several food items simultaneously, saving both time and energy. The ideas combine recipes from various parts of the book and will inspire you to try other combinations.

FREEZER: The last chapter in the book is entitled "From The Freezer". It contains information about the variety of foods that you may be taking from your freezer and defrosting, heating or cooking with some form of microwave or combination cooking. There are several "large-batch" freezer sauces that you

can make ahead and store in the freezer for later use. At serving time, they are heated along with some simple additions for a variety of casseroles. This chapter also contains a complete Defrost Chart for frozen meats, fish and poultry. Whenever you have any questions about a frozen food, home-prepared or commercially-frozen, refer to this chapter.

TIME CHART: Once you have become familiar with the recipes in the book, you will find the concise Cooking Time Chart on pages 14 and 15 to be a handy reference. Included are the times and cooking techniques for a variety of foods. Since they only summarize the times, the recipes in other parts of the book should be referred to until the techniques are easily remembered.

INDEX: The index (in the back of the book) should be consulted for whatever type of recipe or combination cooking information desired. Recipes have been indexed according to the name, food category and primary ingredient so that you will find a given recipe listed several ways. It may be listed under a general category such as cakes or cookies or it may be found under a special ingredient heading such as chocolate or carrots. And, it will probably be listed according to the recipe title.

SUBSTITUTION GUIDE: The last page of the book has a handy substitution guide. In many instances, various forms of a seasoning or ingredient can be used interchangeably in the recipes. Or, you may wish to know how much cheese to buy for 2 cups. You'll find all this and more in the guide.

NON-MICROWAVE OR COMBINATION FOODS: There is a wide variety of recipes in this book. A few foods and dishes that do not benefit from either microwave or combination cooking are omitted. These include: soufflés; fried eggs; hard-cooked eggs; quick-cooking, high-temperature foods such as pastry shells and biscuits; and quick-to-broil foods such as toast or thinly-cut steaks. Be assured that they will cook beautifully using other features of your combination range.

About Combination Microwave Range

The combination microwave range has all the cooking, baking and broiling features of a conventional range. Besides all these usual features, the combination range also includes microwave cooking which can be used alone or in a variety of combinations with bake or broil heat. The result is a new kind of flexibility for meal preparation. The combination microwave range includes the following cooking features:

TOP-OF-THE-RANGE COOKING: This is the familiar type of cooking done on the burners on top of the range and includes boiling, simmering, frying, stewing and sautéing. And it is sometimes utilized to brown foods before they are subjected to microwave or combination cooking. The combination range accomplishes all of these things in the same way a regular range performs.

OVEN-BAKING: The oven can be used as a regular bake oven and can bake or heat a variety of foods, achieving maximum browning. Use your favorite recipes or cook book for this oven baking. There is one difference in the heating process of this oven even though the end results are the same as with a conventional range. Normally, when the bake element is on, only the lower heating coils heat. When the bake element is on in this oven, both the upper and lower coils heat.
You may also notice that this oven preheats in a shorter time than the oven you have been using.

OVEN-BROILING: The broiler is similar to any broiler in an electric oven. It is equipped with a broiler pan used for much of the broiling, especially where fats will accumulate. If meats are broiled in a regular pan, the fats which cook from the meat are exposed to the intense heat of the broiler and can flare up.

MICROWAVE COOKING: The oven cavity is equipped to provide microwave cooking as well as conventional baking and broiling. The microwaves enter the oven through the glass ceramic panel in the bottom of the oven and then bounce from surface to surface in the oven, passing through the food and causing it to heat or cook. Microwave cooking can be used for defrosting foods, heating, simmering, boiling, or in combination with bake and broil heat. A special indicator light is on when microwave cooking is being used. A build-up of food on the glass ceramic panel in the bottom of the oven can affect the cooking pattern of the microwaves. Therefore, this panel should be wiped clean whenever necessary.

COMBINATION COOKING: Combination cooking is like adding microwave cooking to normal oven baking or broiling. Microwave cooking can be used throughout the entire baking or broiling time. This technique is referred to as microwave-bake or microwave-broil. Or, the microwaves can be added during the first or last part of the bake or broil. They can also precede or follow the bake or broil.
Since different techniques are applied to different foods, it is important to use this book as a guide. Although the book is devoted entirely to combination and microwave cooking, the flexibility of your oven allows you to cook combination or conventionally depending upon which is more convenient at the time.

About Microwave Cooking

Microwave cooking heats or cooks foods by activating the molecules inside these foods. This, in turn, creates heat from the activity or friction. This differs from the other means of heating on your new range. With the burners, electricity is converted into the heating element which becomes hot and, in turn, heats the saucepan and then the saucepan contents. With the oven, the element heats the cavity of the oven. Then this heat surrounds the dish of food placed in the oven and gradually heats it and the food it contains.

The door of the oven must be securely latched when microwaves are being used, or cooking will not begin. When you turn on your microwave oven, electrical energy is converted to electromagnetic energy by means of an electron tube, or magnetron, contained inside the oven. When microwaves enter the food, they simply cause the liquid or moisture molecules in the food to vibrate at a fantastic rate . . . friction caused by this vibration produces heat energy which is conducted throughout the food.

Microwaves are electromagnetic waves that are classified as being of a "non-ionizing" frequency, meaning they do not cause a chemical change. (X-rays are of an "ionizing" frequency and can cause chemical change.)

Since the microwave energy works directly inside the food, the food is heated very quickly. The only heat in the oven cavity is that which comes from the food as it heats.

Microwave cooking is used for 3 purposes: defrosting, heating and cooking.

DEFROSTING: Defrosting is the gradual heating of foods which change the ice molecules into water. Since this process needs to happen slowly so that the food does not become hot and begin cooking, it is necessary to occasionally turn the oven off, allowing the food to rest. The defrost feature, available on some ranges, performs this on-off cooking automatically.

HEATING: Heating is when the microwaves enter the food and heat the moisture molecules causing the food to become hot. Porous items, like bread, heat very quickly. Dense items, like meat, heat more slowly and need to be thinly sliced to avoid overcooking while heating. With heating, there is no change in the food other than it becomes hot.

COOKING: With cooking, the food becomes hot and the texture of the food changes from a raw or uncooked state to a cooked state. Usually, this takes additional time beyond that needed to heat the food.

The result desired — defrosting, heating or cooking — determines the time, technique and utensils used for microwave cooking.

With baking, certain factors affect the time it takes to heat or cook a food. For example, a larger roast takes longer than a smaller one, a covered casserole heats faster than an uncovered and a dinner roll heats more quickly than a meat patty. These same factors affect microwave cooking, often more noticeably because the heating or cooking takes place so quickly. Also, with baking, you set a temperature as well as a timer. With microwave cooking, a timer is the sole control over the cooking. Factors which affect cooking time include:

VOLUME: As the volume of food increases, the cooking time also increases. One cup of a casserole mixture will heat more quickly than 2 cups of the same mixture. This difference, sometimes unnoticed with conventional cooking, is quite evident with microwave cooking. For instance, 3 potatoes take a little longer to cook with microwaves than 1 potato. However, in the regular oven, 3 potatoes or 1 potato bake in about the same time. This is because the oven is always filled with heat to surround the food items, gradually heating and cooking them. With microwave cooking, only a certain amount of microwaves are available. As additional food items are added, the concentration in a given food item decreases. The large oven cavity of the combination range minimizes differences in cooking additional items. With only 1 item in the oven, there are microwaves which are not utilized because their normal path does not pass through the small area where the food is. Thus, additional items often make it possible to better utilize the microwaves available.

STARTING TEMPERATURE: The colder a food is, the longer it will take to heat or cook. Milk from the refrigerator will take longer to heat than lukewarm tap water. A room temperature roll will heat more quickly than one refrigerated or frozen.

DENSITY: As with conventional cooking, denser, more compact items take longer to heat than porous food items. The latter allows the microwaves to penetrate deeper, creating instant heat throughout. With these denser items, the microwaves often penetrate only the outer portion, and then the center must be heated by conduction from the heated outer portion. For example, a serving of mashed potatoes will take 5 to 6 minutes to heat and a serving of bread, 1 to 2 minutes.

ARRANGEMENT: When heating several items together, it is possible to minimize differences in density, volume or starting temperature by the way the foods are arranged. A more dense item should be shaped like a ring, if possible, so there is no center that will take additional time for the microwaves to penetrate. Slower-to-heat foods, like meat and potatoes, are placed near the outside of the dish where heating takes place first, and the quicker-to-heat foods, like vegetables and rolls, are placed near the center.

STIRRING: For foods that can be stirred, the heating or cooking time can be reduced by moving the heated portion to the center and the cooler portion from the center to the outside. Thus, a casserole that is stirred during cooking will probably heat in less time than the same amount of casserole not stirred during cooking.

STANDING TIME: Microwave cooking is a rapid process and so the food continues to cook even after removal from the oven. For this reason, it is often advisable to undercook the food just slightly since it will finish cooking during the standing time that takes place before it is served. The timing in the recipes in this book allows for this.

About Cooking Utensils

Your regular cooking and baking utensils can be used for normal baking, broiling, and top-of-the-range cooking. However, microwave cooking requires certain cooking utensils to assure the optimum use of the available microwaves. This section includes the utensils and equipment necessary when microwave cooking is being used alone or in combination with bake or broil.

Microwaves react differently with different substances. When microwaves come in contact with a substance, they can be ABSORBED, TRANSFERRED or REFLECTED. Food absorbs microwaves because of the moisture molecules present.

Glass, paper and plastics are transparent to microwaves so they transfer microwaves through their surface without absorbing. They do not absorb the microwaves because they do not contain moisture molecules. This is why you can microwave foods on a paper napkin or glass plate. The microwaves pass through the paper or plate to the food, causing it to heat or cook.

Metal reflects microwaves. The oven walls are made of metal so the microwaves will bounce from wall to wall and into the food. Because metal reflects microwaves, the cooking is slowed where metal covers any part of the food item. The amount of interference depends upon how deep the metal container is and to what degree the food depends upon microwaves for heating or cooking. For instance, cookies on a metal baking sheet would remain doughy on the bottom when cooked with just microwave cooking. However, when microwave-bake is used, the cookies are cooked evenly, even on the metal baking sheet. (The metal absorbs the heat.)

Here are some of the cooking utensils you will be using with your combination oven:

GLASS: Oven-proof glass or glass ceramic oven baking dishes are the most common and often used utensils for the recipes in this book. They allow the microwaves to pass through their surface freely, yet are designed for the oven heat present when combination cooking is used.

Glass and china serving dishes can be used when just microwave cooking is used for heating. Whenever bake or broil heat is also used, the dishes should be oven-proof.

Some glass containers may have a metallic trim or signature on the underside. These dishes are not recommended for microwave cooking because microwaves may damage them.

PLASTIC: Dishwasher safe plastics can be used in the oven when microwave cooking is being used. However, if bake or broil heat is added, use of plastic should be avoided since it may melt from the heat. Plastic should be used only for heating foods. When cooking foods, the prolonged exposure to the hot food can distort and melt it.

Plastic wrap can be used as a covering when heating or cooking foods with microwaves. When steam will develop from the food, it is best to make a small slit in the plastic for its escape. Otherwise the steam may cause the plastic to burst.

Plastic cooking pouches can be used in the oven for microwave cooking. They, too, should be slit when the contents will become steaming hot.

PAPER: Paper cups, plates, towels, wax paper and paper cartons can be used in the oven only when microwave cooking is being used. If bake or broil is also being used, the paper may scorch or burn. Paper products should be used only when defrosting or, heating foods with only microwave cooking. For cooking foods, a heavier container is usually desirable. Wax paper or paper towels can be used for a covering when either heating or cooking foods as long as bake or broil is not being used.

METAL: Metal can be used for any conventional baking or broiling. When microwaves are combined with this cooking, care should be taken in selecting metal cooking containers. In this book, we recommend metal only when a suitable glass baking container is not available. And, in almost all instances, there is bake or broil heat available too, helping to overcome the cooking interference that takes place when foods are placed in metal. TV dinners are the only exception where metal is used with only microwave cooking. Here the tray is very shallow, and the convenience of the tray justifies the slightly longer heating time compared with cooking it in a glass dish.

Metal can be used to advantage in some recipes. It is very effective if you wish to slow the cooking process or prevent cooking in some areas of a food. If one end of a roast is much thinner than the other, foil can be placed over the thinner end for part of the cooking time. This causes the two areas to cook more evenly. When thawing only a portion of a food, foil can be placed over the part you wish to remain frozen.

Small metal utensils can be used with fairly large food masses. For instance, metal skewers can be used to close the cavity of stuffed poultry or for kabobs when well filled with food.

MEAT AND CANDY THERMOMETERS: Microwaves are attracted to the mercury in most meat and candy thermometers causing them to become inaccurate. Therefore, these thermometers should not be left in the food when microwaves are being used. A few thermometers are available that can be used with microwaves and if they are also heat resistant, they can be used when microwave-bake is being used. Many of the meat recipes finish the cooking with just a bake setting. This makes it convenient to have the thermometer in the meat during the final minutes when it is necessary to determine proper doneness. It also slows the final cooking, giving a more juicy end product that slices easily.

About The Recipes

All the recipes in this book have been tested several times to establish the time and technique necessary to achieve the best possible finished product. As with any recipe, the suggested timings should be used as guides along with the doneness tests to insure accuracy. There can be variances in power levels and other factors which may cause recipes to take a little more or less time than specified.

With all recipes, unless otherwise specified, it is assumed the oven rack is in the third position from the top of the oven. You will note a few recipes that direct you to move the rack to the higher second position or the lower fourth position. A position change is especially important when microwave cooking is being used. The distance from the source of the microwaves can affect the cooking pattern and speed.

Unless covering is specified, it is assumed that foods are left uncovered during cooking. With a few foods where the covering might be questioned, it does specify uncovered in the recipe. Where there are two cooking steps, one immediately following the other without a need to open the oven, it is assumed that the covering remains the same in both steps. For instance, if a stew starts with a microwave-bake setting in a covered casserole for 15 minutes and then switches to a bake setting for 45 minutes, the casserole should remain covered even though this is not specified the second time.

Recipes which begin with a bake setting and then go to a microwave-bake setting are marked with the symbol ✿. This is to alert you to set the microwave-delay timer if your range is equipped with this feature.

A few recipes mention defrost as a cooking technique. Some ranges are equipped with a defrost feature. This automatically turns the microwave cooking on and off to allow the slow heating necessary for defrosting meat and other large or dense items. When defrost is used in a recipe, there is an alternate method in the "Tips" for those ranges not equipped with this feature.

Cooking Techniques

There are five basic techniques used throughout this book, each with its own particular characteristics and certain end results. The next five pages are devoted to these techniques.

When learning to use the oven, keep in mind the results from baking or broiling a food. If you add microwave cooking at the beginning, you speed that portion of the cooking; if you add it at the end of the cooking, you speed that part. Or if you add microwave cooking for the whole time, the entire cooking time is hastened.

Sometimes there are other variations of these five basic techniques. The defrost feature, for example, may be used in combination with the bake setting. This provides a faster cooking than just baking, but slower than a microwave-bake. Sometimes both microwave and bake are used; rather than being used simultaneously, one cooking technique precedes the other. These are foods that are quite sensitive to heat — roast beef is a good example. Normally it is desirable to have the meat cooked to a rare or medium rare doneness. If the heat is too intense, only the very inner portion will have this degree of doneness while the outside portion will be well done. By going to a microwave and then a bake setting, the doneness desired can be evenly distributed throughout the interior of the meat with the cooking time reduced as well.

Once you have become familiar with the recipes in this book, you may wish to adapt some of your favorite recipes to combination cooking. First, find a similar type recipe in this cook book and note the technique and recommended time. Then compare the two recipes to see if the quantities are similar. If they are, the times and techniques will be much the same. If one is larger than the other, the time should be adjusted accordingly.

There is one thing to keep in mind when comparing mix and home recipe techniques. Mixes often have ingredients added to enhance the browning, and thus will brown better at a lower temperature with combination cooking than their home recipe companion. For this reason, many home recipe cakes, biscuits, and muffins call for a higher baking temperature than mix products.

Microwave

Microwave cooking heats foods by agitating the moisture molecules present in all food. Since there is no heat surrounding the food, there is no drying or crisping from the outside. When foods are covered during microwave cooking, the steam from the food is trapped inside the dish. This results in a type of cooking similar to simmering or steaming in a regular saucepan. Since microwaves come from all sides to penetrate the food, the heating is faster than with a burner where the heat source comes from only one side and remains on the outside of the cooking container. The bottom of the oven should not be foil-lined, as the foil impedes microwaves from entering the oven.

RESULTS OF MICROWAVE COOKING: Steamed, simmered or boiled foods are easily achieved with the addition of only minimal additional liquid. Quick defrosting or heating of foods is possible without the need to stir or change the original shape or flavor of the food.

COOKING UTENSILS: Glass, paper and plastic allows microwaves to pass through and reach the food. As mentioned earlier, metal reflects microwaves and interferes with the quick heating of the food. The food will heat, but microwaves can enter the food only where metal does not shield it. Coverings such as casserole covers, overturned plates or plastic wrap hold in the heat and speed heating.

TIMING: Heating and cooking times are usually faster than with conventional cooking methods. Since additional food items reduce the concentration of microwaves for individual food pieces, the cooking time increases somewhat with additional food items.

USES:
- Defrosting frozen items.
- Heating beverages, leftovers, cooked foods, sandwiches, breads and soups.
- Cooking sauces, puddings, salad dressings, candies, rice, scrambled eggs, soups, fruits, vegetables and bacon.
- Poaching or steaming fish, poultry, meats, vegetables and eggs.
- Melting chocolate, marshmallows, candies and butter.
- Softening butter, cream cheese and ice cream.

Pictured: Peas Mandarin, page 109.

Microwave-Bake

Microwave-bake refers to the cooking technique when microwave cooking and baking are used simultaneously. This offers a type of cooking similar to regular baking, but faster. The microwaves help to quickly heat the outside of the food so browning begins earlier in the cooking. However, sometimes the end product is a little lighter in color than when baked conventionally because the total bake time is shortened. Microwaves also penetrate the interior of the food and cause it to heat and cook quickly while the bake setting dries, crisps and browns the crust or food exterior.

Since this technique is actually cooking with 2 processes simultaneously, the concentration of heat or cooking can be a disadvantage in foods sensitive to too much heat. Sometimes a food starts with a microwave-bake setting but is finished with a slower bake setting. For instance, poultry cooks very well with microwave-bake, but a dense pork roast needs to be finished with the slower bake setting.

RESULTS OF MICROWAVE-BAKE COOKING:
The results of this technique are similar to a conventional bake setting except faster. The time is shorter and sometimes the temperature is increased 25° to compensate for the shorter time the food is exposed to the bake heat. Some foods tend to be more moist because they are not exposed to the drying bake setting as long as usual.

COOKING UTENSILS: Oven-proof glass baking dishes are best for this type of cooking because they allow the microwaves to pass into the food from all sides without any interference. Paper and plastic should not be used when the bake heat is being used. For a few foods where glass baking dishes are not yet available, metal is suggested. These include baking sheets, muffin pans and jelly roll pans. Most of these foods are either very quick cooking or else the microwave cooking plays a minor role in the cooking.

TIMING: The addition of microwave to bake cooking usually reduces the cooking time by ⅓ to ½. Additional food items do not greatly affect the times.

Pictured: Roast Poultry, page 47, with Wild Rice and Chestnut Stuffing, page 47.

USES:
- Heating appetizers and sandwiches when some crisping or browning is desired.
- Small meat items like meatballs, ribs and hamburgers.
- Oven-baked chicken and fish.
- Casseroles with toppings that need browning.
- Meatloaves and roast poultry.
- Potatoes and squash.
- Fruit crisps and cobblers.
- Cookies and small pastries.

Microwave-Broil

This cooking technique combines microwave cooking with traditional broiling, resulting in a faster broil heating or cooking. When it is not desirable to turn foods over during broiling the foods do not need to be turned. The broiler cooks and browns the top side while the microwaves cook the underside. Occasionally this technique is used near the end of the cooking process when the top is to be browned after the contents have been heated with just microwave cooking.

This technique is especially convenient for foods that might otherwise dry out and overbrown before the interior is heated. Thick grilled sandwiches or broiled meats are often more moist when broiled with the addition of microwaves.

RESULTS OF MICROWAVE-BROIL COOKING:

The results are similar to conventional broil except faster. Since the food is exposed to the intense heat of the broiler for a shorter period of time, there is less chance of overbrowning.

Usually the broiler is not preheated for this type of cooking. Since microwave-broil must always have the oven door closed, the broiler will heat up the oven and shut off after a while in the same way that the bake element does upon reaching a set temperature. Foods are exposed to the heated element longer and brown more when the broiler is not preheated.

COOKING UTENSILS: The metal broiler pan is used for many broiled foods. It is really designed for the high heat of the broiler and for the removal of fat from the intense heat areas. When the food does not need the broiler pan and when the dish is exposed to the heat for a very short time, a glass casserole or baking dish can be used. Such foods are always cooked on the regular shelf position. Many recipes using the broiler pan, direct you to move the oven rack to the higher second position.

TIMING: The addition of microwave cooking to the broil reduces the time by about ⅓. The number of food items do not greatly affect the cooking time required.

Pictured: Tangy Turkey Combos, page 96.

USES:
- Broiling chicken, chops and fish.
- Grilling sandwiches.
- Heating open-faced sandwiches.
- Broiling kabobs.
- Browning casserole toppings.
- Broiling thick-cut steaks.
- Broiling frozen steak and chops.
- Heating sausages and bratwurst.

Bake, Microwave-Bake

This cooking technique allows the food to start cooking slowly. Once the shape and crust are developed, the cooking can be quickly finished with microwave-bake. This type cooking is often used on leavened breads, cakes and desserts — foods which need time for the leavening to act before the structure is set with the microwave cooking.

RESULTS OF BAKE, MICROWAVE-BAKE COOKING: Breads and cake-like products are beautifully shaped, yet browned and cooked in minimum time.

COOKING UTENSILS: Glass is the best type of cooking utensil because the microwaves can easily reach all sides of the food. When foods are usually baked in pans unavailable in glass, the traditional metal pan is used. These include muffin pans, baking sheets and bundt, angel food and jelly roll pans. With deeper pans, the time is increased slightly because metal slows the effectiveness of the microwave cooking.

TIMING: The time saved with this type of cooking depends upon the food. Breads and cakes are usually cooked in about half the time and for some desserts, like cream puffs and meringues, times are reduced by about ¼.

The microwave-delay feature was designed for this cooking technique. If your oven has this feature, it allows you to set both the bake and microwave times before starting the cooking. Then the oven automatically turns on the microwave cooking at the end of the initial bake time. The recipes in the book that utilize this feature are marked with the symbol ✤ after the first bake time. This will alert you to use this delay timer feature.

USES:

- Cakes.
- Cake-like desserts.
- Yeast breads.
- Coffee cakes, muffins, nut breads and other quick breads.
- Cream puffs and meringues.
- Cheese cakes.
- Bar cookies.

Pictured: White Bread, page 135.

Microwave-Bake, Bake

This technique allows you to quickly start the food cooking and then once it reaches a certain point, allows you to slow the cooking and maintain a simmer or slow finish. It may be a soup or stew that can use quick heating to reach a simmer temperature, but then requires a slower bake setting to simmer and become tender. Or, it may be a custard-type mixture that can begin cooking quickly, but needs a slower setting finish so the edges do not overcook before the center is set. It could also be a fruit pie that needs the faster cooking to cook and thicken the filling before it soaks into the crust, but then requires a short bake setting to finish the browning without the filling boiling over.

Many roasts are started with the fast microwave-bake setting. Then, when about ⅔ cooked, the microwaves are turned off and the roast is allowed to finish cooking with the slower bake setting. This allows the meat juices to "set" in the meat, avoids overcooking any of the outside areas, and makes it possible to use the meat thermometer in the meat during the final minutes of cooking.

RESULTS OF MICROWAVE-BAKE, BAKE

COOKING: Simmered and stewed foods cook in somewhat shorter time because they start faster. Custard mixtures cook more quickly and fruit pies cook in about ⅓ the normal time. Roasts are evenly cooked with a minimum of shrinkage in about ½ the time.

COOKING UTENSILS: With some of these foods, microwaves are used for a very short time. However, it is still recommended that glass baking dishes be used if available. Metal does not contribute to an efficient use of the available energy in the oven, especially during the microwave-bake timing, because it reflects microwaves so they cannot enter the food.

TIMING: The timing for foods requiring long slow simmering is reduced less than for most foods. These foods need this long slow cooking to become tender and any attempts to speed this simmering may result in toughness. The cooking of custard mixtures and pies is reduced by ½ to ⅔; roasts are cooked in about ½ the time.

Pictured: Beef Bourguignon, page 65.

USES:
- Simmered stews, soups and baked beans.
- Less tender meats.
- Pork, lamb and veal roasts.
- Custard-type pies and dishes.
- Fresh fruit pies.

Use this quick reference chart for a comparison of cooking techniques and times, or, for a quick double check once you are familiar with the other details of the recipe. Refer to the recipes in the other parts of the book for type of baking dish, covering, preheating and other preparation details.

COOKING TIME CHART

Item	Amount	Technique	Time		
Appetizers:					
Bacon-Wrapped	20	M-Bake 400°	12	to 16	minutes
Cracker-based	24	Microwave	2	to 4	minutes
Beverages	1 cup	Microwave	4	to 5	minutes
	6 cups	Microwave	13	to 15	minutes
Fish:					
Broiled Fish	1 lb.	M-Broil	6	to 8	minutes
Oven-Baked Fish	1 lb.	M-Bake 400°	5	to 6	minutes
Salmon Loaf	1 lb.	M-Bake 350°	9	to 11	minutes
Poultry:					
Broiled Chicken	2½ lb.	M-Broil	15	to 17	minutes
Oven-Baked Chicken	2½ lb.	M-Bake 400°	20	to 25	minutes
Cornish Hens	4	M-Bake 425°	20	to 25	minutes
Roast Chicken	4 lb.	M-Bake 400°		6	minutes/lb.
Roast Duck	5 lb.	M-Bake 375°		5	minutes/lb.
Roast Capon	6 lb.	M-Bake 350°		7	minutes/lb.
Roast Goose	9 lb.	M-Bake 375°		7	minutes/lb.
Roast Turkey	14 lb.	M-Bake 325°		7	minutes/lb.
Cooked Chicken	2 pieces	Microwave	2	to 3	minutes
(refrigerated)	8 pieces	Microwave	6	to 7	minutes
Beef:					
Meatballs	1 lb.	M-Bake 400°	6	to 8	minutes
Patties	1 lb.	M-Bake 450°	6	to 8	minutes
Meatloaf	1½ lb.	M-Bake 350°	22	to 25	minutes
Broiled Steak	4 lb. (2″)	M-Broil	20	to 22	minutes
Rib or Rump		Microwave		20	minutes
Roast	4 to 5 lb.	Bake 350°		9	minutes/lb.
Pot Roast	4 lb.	M-Bake 325°		20	minutes
		Bake	75	to 90	minutes
Stew	2 lbs.	M-Bake 350°		10	minutes
		Bake	60	to 90	minutes
Pork:					
Broiled Chops	4 to 6	M-Broil	8	to 9	minutes
Ribs	2½ lbs.	M-Bake 400°	20	to 25	minutes
Roast	3 lb.	M-Bake 325°		4	minutes/lb.
		Bake	15	to 25	minutes
Ham	4 lb.	Microwave		20	minutes
		Bake 350°		10	minutes/lb.
Bacon	2 strips	Microwave	4	to 5	minutes
	12 strips	Microwave	12	to 14	minutes
Canadian Bacon	1 lb.	Microwave	15	to 18	minutes
Sausages	1 lb.	M-Broil	6	to 9	minutes
Wieners	1	Microwave	¾	to 1	minute
	8	Microwave	3	to 4	minutes
Lamb:					
Broiled Chops	1½ lbs.	M-Broil	8	to 9	minutes
Roast	3 lb.	M-Bake 325°		9	minutes/lb.
		Bake	10	to 15	minutes
Veal:					
Roast	4 lb.	M-Bake 350°		20	minutes
		Bake	75	to 90	minutes

Item	Amount	Technique	Time		
Cooked Meats	1 slice	Microwave	1	to 2	minutes
(refrigerated)	12 slices	Microwave	5	to 6	minutes
Cooked Casseroles	2 cups	Microwave	10	to 12	minutes
(refrigerated)	6 cups	Microwave	15	to 17	minutes
Soups	1 cup	Microwave	3	to 4	minutes
	4 cups	Microwave	7	to 9	minutes
Sandwiches	1	Microwave	1	to 2	minutes
	4	Microwave	3	to 4	minutes
Grilled Sandwiches	4	Broil	3	to 4	minutes
		M-Broil	1	to 2	minutes
Pizza	14-inch	M-Bake 475°	8	to 9	minutes
Eggs, Scrambled	2	Microwave	2	to 3	minutes
	6	Microwave	7	to 8	minutes
Rice	1 cup	Microwave	13	to 15	minutes
Vegetables, Frozen	1 package	Microwave	10	to 12	minutes
	2 packages	Microwave	14	to 16	minutes
Potatoes	1	M-Bake 450°	8	to 10	minutes
	4	M-Bake 450°	14	to 16	minutes
	8	M-Bake 450°	18	to 20	minutes
Breads:					
Coffee Cake	12 x 7-inch	Bake 350°		15	minutes
		M-Bake	5	to 5½	minutes
Muffins (mix)	12	Bake 425°		5	minutes
		M-Bake	2½	to 3	minutes
Yeast	2 loaves	Bake 400°		15	minutes
		M-Bake	5	to 5½	minutes
Desserts:					
Pudding	4-serving	Microwave	9	to 11	minutes
Baked Apples	4	Microwave	10	to 12	minutes
Apple Crisp	8 x 8-inch	M-Bake 400°	12	to 15	minutes
Cheese Cake	8-inch	Bake 400°		15	minutes
		M-Bake	9	to 10	minutes
Cakes:					
Mix	13 x 9-inch	Bake 375°		15	minutes
		M-Bake	3	to 4	minutes
Pound	8 x 4-inch	Bake 350°		20	minutes
		M-Bake	5	to 6	minutes
Cookies	one panful	M-Bake 425°	4	to 4½	minutes
Bars:					
Brownies (mix)	8 x 8 or				
	13 x 9-inch	Bake 350°		10	minutes
		M-Bake	4	to 4½	minutes
Brownies (homemade)	8 x 8-inch	Bake 350°		5	minutes
		M-Bake	3	to 3½	minutes
Pies:					
Pastry Shell	9-inch	Microwave	8	to 10	minutes
2-Crust Fruit	9-inch	M-Bake 450°		10	minutes
		Bake	5	to 7	minutes
Pumpkin	9-inch	M-Bake 450°		9	minutes
		Bake	7	to 9	minutes
Cooked Pies	1 piece	Microwave	2	to 2½	minutes
(refrigerated)	3 pieces	Microwave	4	to 4½	minutes

Appetizers and Beverages

HEATED APPETIZERS: With many appetizers, just microwave cooking is necessary to give a fresh, piping hot taste and appearance. In this chapter we have used the method with cracker-based appetizers, appetizers on toothpicks, hot dips and filled vegetable appetizers. When a crisp crust or toasted effect is desired, conventional heat is necessary along with the microwave cooking.

Timing for heating appetizers varies depending upon the end result desired — melted, hot, or boiling; the starting temperature; the size of appetizers and the amount being heated at one time.

When the oven is cool and only microwave cooking is required, the serving dish or a paper plate can often be used for both heating and serving. Just be sure it is made of a material that can be used with microwave cooking.

Ham and cheese on a cracker — always a favorite.

HAM ROLL-UPS

Five 3½ x 3½-inch slices cooked ham (4 ozs.)
2 tablespoons salad dressing or mayonnaise
5 slices processed Swiss cheese (4 ozs.)
20 stuffed olives
20 crackers

1. Spread ham slices with salad dressing; top each with a cheese slice. Place 4 olives, end-to-end, on one end of each ham slice; roll up jelly-roll fashion. Secure with toothpicks.

2. Cut into four sections, slicing between olives. Place each piece on a cracker, cut-side-down; arrange in 2-quart (12x7) glass baking dish.

3. MICROWAVE 1½ to 2 minutes or until cheese is melted. Remove picks before serving. 20 Appetizers

Pictured, clockwise: Rosy Apple Punch, page 26, Coquilles St. Jacques, page 25 and Polynesian Tidbits and Ham Roll-Ups, this page.

DEVILED CRAB APPETIZERS

1 can (7 oz.) crabmeat, drained
1 egg, beaten
⅓ cup mayonnaise or salad dressing
1 tablespoon finely chopped green onion
1 teaspoon Worcestershire sauce
½ teaspoon dried parsley flakes
24 wheat wafers or crackers
Paprika

1. Combine crabmeat, egg, mayonnaise, green onion, Worcestershire sauce and parsley in medium mixing bowl; mix with fork.

2. Arrange crackers in 3-quart (13x9) glass baking dish. Top each cracker with rounded teaspoonful of crab mixture. Sprinkle with paprika.

3. MICROWAVE 3 to 4 minutes or until hot.
24 Appetizers

Kabobs of chicken, pineapple, onion, green pepper and olives.

POLYNESIAN TIDBITS

¼ cup soy sauce
1 can (13¼ oz.) pineapple chunks
1 tablespoon sugar
1 tablespoon cooking oil
½ teaspoon ground ginger
1 clove garlic, sliced
1 lb. chicken breasts, boned and cut into ¾-inch cubes
4 to 5 green onions, cut into 1-inch pieces
¼ green pepper, cut into ½-inch pieces
8 to 10 stuffed green olives

1. Combine soy sauce, syrup from pineapple (set aside chunks), sugar, oil, ginger, garlic and chicken in 2-cup glass or plastic measure. Marinate about 30 mintues.

2. Alternate pineapple chunks, green onions, chicken, green pepper, and olives on wooden kabob sticks. Arrange in 2-quart (12x7) glass baking dish. Brush with marinade.

3. MICROWAVE 6 to 7 minutes or until chicken is done, brushing occasionally with marinade.
8 to 10 Kabobs

Wieners or meatballs? Whichever your choice, this sauce makes them special.

SWEET-SOUR APPETIZERS

   2 tablespoons cornstarch
   ⅓ cup packed brown sugar
   1 can (13¼ oz.) chunk pineapple, undrained
   1 tablespoon soy sauce
   ¼ cup vinegar
   ½ green pepper, cut into 1-inch pieces
   1 lb. wieners, cut crosswise into 1-inch pieces

1. Combine cornstarch and brown sugar in 1½-quart glass casserole. Stir in remaining ingredients.
2. MICROWAVE, covered, 13 to 15 minutes or until mixture boils and thickens, stirring once during last half of cooking time. Serve with toothpicks.   10 to 12 Servings

TIP ● Substitute for wieners: cooked appetizer-size meatballs.

Mushroom caps are crowned with a savory crab filling. Impressive looking.

CRAB-STUFFED MUSHROOMS

   1 lb. fresh mushrooms (largest size available)
   1 tablespoon butter or margarine
   3 green onions, sliced
   1 can (7 oz.) crabmeat, drained
   ¼ cup sour cream
   3 tablespoons Parmesan cheese
   Dash salt and pepper

1. Wash mushrooms; remove stem from each cap by twisting. Arrange caps, stem-side-up, in 3-quart (13x9) glass baking dish. Chop stems finely. Combine stems, butter and onions in medium glass mixing bowl.
2. MICROWAVE 4 to 5 minutes or until onions are tender, stirring once. Stir in remaining ingredients.
3. Preheat oven to 400° F.
4. Fill mushroom caps with crab mixture, piling the mixture high.
5. MICROWAVE-BAKE 6 to 7 minutes or until hot.   About 36 Mushrooms

TIP ● To Make Ahead, prepare through step 4 and refrigerate. Cook when ready to serve.

A favorite snack for munching — quickly prepared with microwave cooking.

NUTS AND BOLTS

   ½ cup butter or margarine
   1 package (0.6 oz.) Italian salad dressing mix
   1 package (12 oz.) salted peanuts (about 2 cups)
   2 cups broken pretzel sticks
   1 cup pecan halves
   2 cups toasted oat cereal

1. MICROWAVE butter in 3-quart glass casserole 2½ to 3 minutes or until butter is melted. Stir in seasoning mix and remaining ingredients.
2. MICROWAVE 4 to 5 minutes or until heated through, stirring once.   7 Cups

TIP ● Substitute for seasoning mix: ½ teaspoon garlic salt, ½ teaspoon celery seed and ½ teaspoon Worcestershire sauce.

Appetizers on sticks. Prepare early and just heat with microwaves before serving.

VIENNESE KABOBS

   1 can (5 oz.) Vienna sausages
   Cherry tomatoes
   Fresh mushrooms
Glaze
   1 tablespoon catsup
   1 tablespoon cooking oil
   1 tablespoon vinegar
   1 teaspoon sugar
   ¼ teaspoon cornstarch

1. Cut sausages in half, crosswise. Alternate tomatoes, mushrooms and sausages on wooden kabob sticks; place in 8-inch square glass baking dish. Mix together ingredients for Glaze; brush over kabobs.
2. MICROWAVE 3 to 4 minutes or until hot.
          6 to 7 Kabobs

TIPS ● Substitute for Glaze: 3 tablespoons French dressing.
   ● Substitute for Vienna sausages: wieners, cut crosswise into 1-inch pieces.

Raclette is a French word meaning "scraping". Originally the cheese was heated next to a hearth, and the melted edges scraped off and eaten as the cheese softened.

RACLETTE

8 ozs. Raclette, Monterey Jack, Gruyère or Port du Salut cheese
Paprika
Dill Pickles
Hot boiled potatoes
Corn chips

1. Cut cheese into ¼ inch slices. Overlap slices in 8 or 9-inch round glass baking dish.
2. MICROWAVE 2½ to 3½ minutes or until melted. Sprinkle with paprika. Use pickles, potatoes and corn chips to "scrape" or dip into the melted cheese.

8 to 12 Appetizer Servings

For a pleasant change, serve a hot dip. With microwave cooking you can often heat the dip in the serving dish.

HOT BEEF DIP

1 jar (2½ oz.) dried beef
1 cup cold water
½ cup Parmesan cheese
¼ cup chopped green onion
¼ cup sour cream
¼ cup salad dressing or mayonnaise
1 package (8 oz.) cream cheese
1 tablespoon dried parsley flakes

1. Cut beef into small pieces, using kitchen shears. Combine beef and water in 4-cup glass measure.
2. MICROWAVE 4 minutes; drain well. Mix in remaining ingredients.
3. MICROWAVE 4 to 5 minutes or until hot, stirring once. Serve with crackers, vegetable sticks or chunks of bread.   2 Cups Dip

Go Mexican this quick and easy way!

HOT CHILI DIP

1 can (15 oz.) chili with beans
1 can (10¾ oz.) condensed tomato soup
1 teaspoon dried parsley flakes
½ teaspoon garlic salt
Dash Tabasco sauce

1. Combine all ingredients in 1-quart glass serving dish; mix well.
2. MICROWAVE 5 to 6 minutes or until hot. Serve with corn chips or crackers.

3 Cups Dip

Everyone can assemble his own pizza on an English muffin half. They are heated quickly with combination cooking.

TEEN'S PIZZA

3 English muffins, halved
About ½ cup catsup
Leaf oregano
½ cup sliced pepperoni, sliced olives, sliced mushrooms, green pepper strips and/or shrimp
1 cup shredded Mozzarella cheese

1. Preheat oven to 400° F.
2. Arrange muffin halves, cut-side up, in 3-quart (13x9) glass baking dish. Spread about 1 tablespoon catsup on each muffin half. Season with oregano; top with pepperoni or other topping. Sprinkle with cheese.
3. MICROWAVE-BAKE 3 to 4 minutes or until cheese is melted and pizzas are hot.

6 Pizzas

TIP • Substitute for catsup: tomato sauce, chili sauce or favorite pizza sauce.

A colorful addition to any appetizer tray — cherry tomato flowers with rolled anchovy centers.

CHERRY TOMATOES WITH ANCHOVIES

8 to 12 cherry tomatoes
1 can (2 oz.) rolled anchovies, drained
Garlic powder
Chopped chives

1. Remove stems from tomatoes. Place stem-end-down and cut into fourths, cutting to within ¼ inch of bottom. Spread sections open carefully to form a flower. Center an anchovy in each tomato and arrange in 8-inch square glass baking dish. Sprinkle with garlic powder and chives.
2. MICROWAVE 1 to 1½ minutes or until hot.

8 to 12 Appetizers

TIP • To Make Ahead, prepare through step 1 and refrigerate; heat when ready to serve.

BACON-WRAPPED APPETIZERS: The bacon determines the cooking time necessary for this type of appetizer. Thicker-sliced bacon takes longer than thin-sliced. The cooking times specified on these recipes are longer than most due to differences in cooking required by various brands and types of bacon.

With combination cooking, the bacon cooks quickly on all sides, thus eliminating turning during cooking.

Bacon drippings will accumulate in the baking pan. If you have a roasting rack for use with combination cooking, you can use it to keep the appetizers above the drippings.

These recipes can be a guide for preparing your other favorite bacon-wrapped appetizers.

TUNA MORSELS

    1 can (6½ oz.) tuna, drained
    1 cup dry bread crumbs
    ½ cup chili sauce or catsup
    1 egg
    1 teaspoon dried parsley flakes
    12 slices bacon

1. Preheat oven to 400° F.
2. Combine all ingredients except bacon in medium mixing bowl. Shape into 36 (¾-inch) balls.
3. Cut bacon slices into thirds; wrap a slice around each ball and secure with toothpick. Arrange in 3-quart (13x9) glass baking dish.
4. MICROWAVE-BAKE 12 to 16 minutes or until bacon is crisp.   36 Appetizers

TIPS • Tuna mixture may be shaped into 2-inch long rolls, about ½ inch in diameter. Wrap bacon around each, cook as directed.

• To Make Ahead, prepare through step 3 and refrigerate. Cook when ready to serve.

Pictured: Rumaki and Tuna Morsels, this page and Cherry Tomatoes with Anchovies, page 19.

Even our tasters not fond of chicken livers thought these delicious.

RUMAKI

    ⅓ cup soy sauce
    2 tablespoons lemon juice
    ⅛ teaspoon garlic powder
    8 ozs. chicken livers, halved
    24 small water chestnuts*
    12 slices bacon, halved

1. Combine soy sauce, lemon juice, garlic powder and chicken livers in 2-cup glass or plastic measure. Marinate 30 minutes.
2. Preheat oven to 400° F.
3. Remove chicken livers from marinade; drain. Wrap 1 piece chicken liver and 1 water chestnut in each half slice bacon; secure with toothpick. Place in 2-quart (12x7) glass baking dish.
4. MICROWAVE-BAKE 12 to 16 minutes or until bacon is crisp.   24 Appetizers

TIPS • *A 6-oz. can water chestnuts is more than sufficient for this recipe. Larger water chestnuts can be cut into halves or thirds.

• To Make Ahead, prepare through step 3 and refrigerate. Cook when ready to serve.

The bacon adds a homemade touch to these frozen seafood snacks.

BACON-WRAPPED SEAFOOD SNACKS

    8 slices bacon
    24 frozen breaded seafood snacks

1. Preheat oven to 400° F.
2. Cut bacon slices into thirds. Wrap each snack in a piece of bacon, securing with toothpick. Arrange in 2-quart (12x7) glass baking dish.
3. MICROWAVE-BAKE 10 to 12 minutes or until bacon is crisp.   24 Snacks

TIP • If you have a roasting rack for combination cooking, you can use it to keep the snacks above the drippings during cooking.

RIB, CHICKEN & MEATBALL APPETIZERS:

Ribs are partially cooked before the sauce is added. This allows the fat to be drained and prevents the sauce from overcooking before the meat is done.

Chicken cooks quickly with little fat to be drained; thus the sauce is added at the beginning of the cooking time.

Meatballs cook quickly, but it is often desirable to precook them so the fat can be drained before a sauce is added. If precooking is omitted, lean ground beef should be used.

A turn or two during cooking helps season the meat evenly. When the broiler is used, turning is necessary to achieve browning on both sides of the meat.

Use both parts of the chicken wing for these delicious snacks. The unique "drumstick" shape is sure to be a conversation piece and handles easily.

SOY-DIPPED CHICKEN SNACKS

   2 lbs. chicken wings
  ¼ cup soy sauce
  ¼ cup vegetable and fruit chutney
   2 tablespoons cooking oil

1. Cut chicken wings at joints, separating single-bone section (drumstick), double-bone section and tip. Discard tips (or save for soup stock) and set aside double-bone sections.

2. Slit drumstick meat along bone, cutting to within ½ inch of wide end. Separate meat from bone on narrow end; pull meat over larger end forming a ball.

3. Combine soy sauce, chutney and oil in small bowl. Dip drumstick and double-boned chicken pieces in mixture; arrange in 2-quart (12x7) glass baking dish.

4. Move oven rack to second position.

5. **MICROWAVE-BROIL** 4 minutes. Turn wings over and brush with some of remaining sauce.

6. **MICROWAVE-BROIL** 2 to 3 minutes more or until done.   About 16 Snacks

TIPS • Substitute for chutney: 2 tablespoons honey and 1 tablespoon lemon juice.

   • To Make Ahead, prepare through step 3 and refrigerate. Cook when ready to serve, increasing time about 1 minute on each side.

Pictured: Soy-Dipped Chicken Snacks, this page.

The zippy flavor of these meatballs makes them good for appetizers. If you prefer, substitute your favorite meatball recipe, shape and cook as directed here.

DEVILED MEATBALLS

 1 lb. lean ground beef
 1 can (4½ oz.) deviled ham
 ¼ cup dry bread crumbs
 2 tablespoons chili sauce
 1 tablespoon prepared horseradish
 ½ teaspoon dry mustard
 ¼ teaspoon garlic salt
 ¼ teaspoon pepper
 1 egg

1. Preheat oven to 400° F.
2. Combine all ingredients in medium mixing bowl until well blended. Shape into 36 (1-inch) balls. Place in 2-quart (12x7) glass baking dish.
3. MICROWAVE-BAKE 7 to 8 minutes or until done; drain.   About 36 Meatballs

TIPS • Serve in chafing dish with your favorite sauce. Or, try a sauce from page 118.

  • Keep extra meatballs in the freezer for quick thawing and heating in the oven — see page 191.

GLAZED COCKTAIL MEATBALLS

 Deviled Meatballs, this page
 2 tablespoons cornstarch
 2 tablespoons currant or grape jelly
 1 can (10½ oz.) condensed beef
  consommé
 1 teaspoon dry mustard
 ¼ teaspoon ginger

1. Prepare and cook meatballs as directed; drain.
2. Combine remaining ingredients in small mixing bowl; pour over meatballs.
3. MICROWAVE-BAKE at 400° F. for 10 to 11 minutes or until browned and glazed, stirring once during last half of cooking time.
                    About 36 Meatballs

Spareribs are quick and easy when using combination cooking.

SOY-GLAZED SPARERIBS

 2½ to 3 lbs. spareribs
Sauce
 1 tablespoon cornstarch
 2 tablespoons honey
 3 tablespoons soy sauce
 ¼ cup dry sherry
 ¼ cup orange juice

1. Cut spareribs into individual rib pieces; arrange in 3-quart (13x9) glass baking dish.
2. MICROWAVE-BAKE at 400° F. for 15 minutes.
3. Drain fat. Combine sauce ingredients; pour over ribs.
4. MICROWAVE-BAKE 10 to 15 minutes or until done, turning ribs once.   About 20 Ribs

TIPS • Substitute for sherry: omit sherry and increase orange juice to ½ cup.

  • If you prefer a barbecue sauce flavor with ribs, prepare ribs as directed above, but use the sauce in the Oven-Barbecued Ribs Recipe, page 70.

The heating of these first course delicacies uses microwave cooking only.

ESCARGOTS A LA BOURGUIGNONNE

 18 snail shells
 ¾ cup butter or margarine
 3 cloves garlic, finely chopped
 1 tablespoon dried parsley flakes
 2 tablespoons chopped green onion
 1 tablespoon dry white wine, if desired
Dash pepper
 18 (7½-oz. can) snails, drained

1. Cover shells with water in medium glass mixing bowl.
2. MICROWAVE 15 minutes to sterilize. Drain shells on paper towels. Combine remaining ingredients except snails in small glass mixing bowl.
3. MICROWAVE about 2 minutes or until butter is soft.
4. Place 1 teaspoon butter mixture in each shell; add the snail. Fill shells completely with butter. Place on glass escargot plates.
5. MICROWAVE 2 to 2½ minutes or until heated through. Serve with French bread.
                    18 Escargots

PASTRY-TYPE APPETIZERS: Pastry is usually cooked wtih combination cooking. Sometimes the pastry crust and the filling are cooked together — the heat browns and crisps the crust while the microwaves heat or cook the filling.

When the filling is only a thin layer and will cook more quickly than the pastry crust, the crust is usually partially cooked before the filling or topping is added.

Individual pastry-type appetizers are best cooked by conventional methods. They normally cook very quickly and require a large baking sheet for cooking.

Bite-size cheese and ham sandwiches. The broiler makes them toasty; microwave cooking quickly heats the filling.

CROQUE-MONSIEUR

  10 slices white bread
  ¼ cup salad dressing or mayonnaise
  5 slices Swiss cheese (4 ozs.)
  5 slices cooked ham (4 ozs.)
  ⅓ cup butter or margarine

1. Spread one side of bread slices with salad dressing. Place a slice of cheese and ham on 4 of the slices. Top with remaining bread slices, plain side up.
2. MICROWAVE butter in small glass mixing bowl about 1 minute or until softened; spread on outside of sandwiches. Arrange sandwiches on metal broiler pan.
3. Move oven rack to second position.
4. BROIL 3 to 4 minutes or until toasted. Turn sandwiches over.
5. MICROWAVE-BROIL 1 to 1½ minutes or until toasted. Cool about 5 minutes.
6. Remove crusts and cut each sandwich into four portions. If desired, garnish each with a pickle slice or olive, secured with toothpick.
          16 Party Sandwiches

Frozen puff pastry makes the easy base, cheese and onions the tasty topping.

CHEESE PASTRIES

  1 package (10 oz.) frozen patty shells
  1 small onion, finely chopped
  1 tablespoon butter or margarine
  1 cup shredded Swiss cheese
  1 cup shredded Cheddar cheese
  1 teaspoon dried parsley flakes
  ½ teaspoon salt

1. Preheat oven to 450° F.
2. Arrange frozen patty shells in 3-quart (13x9)

glass baking dish.
3. MICROWAVE-BAKE 9 to 10 minutes or until puffed and golden brown. Remove puffs and turn oven off.
4. MICROWAVE onion and butter in 1-quart glass casserole 5 minutes or until onion is limp; set aside.
5. Divide each puff pastry into four layers, separating with fork. Arrange pastries in same baking dish, overlapping if necessary.
6. Stir cheeses and seasonings into onion mixture; spoon over pastries.
7. MICROWAVE 1 to 2 minutes or until cheese is melted.   24 Pastries

TIPS • Try the cheese topping on crackers, too.
    • The puff pastry shells may tip during cooking. If you want them to remain upright, place each in a custard cup when baking.

Looking for an easy way to serve quiche? Try this idea that tastes like quiche, but is served in bite-sized squares with toothpicks.

QUICHE HORS D'OEUVRES

  1 cup unsifted all-purpose flour
  1 teaspoon celery seed
  ½ teaspoon salt
  ¼ teaspoon dry mustard
  ⅓ cup butter or margarine
  ⅓ cup milk

Filling
  5 slices bacon
  1 cup shredded Cheddar cheese
  3 eggs
  ½ cup milk
  ¼ teaspoon salt

1. Arrange bacon for Filling in 8-inch square glass baking dish.
2. MICROWAVE-BAKE at 450° F. for 6 to 7 minutes or until crisp; set aside.
3. Combine flour, celery seed, salt and mustard in medium mixing bowl. Cut in butter until crumbly; stir in milk to form a dough. Press in bottom of 2-quart (12x7) glass baking dish.
4. MICROWAVE-BAKE 3 to 3½ minutes or until no longer doughy.
5. Sprinkle cheese over crust; crumble bacon over top. Beat eggs, milk and salt in small mixing bowl; pour over bacon.
6. MICROWAVE-BAKE 3½ minutes.
7. BAKE 2 to 3 minutes or until set. Cool 10 minutes. Cut into squares and serve with toothpicks.   About 36 Hors d'oeuvres

TIP • To Make Ahead, prepare through step 4 and refrigerate. Complete and cook when ready to serve.

APPETIZERS IN SHELLS: Shells can be used in both microwave and combination cooking. They are placed directly on the oven rack just like individual baking dishes.

With most appetizers in shells, the purpose of the final cooking is to heat the mixture and brown the topping. Microwaves quickly heat the filling mixture while the broiler browns the topping. The length of heating time depends upon the starting temperature and quantity of the mixture and the depth of the shells. When longer heating is necessary, the shells are placed further from the broiler so that the topping will brown more slowly and not overcook before the microwaves heat the filling mixture.

When crispness of the topping is not important, the shells can be heated with microwaves only. This method will take 1 or 2 minutes longer than the microwave-broil method.

A festive appetizer that is easy on the budget.

TUNA-IN-A-SHELL

  1 can (6 oz.) tuna, drained
  ½ cup shredded Cheddar cheese
  ½ cup finely chopped celery
  ¼ cup finely chopped onion
  ¼ cup salad dressing or mayonnaise
  2 tablespoons chopped pimiento
  1 teaspoon chopped chives
  1 teaspoon lemon juice
  ⅛ teaspoon salt
Dash pepper
  2 tablespoons dry bread crumbs
  ½ tablespoon butter or margarine

1. Combine all ingredients except bread crumbs and butter in medium mixing bowl; mix with fork.
2. Spoon into four ½-cup shells. Sprinkle with bread crumbs; dot with butter.
3. MICROWAVE 4 to 5 minutes or until mixture is heated through and bubbly.   4 Servings

TIP • Tuna mixture may be heated in 4 individual ½-cup glass baking dishes or ramekins. Increase time to 7 to 8 minutes.

Scallops in a creamy sauce are especially elegant served in shells.

COQUILLES ST. JACQUES

  ¼ cup butter or margarine
  ¼ cup chopped celery
  1 cup sliced fresh mushrooms
  2 medium green onions, sliced
  2 tablespoons finely chopped green pepper
  2 tablespoons all-purpose flour
  ½ teaspoon salt
  ⅛ teaspoon pepper
  1 package (12 oz.) fresh or frozen sea scallops, thawed
  ⅓ cup whipping cream
  1 egg yolk
  1 tablespoon chopped pimiento
  2 tablespoons dry bread crumbs
  2 tablespoons Parmesan cheese
  2 tablespoons butter or margarine

1. MICROWAVE butter, celery, mushrooms and green onions in medium glass mixing bowl 6 to 7 minutes or until vegetables are limp. Stir in green pepper, flour, salt, pepper and scallops.
2. MICROWAVE 5 to 6 minutes or until scallops are almost cooked and sauce is thickened. Blend in cream, egg yolk and pimiento.
3. MICROWAVE 3 to 4 minutes or until mixture boils.
4. Move oven rack to second position; turn on broiler.
5. Spoon scallop mixture into six ½-cup shells Sprinkle with mixture of bread crumbs and Parmesan cheese; dot with butter.
6. MICROWAVE-BROIL 1½ to 2½ minutes or until topping is golden brown.   6 Servings

TIPS • Scallop mixture may be heated in individual ½-cup glass baking dishes or ramekins.

• Dry white wine may be added when adding cream and egg yolk — use 2 to 3 tablespoons.

• Keep extras in the freezer for last minute special dinners. See page 191 for reheating directions.

BEVERAGES: Microwave cooking is used effectively for heating beverages.

They can be heated in individual cups or mugs or in a large container such as a glass bowl, casserole or pitcher.

The time needed is determined by the amount of liquid being heated, the starting temperature and the end temperature desired.

When heating several cups at one time, place them on a glass tray or in a shallow baking dish. This simplifies getting them in and out of the oven.

Use these times for heating individual cups or mugs of beverages, starting with the temperature of liquid indicated. When the same quantity is in just one container, the times may be slightly longer.

BEVERAGE HEATING CHART

Amount	Room Temperature	Chilled Temperature
1 cup	4 to 5 minutes	6 to 8 minutes
4 cups	10 to 12 minutes	12 to 14 minutes
6 cups	13 to 15 mniutes	14 to 16 minutes
8 cups	16 to 18 minutes	18 to 20 minutes

Coffee reheats very well using microwave cooking. The times are shorter than in the regular beverage chart so that the coffee heats to drinking temperature, but does not develop a bitter reheated flavor.

COFFEE HEATING CHART

Amount	Time
1 cup	2 to 2½ minutes
2 cups	3 to 3½ minutes
3 cups	4 to 4½ minutes
4 cups	5 to 6 minutes

This delicious hot punch contains mint and ginger ale. Also good cold.

SPARKLING MINT PUNCH

1 can (46 oz.) unsweetened pineapple juice
4 cups (1 quart) apple juice or cider
3 sprigs fresh mint
1 bottle (32 oz.) ginger ale
(room temperature)

1. Combine all ingredients except ginger ale in large glass bowl or casserole; mix well.
2. MICROWAVE 22 to 24 minutes or until very hot.
3. Add ginger ale. Serve immediately.
                                    Fourteen 1-cup Servings

TIP ● To serve cold, prepare through step 2 and chill. Remove mint and add chilled ginger ale. Serve over ice garnished with additional fresh mint.

AUTUMN CIDER

8 cups (2 quarts) apple cider
2 tablespoons packed brown sugar
4 cinnamon sticks
5 whole cloves
10 whole allspice
2 oranges, sliced
1 lemon, sliced

1. Combine all ingredients in large glass bowl or casserole; mix well.
2. MICROWAVE 18 to 20 minutes or until hot. Remove whole spices before serving, if desired.   Eight 1-cup Servings

ROSY APPLE PUNCH

8 cups (2 quarts) apple cider
1 cup orange juice
¼ cup red cinnamon candies
10 whole cloves
1 orange, sliced

1. Combine all ingredients except orange in large glass bowl or casserole; mix well.
2. MICROWAVE 20 to 22 minutes or until hot. Remove cloves; garnish with orange slices.
                                    Nine 1-cup Servings

WINTER-WARMER BOUILLON

**2 cans (10½ ozs. each) condensed beef
broth**
1½ cups water
¼ cup dry sherry
1 teaspoon dried parsley flakes

1. Combine all ingredients in 4-cup glass
   measure; mix well.
2. MICROWAVE 15 to 17 minutes or until hot.
   Four 1-cup Servings

TIP • If desired, combine ingredients in
individual mugs. Use times in Beverage
Heating Chart for heating.

*A hot before-dinner drink to serve in mugs or
demi-tasse cups.*

TOMATO BOUILLON

1 can (46 oz.) tomato juice
1 can (10½ oz.) condensed beef broth
1 teaspoon Worcestershire sauce
½ teaspoon salt
½ teaspoon leaf oregano
Dash Tabasco sauce

1. Combine all ingredients in large glass bowl or
   casserole; mix well.
2. MICROWAVE 18 to 20 minutes or until hot.
   Seven 1-cup Servings

HOT SPICY SANGRIA

1 bottle (26 oz.) dry red wine
1 cup water
½ cup sugar
½ cup orange juice
5 whole cloves
2 cinnamon sticks
1 lemon, sliced

1. Combine all ingredients except lemon in
   large glass bowl or casserole; mix well.
2. MICROWAVE 15 to 17 minutes or until hot.
   Garnish with lemon slices.
   Five 1-cup Servings

*Make up this chocolate mixture and refrigerate
it for up to a week. To serve, just heat the
desired amount of milk and make hot
chocolate as needed.*

FRENCH CHOCOLATE

**3 squares or envelopes (1 oz. each)
unsweetened chocolate**
½ cup water
½ cup sugar
Dash salt
½ cup whipping cream, whipped
Milk
Nutmeg

1. MICROWAVE chocolate and water in 2-cup
   glass measure 3 to 3½ minutes or until
   chocolate is melted. Blend in sugar and salt.
2. MICROWAVE 2 minutes or until hot and well
   combined. Cool. Fold in whipped cream.
   Refrigerate until served.
3. MICROWAVE desired amount of milk in
   individual glass cups or mugs using times in
   the Beverage Heating Chart. Add about 1
   heaping tablespoonful chocolate mixture to
   each cup; stir to mix. Sprinkle with nutmeg.
   About 12 Cups

TIP • Substitute for whipping cream: 1 cup
whipped topping.

*Spices and fruit slices make this tea delicious,
hot or cold.*

SPICED TEA

5 cups water
⅓ cup packed brown sugar
4 cinnamon sticks
5 whole cloves
1 orange, sliced
½ lemon, sliced
4 tea bags

1. Combine all ingredients in large glass bowl
   or casserole.
2. MICROWAVE 15 to 17 minutes or until hot.
   Six 1-cup Servings

TIP • Substitute for tea bags: 4 rounded
teaspoons instant tea added after heating
liquid.

Fish and Seafood

OVEN-BAKED OR BROILED FISH: Conventional baking or broiling heat is combined with microwave cooking to lightly brown and crisp the fish while microwaves cook the interior. Because the fish cooks quickly and the microwaves help to cook the underside, turning is unnecessary.

A glass baking dish is suitable for broiling when the regular third rack position is used for a short cooking time.

Before cooking, the fish can be coated with a crumb mixture, a glaze or a buttery sauce to add flavor and texture to the fish.

OVEN-FRIED FISH

¼ cup butter or margarine
1 lb. fish fillets, cut into serving pieces
1 egg, beaten
½ tablespoon lemon juice
½ teaspoon salt
Dash pepper
½ cup dry bread crumbs

1. MICROWAVE butter in 2-quart (12x7) glass baking dish 2 to 2½ minutes or until melted; set aside.
2. Preheat oven to 400° F.
3. Dip fish fillets in mixture of egg, lemon juice, salt and pepper. Coat with bread crumbs. Arrange in baking dish, turning to coat with butter.
4. MICROWAVE-BAKE 5 to 6 minutes or until fish flakes easily with fork.   4 to 6 Servings

BROILED SALMON STEAKS

1. Arrange 4 salmon steaks, cut ¾ inch thick, in 2-quart (12x7) glass baking dish; brush with melted butter.
2. MICROWAVE-BROIL 5 to 5½ minutes or until fish flakes easily with fork.   4 Servings

GLAZED SALMON STEAKS

Combine ¼ cup mayonnaise or salad dressing, 2 tablespoons lemon juice and 1 teaspoon dried parsley flakes. Spread sauce over 4 salmon steaks before cooking. Broil as directed for Broiled Salmon Steaks.

BROILED FISH FILLETS

2 tablespoons butter or margarine
1 lb. fish fillets or steaks, cut into serving pieces
Salt and pepper

1. MICROWAVE butter in 8-inch square glass baking dish about 2 minutes or until melted.
2. Arrange fillets in baking dish, turning to coat with butter. Sprinkle with salt and pepper.
3. MICROWAVE-BROIL 6 to 8 minutes or until lightly browned and fish flakes easily with fork.   4 to 5 Servings

LEMON-BROILED FISH WITH ONION

1 medium onion, sliced
1 clove garlic, finely chopped
1 teaspoon dried parsley flakes
1 teaspoon Worcestershire sauce
1 tablespoon lemon juice
¼ cup butter or margarine
1 lb. fish fillets, cut into serving pieces

1. MICROWAVE all ingredients except fish in small glass mixing bowl 4 to 5 minutes or until onion is partially cooked.
2. Arrange fish fillets in 8-inch square glass baking dish. Spoon sauce over fillets.
3. MICROWAVE-BROIL 6 to 8 minutes or until fish flakes easily with fork.   4 to 5 Servings

FILLET OF SOLE IN ALMOND BUTTER

⅓ cup butter or margarine
2 tablespoons lemon juice
2 tablespoons dry white wine or sherry
½ teaspoon dill weed
½ teaspoon salt
1 lb. fish fillets, cut into serving pieces
⅓ cup slivered or sliced almonds

1. Combine butter, lemon juice, wine, dill weed and salt in 8-inch square glass baking dish.
2. MICROWAVE 2 to 2½ minutes or until butter is melted.
3. Arrange fish fillets in butter mixture, turning to coat fillets with butter. Sprinkle with almonds.
4. MICROWAVE-BROIL 6 to 8 minutes or until fish flakes easily and almonds are lightly browned.   4 to 5 Servings

Pictured: Shrimp-Stuffed Trout, page 30, Oven-Fried Fish, this page and Lobster Tails, page 32.

FISH STICKS ITALIANO

2 packages (8 ozs. each) frozen fish sticks
¼ cup butter or margarine
¼ cup finely chopped green pepper
½ cup finely chopped celery
1 small onion, finely chopped
2 tablespoons all-purpose flour
½ teaspoon salt
½ teaspoon leaf oregano
¼ teaspoon sugar
⅛ teaspoon garlic powder
1 can (16 oz.) tomatoes, undrained

1. Arrange frozen fish sticks in 2 or 3-quart (12x7 or 13x9) glass baking dish; set aside.
2. Combine butter, green pepper, celery and onion in 1-quart glass casserole.
3. MICROWAVE, covered, 4 minutes or until vegetables are partially cooked; stir in remaining ingredients. Cover; place sauce and dish of fish sticks in oven.
4. MICROWAVE-BAKE at 425° F. for 7 to 8 minutes or until fish is hot and sauce is thickened. Stir sauce before serving. Serve sauce over hot fish sticks.   5 to 6 Servings

LEMON-MUSTARD BAKED FISH

1 lb. fish fillets, cut into serving pieces
¼ cup lemon juice
1 tablespoon cooking oil
2 teaspoons dried parsley flakes
1 teaspoon prepared mustard
½ teaspoon leaf basil
¼ teaspoon salt
¼ teaspoon garlic salt
Dash pepper

1. Preheat oven to 375° F.
2. Arrange fillets in 8-inch square glass baking dish. Combine remaining ingredients and pour over fish.
3. MICROWAVE-BAKE 9 to 11 minutes or until fish flakes easily with fork.   4 to 5 Servings

BROILED SMELTS

½ cup butter or margarine
1 lb. fresh or frozen smelts, cleaned
Salt
¼ cup dry bread crumbs

1. MICROWAVE butter in 3-quart (13x9) glass baking dish 2½ to 3 minutes or until melted. Add smelts, coating with butter; sprinkle with salt and bread crumbs.
2. MICROWAVE-BROIL 5 to 5½ minutes or until fish flakes easily with fork.

5 to 6 Servings

TROUT MEUNIERE

1 package (14 to 16 oz.) frozen trout
fillets, thawed
¼ cup all-purpose flour
1 teaspoon salt
¼ teaspoon pepper
¼ cup butter or margarine
1 teaspoon dried parsley flakes
Juice of 1 lemon (about 3 tablespoons)

1. Coat fillets with mixture of flour, salt and pepper.
2. MICROWAVE butter in 2-quart (12x7) glass baking dish 2 to 2½ minutes or until melted.
3. Arrange fillets in baking dish, turning to coat with butter.
4. MICROWAVE-BROIL 4 to 5 minutes or until lightly browned and fish flakes easily with fork.
5. Remove trout to serving platter; sprinkle with parsley. Stir lemon juice into pan drippings and pour over fish.   4 to 5 Servings

SHRIMP-STUFFED TROUT

10 ozs. fresh spinach (8 cups)
¼ cup butter or margarine
1 medium onion, finely chopped
1 can (4½ oz.) tiny shrimp, drained
½ teaspoon salt
Dash pepper
2 tablespoons butter or margarine
1 tablespoon lemon juice
½ teaspoon dill weed
6 rainbow or brook trout (about
12 ozs. each)

1. Cook spinach as directed on page 114. Drain well.
2. MICROWAVE ¼ cup butter and the onion in medium glass mixing bowl 4 to 4½ minutes or until onion is partially cooked. Stir in spinach, shrimp, salt and pepper; set aside.
3. MICROWAVE 2 tablespoons butter in small glass dish about 2 minutes or until melted. Stir in lemon juice and dill weed; set aside.
4. Stuff trout using about ¼ cup shrimp filling for each fish. Secure openings with string, toothpicks or metal skewers. Place in two 2-quart (12x7) glass baking dishes. Brush with lemon butter mixture.
5. MICROWAVE-BROIL 9 to 10 minutes or until fish flakes easily with fork.   6 Servings

TIP • Substitute for fresh spinach: 10-oz. pkg. frozen chopped spinach. Cook as directed on page 101.

FISH STICKS

1. Arrange about 1 lb. frozen fish sticks in 2 or 3-quart (12x7 or 13x9) glass baking dish.
2. MICROWAVE-BAKE at 425° F. for 8 to 10 minutes or until hot.   4 to 6 Servings

STEAMED (POACHED) FISH: Traditionally, poached fish is cooked in hot liquid. With a microwave oven, fish can be covered and steamed without the addition of liquid, creating an end product like poached fish.

As with any fish, care should be taken not to overcook as this results in tough, dry fish. Just cook until the fish flesh flakes apart when separated with a fork.

With many of these recipes, a butter or other seasoned sauce is added to the fish to give additional flavor.

FISH FILLETS IN MUSHROOM-TOMATO SAUCE

    ¼ cup butter or margarine
     1 lb. fish fillets, cut into serving pieces
    ½ cup dry bread crumbs
     3 green onions, sliced
     1 can (4 oz.) mushroom stems and
       pieces, drained
     1 can (16 oz.) tomatoes, undrained
    ¼ cup light cream
     2 tablespoons lemon juice
    ½ teaspoon salt
    ¼ teaspoon pepper
    ¼ cup toasted slivered almonds, if desired

1. MICROWAVE butter in medium glass mixing bowl 2 to 2½ minutes or until melted.
2. Dip fillets in butter; coat with bread crumbs. Arrange in 8-inch square glass baking dish.
3. Combine remaining ingredients except almonds in medium mixing bowl. Pour over fish.
4. MICROWAVE, covered with cover or plastic wrap, 11 to 13 minutes or until fish flakes easily with fork. Sprinkle with almonds before serving.   4 to 6 Servings

ASPARAGUS FISH ROLL-UPS

     1 package (8 oz.) frozen asparagus spears
     2 lbs. fish fillets, cut into serving pieces
     1 can (10¾ oz.) condensed cream of
       shrimp soup
     1 jar (2½ oz.) sliced mushrooms, drained
     1 teaspoon chopped chives
    ½ teaspoon salt
    ¼ teaspoon pepper
    ¼ cup Parmesan cheese

1. MICROWAVE frozen asparagus in package 3 to 3½ minutes or until thawed. Arrange asparagus crosswise on fillets. Roll up fillets with asparagus in the center; fasten with toothpicks. Place in 3-quart (13x9) glass baking dish.
2. Preheat oven to 375° F.
3. Combine soup, mushrooms, chives, salt and pepper in medium mixing bowl. Spoon mixture over fish fillets. Sprinkle with Parmesan cheese.
4. MICROWAVE-BAKE 12 to 14 minutes or until fish flakes easily with fork.   6 to 8 Servings

Like a fondue, but served over toast.

COD FONDUE

     1 lb. cod fillets (torsk)
    1½ cups milk
    ¼ cup butter or margarine, cut into pieces
    ½ cup unsifted all-purpose flour
    ½ teaspoon salt
    ½ teaspoon dried parsley flakes
    ¼ teaspoon leaf basil
     2 tablespoons lemon juice
    ½ cup dry white wine
     1 cup shredded Swiss cheese
     2 tomatoes, quartered
    Buttered toast

1. Place fillets in 1½-quart glass casserole; add 1 cup milk and the butter.
2. MICROWAVE, uncovered 8 to 10 minutes or until fish flakes easily with fork. Break fish into large pieces.
3. Combine flour with remaining ½ cup milk. Add to fish along with remaining ingredients except tomatoes and toast. Stir carefully to combine.
4. MICROWAVE-BROIL 5 to 6 minutes or until sauce bubbles and top is golden brown. Arrange tomatoes on top.
5. MICROWAVE 1 minute to heat tomatoes. Serve over toast.   5 to 6 Servings

SEAFOOD NEWBURG

¼ cup butter or margarine
2 tablespoons all-purpose flour
1½ cups light cream
¼ cup sliced green onions
2 egg yolks, beaten
2 tablespoons dry sherry
1 teaspoon lemon juice
½ teaspoon salt
1 cup cooked lobster
1 package (6 oz.) frozen crabmeat,
thawed and drained

1. MICROWAVE butter in 1-quart glass casserole 2 to 2½ minutes or until melted. Stir in flour, cream and green onions.

2. MICROWAVE 4½ to 5 minutes or until mixture boils and thickens, stirring once during last half of cooking time. Blend a little of hot sauce into beaten egg yolks; add to sauce mixture, mixing well. Stir in remaining ingredients.

3. MICROWAVE 2½ to 3 minutes or until bubbly, stirring once. Serve over patty shells, toast points or parslied noodles.

5 to 6 Servings

TIP • Substitute for frozen crabmeat: 6 ozs. cooked fresh crabmeat or 6-oz. can crabmeat, drained.

LIVE LOBSTER

½ cup water
½ teaspoon salt
1½-lb. live lobster

1. MICROWAVE water and salt in 3-quart (13x9) glass baking dish 4 to 5 minutes or until water is hot.

2. Place lobster in water.

3. MICROWAVE, covered with wax paper, 12 to 15 minutes or until tail meat is firm and no longer translucent.   1 Lobster

LOBSTER TAILS

1. Split each 12-oz. thawed lobster tail through top shell. Release lobster meat from shell, leaving meat connected to shell at top end. Place meat on top of shell.

2. Brush with melted butter and sprinkle with paprika.

3. MICROWAVE, covered, in shallow glass casserole or skillet:
        1 tail — 6 to 8 minutes
        2 tails — 10 to 12 minutes
        4 tails — 14 to 16 minutes

Serve with chunks of hot French bread for a complete meal. This traditional meal of Marseille, France will make you feel like you're on the Mediterranean.

BOUILLABAISSE

1 cup chopped onion
1 cup sliced carrot
1 clove garlic, finely chopped
¼ cup olive or cooking oil
1 lb. frozen cod (torsk)
1 lb. frozen sole fillets
8 ozs. frozen small Rock lobster tails
12 ozs. frozen uncooked shrimp
1 can (16 oz.) tomatoes, undrained
4 cups water
1 teaspoon instant beef bouillon
½ cup chopped pimiento
2 tablespoons dried parsley flakes
2 bay leaves
1 tablespoon lemon juice
2 teaspoons salt
½ teaspoon curry powder
⅛ teaspoon pepper

1. MICROWAVE onion, carrot, garlic and oil in covered 4-quart glass casserole 5 minutes or until onion is limp. Stir in remaining ingredients (if desired, cut lobster tails into pieces).

2. MICROWAVE, covered, 45 to 55 minutes or until fish and seafood are done, stirring once. Remove bay leaves and break fish into pieces before serving.   10 to 12 Servings

TIP • Fresh fish and seafood may be used in recipe; microwave 30 to 34 minutes or until fish is done.

Pictured: Bouillabaisse, this page.

Oyster lover or not, you'll relish this dish.

SCALLOPED OYSTERS

½ cup butter or margarine
1½ cups dry bread crumbs or crushed
    soda crackers
½ cup Parmesan cheese
⅛ teaspoon pepper
Dash nutmeg
  2 cups or 1 pint oysters, drained
¼ cup water or liquid from oysters
¼ cup dry sherry

1. MICROWAVE butter in medium glass mixing bowl 2½ to 3 minutes or until melted. Stir in crumbs, cheese, pepper and nutmeg.

2. Preheat oven to 450° F.

3. Sprinkle half of crumb mixture on bottom of 1½-quart (10x6) glass baking dish. Top with mixture of oysters, water and sherry. Sprinkle with remaining crumbs.

4. MICROWAVE-BAKE 6 to 6½ minutes or until oysters are set and top is golden brown.
                    5 to 6 Servings

TIP • 2 cans (8 ozs. each) canned oysters may be substituted for fresh oysters.

STEAMED CLAMS

1 lb. (about 12) fresh clams, thoroughly
    washed
¼ cup water
Melted butter

1. Combine clams and water in 2-quart glass casserole.

2. MICROWAVE, covered, 7 to 8 minutes or until shells open and clam meat is firm. Serve with melted butter.   6 to 8 Servings

TIPS • Clam broth may be strained through several layers of cheese cloth to remove sand. Serve broth with clams.

    • To help remove sand from clams, soak clams in salt water about 30 minutes. Drain and rinse thoroughly.

SCALLOP KABOBS

3 tablespoons cooking oil
2 tablespoons lemon juice
¼ teaspoon salt
¼ teaspoon dill weed
Dash pepper
12 ozs. frozen scallops
8 slices bacon
Olives, pickles, green pepper pieces,
    cherry tomatoes and/or mushrooms

1. Combine oil, lemon juice, seasonings and frozen scallops in 1-quart glass casserole.

2. MICROWAVE, covered, about 6 minutes or until scallops are thawed. Marinate 1 hour.

3. MICROWAVE bacon in 2-quart (12x7) glass baking dish 7 to 8 minutes or until partially cooked but not crisp; drain.

4. Thread drained scallops (if scallops are small, group 2 or 3 together) and other desired vegetables on skewers, interlacing slices of bacon over and under each piece. Place on rack in glass baking dish. Brush with marinade.

5. MICROWAVE-BROIL 4 to 5 minutes or until bacon is crisp and scallops are firm.
                    4 to 5 Servings

TIP • With fresh scallops, omit the cooking in step 2.

FISH AND SEAFOOD CASSEROLES: When cooked fish or seafood is used in casseroles, cooking time is dependent on the time needed to heat the ingredients. Sometimes uncooked vegetables are partially cooked before the cooked seafood is added. Overcooking causes fish and seafood to become tough.

When uncooked fish or seafood is used in casseroles, the casserole must bake long enough to cook the fish and allow the texture to become firm. If other uncooked ingredients and the sauce are combined with the uncooked fish, they all cook together in one step.

Microwave cooking is usually all that is needed with fish and seafood casseroles. Cooking covered and occasional stirring speed the cooking process. When a special browned or crisp topping or crust is desired, conventional heat is added through broiling or baking.

TUNA-NOODLE BAKE

¼ **cup butter or margarine**
1 **small onion, finely chopped**
¼ **cup all-purpose flour**
1 **teaspoon instant chicken bouillon**
1 **cup water**
¼ **cup sour cream**
¼ **cup dry sherry, if desired**
1 **can (4 oz.) mushroom stems and
   pieces, drained**
2 **tablespoons chopped pimiento**
1 **teaspoon dried parsley flakes**
2 **cans (6½ ozs. each) tuna, drained**
3 **cups noodles, cooked**

1. MICROWAVE butter and onion in 1½-quart glass casserole 3½ to 4 minutes or until onion is partially cooked. Stir in remaining ingredients.
2. MICROWAVE, covered, 14 to 16 minutes or until bubbly in the center.   5 to 6 Servings

A family style casserole with an exotic flavor.

CURRIED TUNA CASSEROLE

½ **cup butter or margarine**
1 **package (10 oz.) frozen peas**
2 **tablespoons cornstarch**
1½ **cups water**
½ **tablespoon instant chicken bouillon**
½ **teaspoon curry powder**
¼ **teaspoon onion salt**
2 **cans (7 ozs. each) tuna, drained**

Dumplings
2 **cups biscuit mix**
1 **cup shredded processed cheese**
⅔ **cup milk**

1. MICROWAVE butter and frozen peas in covered 2-quart glass casserole 6 to 7 minutes or until peas are partially thawed and butter melted. Stir in cornstarch, water, bouillon, curry powder, onion salt and tuna.
2. MICROWAVE, covered, 8 minutes; stir with fork.
3. Combine dumpling ingredients in medium mixing bowl; stir just until combined. Drop by tablespoonfuls onto warm tuna mixture.
4. MICROWAVE, covered, 5 to 6 minutes or until filling is bubbly and dumplings are cooked.   6 to 8 Servings

SWEET AND SOUR SHRIMP

¼ **cup packed brown sugar**
3 **tablespoons cornstarch**
⅛ **teaspoon ginger**
1 **teaspoon paprika**
2 **tablespoons soy sauce**
¼ **cup vinegar**
1 **can (13¼ oz.) pineapple tidbits,
   undrained**
12 **ozs. frozen uncooked shrimp**
3 **green onions, sliced**
2 **stalks celery, thinly sliced**
1 **green pepper, sliced**
1 **large tomato, cut into wedges**
Hot cooked rice

1. Combine brown sugar, cornstarch, ginger, paprika, soy sauce and vinegar in 2-quart glass casserole. Mix well. Stir in remaining ingredients except green pepper, tomato and rice.
2. MICROWAVE, covered, 15 to 18 minutes or until shrimp are firm and sauce is thickened. Stir in green pepper and tomato.
3. MICROWAVE, covered, 5 to 6 minutes or until bubbly. Serve over rice.   4 to 5 Servings

TIP • The green pepper in this recipe will still be crisp. If you prefer a softer texture, add in step 1.

FLAMED MUSHROOMS AND SHRIMP

12 **ozs. frozen uncooked shrimp**
1½ **cups (5 ozs.) sliced fresh mushrooms**
¼ **cup butter or margarine**
2 **cloves garlic, finely chopped**
1 **tablespoon cornstarch**
1 **tablespoon dry white wine**
1 **teaspoon dried parsley flakes**
1 **tablespoon chopped chives**
2 **tablespoons brandy**
Hot cooked rice

1. Combine shrimp, mushrooms, butter and garlic in 1½-quart glass casserole.
2. MICROWAVE, covered, 9 to 10 minutes or until shrimp are just about cooked. Dissolve cornstarch in wine; stir into shrimp mixture along with parsley and chives.
3. MICROWAVE, covered, 2½ to 3 minutes or until sauce is thickened.
4. MICROWAVE brandy in 1-cup glass measure about ½ minute or until just warm. Flame and carefully pour over shrimp. Serve over rice.
                    5 to 6 Servings

TIP • Substitute for fresh mushrooms: 1 can (4 oz.) sliced mushrooms, drained.

An elegant seafood dish that's easy to serve from a buffet table.

SHRIMP AND ARTICHOKE CASSEROLE

½ cup butter or margarine
½ cup unsifted all-purpose flour
½ cup Parmesan cheese
½ cup sliced green onion
1 cup milk
1 cup light cream
¼ cup dry sherry
2 tablespoons chopped pimiento
1 tablespoon Worcestershire sauce
1 teaspoon salt
1 teaspoon paprika
1 can (4 oz.) mushroom stems and pieces, drained
2 cans (14 ozs. each) artichoke hearts, drained
12 ozs. frozen uncooked shrimp
6 ozs. spinach noodles, cooked

1. MICROWAVE butter in 3-quart glass casserole 2½ to 3 minutes or until melted. Stir in flour and remaining ingredients except noodles.
2. MICROWAVE, covered, 22 to 25 minutes or until bubbly, stirring once. Serve over spinach noodles.   6 to 8 Servings

SHRIMP NEW ORLEANS

¼ cup butter or margarine
1 cup chopped onion
½ cup chopped celery
½ cup chopped green pepper
2 cloves garlic, finely chopped
1 tablespoon all-purpose flour
1 can (15 oz.) tomato sauce
1 teaspoon dried parsley flakes
1 teaspoon salt
Dash Tabasco sauce
12 ozs. frozen uncooked shrimp
Hot cooked rice

1. Combine butter, onion, celery, green pepper and garlic in 1½-quart glass casserole.
2. MICROWAVE, covered, 4½ to 5 minutes or until vegetables are partially cooked. Stir in flour and remaining ingredients except rice.
3. MICROWAVE, covered, 15 to 16 minutes or until shrimp are firm. Serve over rice.
                5 to 6 Servings

Pictured: Shrimp and Artichoke Casserole, this page.

A company casserole that's easy to prepare ahead.

SCALLOP AND CRAB PARMESAN

3 tablespoons butter or margarine
1 small onion, chopped
⅓ cup all-purpose flour
1 cup water
1 teaspoon instant chicken bouillon
½ teaspoon salt
¼ teaspoon paprika
⅛ teaspoon nutmeg
2 tablespoons dry sherry
1 can (4 oz.) mushroom stems and pieces, drained
12 ozs. scallops
1 package (6 oz.) frozen crabmeat, thawed and drained
7 ozs. spaghetti, cooked
2 tablespoons Parmesan cheese

1. MICROWAVE butter and onion in 2-quart glass casserole 4 to 4½ minutes or until onion is limp. Stir in flour and remaining ingredients except spaghetti and Parmesan cheese.
2. MICROWAVE, covered, 10 to 11 minutes or until sauce is thickened, stirring once. Serve over cooked spaghetti. Sprinkle with Parmesan cheese.   5 to 6 Servings

TIPS • If desired, arrange cooked spaghetti in 2-quart (12x7) glass baking dish. Pour sauce over spaghetti; sprinkle with Parmesan cheese. Broil 5 to 6 minutes or until top is golden brown.

• If scallops and crabmeat are frozen, decrease water to ¾ cup and increase cooking time to 15 to 18 minutes.

CHEESY SALMON LOAF

2 cans (7¾ ozs. each) salmon, drained
3 eggs, beaten
1 cup shredded Cheddar cheese
2 cups (2 slices) fresh bread cubes
1 small onion, finely chopped
1 tablespoon dried parsley flakes
1 tablespoon lemon juice
½ teaspoon salt
⅛ teaspoon pepper

1. Combine all ingredients in medium mixing bowl. Press evenly into greased 1½-quart (8x4) glass loaf dish.
2. MICROWAVE-BAKE at 350° F. for 9 to 11 minutes or until set in the center.
                5 to 6 Servings

TIP • Substitute for salmon: 2 cans (6½ ozs. each) tuna, drained.

Poultry

CHICKEN PARTS: With combination cooking, conventional baking or broiling browns the skin or crust while microwaves cook the interior. For best browning and crispness, cook pieces skin-side-up.

For broiling, the metal broiler pan is used. Metal is best when a pan is exposed for this length of time to the intense heat of the broiler.

With pan-fried chicken, the chicken is first fried in hot oil, then baked with combination cooking. Conventional heat retains the crisp crust and microwave cooking cooks the interior.

Chicken parts cook best if fairly alike in size. A cut-up chicken is approximately uniform in height when placed in a pan, helping to achieve even browning. Quartered chicken can be used; however, the thicker pieces may take slightly longer to cook and the wings and other raised areas will brown faster than the rest of the meat.

OVEN-BAKED CHICKEN

**1 package (2⅜ oz.) seasoned coating mix
for chicken**
2½ to 3-lb. frying chicken, cut up

1. Place seasoned coating mix in plastic bag provided with mix. Add chicken pieces and shake to coat. Arrange chicken skin-side-up in 2-quart (12x7) glass baking dish.
2. MICROWAVE-BAKE at 400° F. for 20 to 25 minutes or until done.   4 to 6 Servings

BATTER-BAKED CHICKEN

**1 package (3¾ oz.) seasoned batter mix
for chicken**
2½ to 3-lb. frying chicken, cut up

1. Prepare seasoned batter mix as directed on package. Dip chicken in batter as directed on package. Arrange skin-side-up in 2-quart (12x7) glass baking dish.
2. MICROWAVE-BAKE at 400° F. for 20 to 25 minutes or until done.   4 to 6 Servings

Pictured, clockwise: Turkey Divan, page 50, Roast Duckling with Orange Sauce, page 46 and Crunchy Oven-Browned Chicken, this page.

Use your combination oven to quickly finish pan or batter-fried chicken.

PAN-FRIED CHICKEN

⅓ cup all-purpose flour
1½ teaspoons salt
1 teaspoon paprika
½ teaspoon pepper
2½ to 3-lb. frying chicken, cut up
½ to ⅔ cup cooking oil or shortening

1. Combine flour and seasonings in paper or plastic bag. Add chicken pieces and shake to coat.
2. Heat oil in large frying pan over medium-high heat. Add chicken and brown on all sides. Arrange skin-side-up in 2-quart (12x7) glass baking dish.
3. MICROWAVE-BAKE at 400° F. for 15 to 17 minutes or until done.   4 to 6 Servings

TIPS • Batter-Fried Chicken: Use your favorite batter to coat chicken pieces. Fry in oil and arrange in baking dish. Finish cooking as in step 3.

• With pan-fried chicken, you can use a freezer-to-range glass ceramic skillet for both frying and microwave-baking. Just drain the fat before placing skillet in the oven.

CRUNCHY OVEN-BROWNED CHICKEN

½ cup butter or margarine
1 clove garlic, finely chopped
1 cup dry bread crumbs
1 tablespoon dried parsley flakes
¼ cup finely chopped almonds
1 teaspoon salt
**¼ teaspoon powdered thyme or poultry
seasoning**
⅛ teaspoon pepper
2½ to 3-lb. frying chicken, cut up

1. MICROWAVE butter and garlic in 2-quart (12x7) glass baking dish 2½ to 3 minutes or until butter is melted.
2. Combine bread crumbs, parsley, almonds, salt, thyme and pepper in shallow bowl; mix well. Dip chicken pieces in garlic butter; coat with crumb mixture. Arrange skin-side-up in baking dish. Sprinkle with any remaining crumbs.
3. MICROWAVE-BAKE at 400° F. for 20 to 25 minutes or until done.   4 to 6 Servings

Serve this Italian specialty with spaghetti.

CHICKEN CACCIATORE

    2 tablespoons olive or cooking oil
2½ to 3-lb. frying chicken, cut up
    1 medium onion, chopped
    1 clove garlic, finely chopped
    2 tablespoons all-purpose flour
    1 can (16 oz.) tomatoes, undrained
    1 tablespoon dried parsley flakes
    1 teaspoon salt
    ¼ teaspoon pepper
    ¼ teaspoon leaf oregano

1. Heat oil in freezer-to-range glass ceramic 10-inch skillet over medium-high heat. Add chicken pieces and brown on all sides. Remove chicken and set aside.
2. Add onion and garlic to pan drippings; cook until tender. Stir in flour, tomatoes, seasonings and chicken pieces.
3. MICROWAVE, covered, 25 to 30 minutes or until chicken is done.   **4 to 6 Servings**

TIP • If a glass ceramic skillet is not available, brown chicken and onion mixture in frying pan. Then transfer to 3 or 4-quart glass casserole.

CALIFORNIA CHICKEN

    2 tablespoons butter or margarine
    3 tablespoons white wine
    1 clove garlic, finely chopped
2½ to 3-lb. frying chicken, cut up
Salt and pepper
    ¾ cup sour cream
    ¼ cup mayonnaise or salad dressing
    1 avocado, peeled and sliced
    1 tomato, cut into wedges

1. MICROWAVE butter in 2-quart (12x7) glass baking dish about 2 minutes or until melted. Stir in wine and garlic. Add chicken; turn to coat with butter and place skin-side-up. Season with salt and pepper.
2. MICROWAVE-BAKE at 425° F. for 20 to 25 minutes or until chicken is done.
3. Remove chicken to serving plate. Add sour cream, mayonnaise, avocado and tomato to pan drippings; stir to combine.
4. MICROWAVE 2 to 3 minutes or until hot. Pour over chicken on serving plate.
    4 to 5 Servings

A delicious combination of flavors — oven-baked chicken in a creamy sauce. Serve with rice or noodles.

CREAMY PARMESAN CHICKEN

    ¼ cup dry bread crumbs
    2 tablespoons Parmesan cheese
    ¼ teaspoon leaf oregano
Dash garlic powder
Dash pepper
2½ to 3-lb. frying chicken, cut up
    1 can (10¾ oz.) condensed cream of mushroom soup
    ½ cup milk
    ¼ cup sour cream
    1 teaspoon chopped chives
    2 tablespoons Parmesan cheese
Paprika, if desired

1. Combine bread crumbs, 2 tablespoons cheese, the oregano, garlic powder and pepper in paper or plastic bag. Add chicken pieces and shake to coat with crumbs. Arrange skin-side-up in 2-quart (12x7) glass baking dish.
2. MICROWAVE-BAKE at 425° F. for 18 to 20 minutes or until chicken is just about done. Combine soup, milk, sour cream and chives; pour evenly over chicken. Sprinkle with 2 tablespoons Parmesan cheese and the paprika.
3. MICROWAVE-BROIL 5 minutes or until golden brown.   **4 to 6 Servings**

CHICKEN WITH STUFFING

    1 package (4½ or 5 oz.) saucepan stuffing mix with seasonings
    1 cup water
    1 can (4 oz.) mushroom stems and pieces, drained
2½ to 3-lb. frying chicken, cut up
    2 tablespoons butter or margarine
Salt and pepper

1. Mix together stuffing mix (with seasonings), water and mushrooms in 2-quart (12x7) glass baking dish. Arrange chicken pieces skin-side-up over stuffing.
2. MICROWAVE butter in small glass dish about 2 minutes or until melted. Brush chicken with butter. Season with salt and pepper.
3. MICROWAVE-BAKE at 425° F. for 20 to 25 minutes or until done.   **4 to 6 Servings**

CHICKEN IN SHERRY-ORANGE SAUCE

⅓ **cup orange marmalade**
⅓ **cup orange juice**
⅓ **cup dry sherry**
 3 **tablespoons brown sugar**
 2 **tablespoons cornstarch**
 2 **tablespoons butter or margarine, cut**
   into pieces
 1 **teaspoon salt**
  Dash pepper
2½ **to 3-lb. frying chicken, cut up**

1. Combine all ingredients except chicken in
   2-quart (12x7) glass baking dish. Arrange
   chicken, skin-side-down, in sauce.
2. MICROWAVE-BAKE at 400° F. for 10
   minutes. Turn chicken pieces over.
3. MICROWAVE-BAKE 10 to 15 minutes or until
   chicken is done. Serve sauce over chicken.
                                    4 to 6 Servings

OVEN-BARBECUED CHICKEN 'N BISCUITS

2½ **to 3-lb. frying chicken, cut up**
 1 **cup barbecue sauce**
 1 **small onion, chopped**
 1 **clove garlic, finely chopped**
½ **teaspoon Italian seasoning**
 1 **can (8 oz.) refrigerated biscuits**
 3 **tablespoons Parmesan cheese**

1. Arrange chicken pieces skin-side-up in
   2-quart (12x7) glass baking dish. Combine
   barbecue sauce, onion, garlic and seasoning;
   pour over chicken.
2. MICROWAVE-BAKE at 400° F. for 17 to
   19 minutes or until chicken is just about
   done. Move chicken to one end of dish. Add
   biscuits, dipping into sauce to coat; sprinkle
   with Parmesan cheese.
3. MICROWAVE-BAKE 5 to 6 minutes or until
   biscuits are done.   4 to 5 Servings

TIP • Substitute for refrigerated biscuits: about
10 favorite homemade biscuits.

OVEN-BROILED BARBEQUED CHICKEN

  Barbecue Sauce, page 70
2½ **to 3-lb. frying chicken, cut up**

1. Combine barbecue sauce ingredients in
   2-cup glass measure.
2. MICROWAVE 4 to 4½ minutes or until hot.
   Arrange chicken pieces skin-side-down on
   metal broiler pan; brush with sauce.
3. MICROWAVE-BROIL 10 minutes or until
   chicken is browned. Turn chicken pieces
   over and brush with sauce.
4. MICROWAVE-BROIL 5 to 7 minutes or until
   chicken is done.   4 to 6 Servings

LEMON-BROILED CHICKEN

2½ **to 3-lb. frying chicken, cut up**

Lemon-Butter Sauce
¼ **cup lemon juice**
 1 **teaspoon salt**
½ **teaspoon paprika**
⅛ **teaspoon pepper**
 2 **tablespoons butter or margarine**

1. Arrange chicken pieces skin-side-down on
   metal broiler pan.
2. MICROWAVE sauce ingredients in 1-cup
   glass measure 2 to 3 minutes or until butter
   is melted. Brush chicken with sauce.
3. MICROWAVE-BROIL about 8 minutes or
   until chicken is browned. Turn chicken pieces
   over and brush with remaining sauce.
4. MICROWAVE-BROIL 6 to 8 minutes or until
   chicken is done.   4 to 6 Servings

MUSTARD-BROILED CHICKEN

¼ **cup butter or margarine**
1½ **teaspoons curry powder**
 2 **tablespoons lemon juice**
¼ **cup prepared mustard**
¼ **cup honey**
2½ **to 3-lb. frying chicken, cut up**

1. Combine all ingredients except chicken in
   shallow glass dish.
2. MICROWAVE 5 to 5½ minutes or until
   bubbly; mix well. Dip chicken pieces in sauce
   and arrange skin-side-down on metal broiler
   pan.
3. MICROWAVE-BROIL about 8 minutes or until
   chicken is browned. Turn chicken pieces
   over.
4. MICROWAVE-BROIL 6 to 8 minutes or until
   chicken is done.   4 to 6 Servings

TIP • For additional flavor, marinate chicken in
   sauce for about 1 hour before cooking.

A company "chicken stew" cooked in a flavorful burgundy wine sauce.

COQ AU VIN

    5 slices bacon
2½ to 3-lb. frying chicken, cut up
2½ tablespoons all-purpose flour
1½ teaspoons salt
1½ teaspoons instant chicken bouillon
    1 teaspoon dried parsley flakes
    ¼ teaspoon leaf thyme
    ⅛ teaspoon pepper
    5 ozs. fresh mushrooms
    5 green onions, sliced
    2 medium carrots, cut into 1-inch pieces
    6 small new potatoes, peeled
    1 clove garlic, finely chopped
    1 cup burgundy wine
1½ cups water

1. MICROWAVE bacon in freezer-to-range glass ceramic Dutch oven 7 to 8 minutes or until crisp. Remove bacon and set aside.

2. Place Dutch oven with bacon drippings over medium-high heat and add chicken pieces; brown on all sides. Remove chicken and set aside. Pour off drippings except for 2 tablespoons. Blend in flour and seasonings; add chicken and remaining ingredients. Crumble bacon and add to mixture.

3. MICROWAVE-BAKE, covered, at 400° F. for 25 minutes. Remove cover and stir.

4. MICROWAVE-BAKE, uncovered, 5 to 7 minutes or until chicken and vegetables are done.   5 to 6 Servings

TIPS • Substitute for green onions: 1 can (16 oz.) whole small onions, drained.

 • If a glass ceramic Dutch oven is not available, cook bacon and chicken in frying pan. Then transfer to 4-quart glass casserole.

Pictured: Paëlla, this page.

Paëlla is a mixture of seasoned rice, vegetables, meats and seafood. You can vary the types of meat and seafood, but keep their total weight about the same as specified in these cooking times. In Spain where this dish is common, it is often cooked over a campfire.

PAELLA

    2 tablespoons olive or cooking oil
10 to 12 chicken drumsticks
    2 cups chopped onion
    2 cloves garlic, finely chopped
    2 cups uncooked long-grain rice
    1 can (28 oz.) tomatoes, undrained
    3 cups water
    ½ cup chopped pimiento
    1 medium green pepper, chopped
    4 carrots, sliced
    ½ cup sliced dill pickle
    ½ cup sliced pepperoni
    2 teaspoons salt
    2 teaspoons instant chicken bouillon
    1 teaspoon paprika
    1 teaspoon curry powder
    ¼ teaspoon saffron, if desired
    ⅛ teaspoon pepper
    ⅛ teaspoon cayenne pepper
    1 can (14 oz.) artichoke hearts, drained and halved, if desired
    1 to 1½ cups frozen peas
    8 ozs. frozen uncooked shrimp

1. Heat olive oil in freezer-to-range glass ceramic Dutch oven; brown drumsticks on all sides. Remove drumsticks and set aside. Add onion and garlic to same pan; cook until tender.

2. Stir in rice, tomatoes, water, pimiento, green pepper, carrots, dill pickle, pepperoni and seasonings. Arrange drumsticks on top.

3. MICROWAVE-BAKE, covered, at 400° F. for 25 to 30 minutes or until rice is just about tender. Turn into 3-quart (13x9) glass baking dish or large metal paëlla pan. Arrange artichoke hearts, peas and shrimp on top.

4. MICROWAVE-BAKE, uncovered, 10 to 12 minutes or until shrimp are pink and firm.
                          8 to 10 Servings

TIP • If a glass ceramic Dutch oven is not available, brown drumsticks, onion and garlic in frying pan. Then transfer to 4-quart glass casserole.

CHICKEN BREASTS: Chicken breasts are cooked similarly to chicken parts, but often are stuffed or seasoned with a special sauce. Cooking time is a little less because total weight is usually less. The type of stuffing in the breast does not affect the cooking time needed. You can sometimes buy already-boned chicken breast; otherwise you can easily bone your own.

To bone chicken breasts:
   a) Remove skin by pulling off and releasing with knife.
   b) Release chicken meat from bone by starting at thickest part and cutting along bone to release meat.

A whole chicken breast means a breast from one chicken, usually then divided into 2 individual breasts.

Swiss and bleu cheeses make the interesting filling for these breaded and browned chicken breasts.

CHEESY CHICKEN ROLLS

   4 whole chicken breasts, halved, skinned and boned
Salt
   4 slices processed Swiss cheese, halved
¼ cup crumbled bleu cheese
⅓ cup all-purpose flour
   1 egg, beaten
½ cup dry bread crumbs
¼ cup butter or margarine

1. Place chicken breasts, one at a time, between pieces of plastic wrap. Using the flat side of a meat mallet or rolling pin, pound to ¼-inch thickness. Sprinkle with salt and place boned-side-up.
2. Place a half slice of Swiss cheese and ½ tablespoon bleu cheese on each chicken breast. Roll up jelly-roll fashion, tucking in ends and fastening with toothpicks.
3. Coat each with flour, then dip in egg and roll in bread crumbs. Refrigerate 1 hour.
4. Preheat oven to 400° F.
5. Melt butter in frying pan over medium-high heat. Add chicken breasts and brown on all sides. Arrange in 8-inch square glass baking dish.
6. **MICROWAVE-BAKE** 8 to 10 minutes or just until chicken is done.   8 Chicken Breasts

CHICKEN BOURGUIGNON

   2 tablespoons butter or margarine, softened
⅔ cup finely chopped mushrooms
⅓ cup finely chopped ham
   3 tablespoons shredded Mozzarella cheese
   1 tablespoon chopped chives
   4 whole chicken breasts, halved, skinned and boned
   2 tablespoons butter or margarine
   2 tablespoons Cognac or brandy
   2 tablespoons all-purpose flour
   1 tablespoon tomato paste or catsup
   1 tablespoon instant beef bouillon
¾ cup water
¼ cup red wine
Snipped parsley

1. Mix together 2 tablespoons butter, the mushrooms, ham, cheese and chives in small bowl. Place 2 tablespoons of mixture on boned side of each chicken breast. Fold over edges of chicken breast and secure with toothpicks.
2. Melt 2 tablespoons butter in freezer-to-range glass ceramic 10-inch skillet over medium-high heat. Add chicken breasts and brown on both sides.
3. **MICROWAVE** Cognac in 1-cup glass measure about ½ minute or until just warm. Flame and carefully pour over chicken. Remove chicken from pan and set aside. Add the flour, tomato paste and bouillon to pan drippings; stir until smooth. Stir in water and wine; bring to boil. Return chicken pieces to skillet.
4. **MICROWAVE-BAKE**, uncovered, at 400° F. for 15 to 20 minutes or until well done, occasionally spooning sauce over chicken. Sprinkle with parsley.   8 Chicken Breasts

TIPS • With large chicken breasts, you can cut a pocket by slitting the thickest part of the breast. Place stuffing in pocket.

   • If a glass ceramic skillet is not available, brown chicken in frying pan. Arrange in 8-inch square glass baking dish. Heat sauce in frying pan and pour over chicken in dish.

Pictured: Chicken Borguignon, this page.

ROASTING WHOLE BIRDS: It is important that whole birds be completely thawed when using the times given. If there are still icy areas when cooking begins, these may not be done when other areas are. This is especially true near the breast bone and the inside part of the thigh.

Birds are prepared for roasting as usual by stuffing, closing the openings, tying legs together and securing wings to body. Stuffings do not affect the cooking time.

A roasting rack helps achieve a crisp skin by elevating the bird above the moist juices.

Metal clips and pop-out doneness indicators may be left in during cooking. However, such indicators are not good tests for doneness because faster cooking of the bird's interior due to microwaves makes it done before the indicator pops out.

For testing doneness, the meat thermometer in the breast should register 165° F. and in the thick part of the thigh, 185° F. Also, the drumstick should move easily.

Upon removal from the oven, a 10 to 20 minute standing time gives the juices time to "set" in the meat so there is less loss of juices during carving. Thus, the meat will be more moist. During the standing time, the bird will continue to cook and the internal temperature may increase 10 to 15 degrees.

Mercury-type thermometers become inaccurate from microwaves, so this type thermometer should not be used in the oven. There are some special meat thermometers available that can be used with microwave cooking.

Large birds are roasted at about the same temperature as conventionally. The use of microwaves decreases the time about one half. Smaller birds use slightly higher temperatures to achieve the browning desired.

With turkey, capon and chicken, turning the bird over during cooking is not necessary. With goose and duck, more fat can be cooked out of the skin area if the bird is turned once.

ROAST DUCKLING WITH ORANGE SAUCE

  4½ to 5-lb. duckling
    1 teaspoon salt
    2 unpeeled oranges, quartered
    1 clove garlic
    3 peppercorns
    3 to 4 tablespoons orange marmalade

Orange Sauce
    ⅔ cup orange juice
    2 tablespoons packed brown sugar
    1 tablespoon cornstarch
    3 tablespoons duck drippings
    2 tablespoons orange-flavored liqueur
      (Cointreau or Grand Marnier)

1. Remove giblets from duckling and set aside to use as desired. Sprinkle cavity with salt. Stuff with oranges, garlic and peppercorns. Secure with toothpicks or metal skewers; tie legs and wings to body with string. Place breast-side-down on rack in 2-quart (12x7) glass baking dish.
2. MICROWAVE-BAKE at 375° F. for 18 minutes. Turn duck breast-side-up, using paper towels to protect hands. Drain fat, saving 3 tablespoons drippings for sauce.
3. MICROWAVE-BAKE 12 to 15 minutes or until duck is done; brush with marmalade.
4. Combine sauce ingredients in 2-cup glass measure; mix well.
5. MICROWAVE-BAKE duckling and sauce 6 to 8 minutes or until duckling is brown and sauce is thickened. Serve sauce with duckling. If desired, garnish with orange wedges.   About 4 Servings

TURKEY STUFFING

    ½ cup butter or margarine
    1 medium onion, chopped
    2 stalks celery, chopped
  10 cups dry bread cubes
    1 tablespoon dried parsley flakes
  1½ teaspoons poultry seasoning
    ½ teaspoon salt
    ¼ teaspoon pepper
    ¼ to ½ cup chicken broth or water

1. Combine butter, onion and celery in large glass mixing bowl.
2. MICROWAVE 7 to 8 minutes or until vegetables are partially cooked.
3. Stir in remaining ingredients.
    Stuffing for 12 to 16-lb. Turkey

ROAST TURKEY, CAPON, OR CHICKEN

1. Wash bird and set aside giblets (use as you prefer). Sprinkle cavity with salt. If desired prepare favorite stuffing and stuff main cavity and neck cavity. Secure openings with toothpicks or metal skewers. Tie legs together and wings to body with string.

2. Place bird, breast-side-up, on rack* in 2 or 3-quart (12x7 or 13x9) glass baking dish. If desired, brush with melted butter.

3. MICROWAVE-BAKE, uncovered, as directed in chart until meat thermometer inserted in thickest part of breast registers 165° F. Let stand 10 to 20 minutes before carving.

COOKING TIMES

BIRD	SIZE	MICROWAVE-BAKE TEMPERATURE	MIN./LB.	TIME
Chicken	4-4½ lbs.	400° F.	6	24-26 min.
Capon	6-6½ lbs.	350° F.	7	42-46 min.
Goose**	9-10 lbs.	375° F.	7	1-1¼ hrs.
Duck**	4½-5 lbs.	375° F.	5	22-25 min.
Turkey (small)	8-12 lbs.	350° F.	7	1-1¼ hrs.
Turkey (med.)	12-16 lbs.	325° F.	7	1¼-1¾ hrs.
Turkey (large)	17-25 lbs.	325° F.	5	1½-2 hrs.

*With large size turkeys, it may be necessary to omit the rack so the turkey sets lower in the oven.

**For crisp skin, cook goose and duck half the time breast down and half the time breast up. You may wish to stuff goose and duck with apples and prunes, or oranges rather than a bread stuffing.

TIP • If necessary, lower oven rack position with larger birds.

A nice flavor combination with turkey.

CORNBREAD STUFFING

½ cup butter or margarine
½ cup sliced green onion
1 teaspoon dried parsley flakes
½ teaspoon salt
½ teaspoon leaf thyme
¼ teaspoon pepper
8 cups coarsely crumbled cornbread
1 package (8 oz.) herb-seasoned bread stuffing mix
¼ cup dry sherry
1½ cups hot tap water
Chopped turkey liver, if desired

1. MICROWAVE butter in large glass mixing bowl about 2½ to 3 minutes or until melted.
2. Stir in remaining ingredients.
Stuffing for 12 to 16-lb. Turkey

WILD RICE AND CHESTNUT STUFFING

1 package (6 oz.) long grain white and wild rice mix
2½ cups water
1 can (6 oz.) water chestnuts, drained and sliced
1 can (4 oz.) mushroom stems and pieces, drained
1 small onion, finely chopped
¼ cup chopped celery
¼ cup butter or margarine

1. Combine all ingredients including seasoning mix from rice in 1½-quart glass casserole.
2. MICROWAVE, covered, 25 to 30 minutes or until rice is almost tender. Use to stuff a 6-lb. capon or 6 cornish game hens.
About 4 Cups Stuffing

TIP • Chopped poultry liver may be added to stuffing after cooking rice mixture.

TURKEY PARTS: Most turkey parts require moist, slow simmering to become tender. Microwaves can be used to bring the mixture to a boil, then slow conventional heat keeps the mixture simmering.

Turkey breasts are roasted similarly to whole birds.

ROAST TURKEY BREAST

1. Place 4 to 5-lb. thawed turkey breast (bone in) on rack in 2-quart (12x7) glass baking dish. Cover thin end with small piece of foil to prevent overcooking.
2. MICROWAVE-BAKE at 325° F. for 30 to 40 minutes or until meat thermometer inserted in thickest part of breast registers 180° F.   10 to 12 Servings

TIP • For a flavorful glaze, prepare Orange-Lemon Sauce page 118; brush over turkey breast during last 5 minutes of cooking. Serve any remaining sauce with turkey.

If your oven has a defrost feature, you can cook and defrost this roast at the same time. If not, the roast must be thawed before cooking (see Tips).

BONELESS TURKEY ROAST

**2 to 2½-lb. frozen turkey roast
Glaze, if desired (see Tips)**

1. Remove frozen turkey roast from original container; place skin-side-down on rack in 2-quart (12x7) glass baking dish.
2. DEFROST-BAKE at 400° F. for 35 minutes. Turn roast skin-side-up.
3. DEFROST-BAKE 25 to 30 minutes or until meat thermometer inserted in center registers 175° F. Brush with glaze during the last 5 or 10 minutes of cooking. Let stand 10 minutes before serving.   8 to 10 Servings

TIPS • If your oven does not have a defrost feature, first thaw the roast completely. Then microwave-bake at 400° for 20 to 25 minutes or until meat thermometer registers 175° F.

• Cinnamon-Apricot Glaze: Combine ¼ cup apricot preserves with 2 tablespoons melted butter or margarine and ½ teaspoon cinnamon.

• Ginger-Peach Glaze: Combine ¼ cup peach preserves with 2 tablespoons melted butter or margarine and ½ teaspoon ground ginger or 2 tablespoons chopped candied ginger.

SPICY TURKEY THIGH

**2 tablespoons butter or margarine
1½ to 2-lb. frozen turkey thigh, thawed
1 medium onion, chopped
2 tablespoons all-purpose flour
1 teaspoon salt
1 teaspoon dried parsley flakes
1 teaspoon cinnamon
¼ teaspoon ground cloves
⅛ teaspoon pepper
Dash Tabasco sauce
1 bay leaf
2 cups water
¼ cup pecan halves**

1. Melt butter in freezer-to-range glass ceramic Dutch oven over medium heat. Add meat and brown on all sides. Stir in onion; cook until golden brown. Blend in flour and seasonings; stir in water and pecans.
2. MICROWAVE-BAKE, covered, at 325° F. for 15 minutes.
3. BAKE 50 to 55 minutes or until meat is fork tender.   5 to 6 Servings

TIP • If a glass ceramic Dutch oven is not available, brown meat and onion in frying pan. Then transfer to 4-quart glass casserole.

RABBIT AND BEER STEW

**¼ cup butter or margarine
2 to 2½-lb. rabbit, cut up
1 medium onion, sliced
4 potatoes, peeled and quartered
4 carrots, cut into chunks
2 cloves garlic, finely chopped
1 tablespoon packed brown sugar
1 teaspoon salt
1 teaspoon caraway seed
1 teaspoon dried parsley flakes
⅛ teaspoon pepper
1 can (12 oz.) beer
¼ cup all-purpose flour
¼ cup cold water**

1. Melt butter in freezer-to-range glass ceramic Dutch oven over medium heat. Brown rabbit on all sides; add onion and cook until limp. Add vegetables, seasonings and beer.
2. MICROWAVE, covered, 30 to 35 minutes or until rabbit is tender. Combine flour and water; stir into sauce-rabbit mixture.
3. MICROWAVE, covered, 5 to 6 minutes or until sauce is thickened.   5 to 6 Servings

TIP • If a glass ceramic Dutch oven is not available, brown meat and onion in frying pan. Then transfer to 4-quart glass casserole.

Pictured: Rabbit and Beer Stew, page 48.

CORNISH GAME HEN: Cornish game hens can be roasted whole or split in half and broiled. Complete thawing is important for even cooking. To check doneness, cut between thigh and body to see that the meat is no longer pink.

ROAST CORNISH GAME HENS

    4 frozen Cornish game hens, thawed
    3 cups favorite stuffing
    Melted butter

1. Stuff cornish hens, using about ¾ cup stuffing for each. Secure openings with toothpicks or metal skewer. Place stuffed hens breast-side-up on rack in 3-quart (13x9) glass baking dish. Brush with melted butter.
2. MICROWAVE-BAKE at 425° F. for 20 to 25 minutes or until done.   **4 Servings**

SHERRY-GLAZED CORNISH HENS

    4 frozen Cornish game hens, thawed

Sherry Glaze
    3 tablespoons butter or margarine
    2 tablespoons sherry or white wine
    1 teaspoon seasoned salt
    ½ teaspoon onion salt
    ⅛ teaspoon paprika
    1 teaspoon soy sauce

1. Split cornish hens in half; place skin-side-up on metal broiler pan. Combine ingredients for glaze in 1-cup glass measure.
2. MICROWAVE glaze 2½ to 3 minutes or until butter is melted. Brush over hens.
3. MICROWAVE-BAKE at 350° F. for 20 minutes or until almost done. Brush with remaining glaze.
4. MICROWAVE-BROIL 5 to 6 minutes or until golden brown and hens are done. **8 Servings**

CASSEROLES USING COOKED POULTRY:
Chicken and turkey can be used interchangeably. Many have most ingredients
already cooked so the final cooking is primarily
for heating. If there is no topping to brown,
these are cooked covered. If there is a topping,
they are cooked uncovered. Other ideas for
using leftover cooked chicken or turkey may be
found in the Sandwich Chapter.

*Super easy, yet with gourmet flavor. Cubed
chicken in wine sauce with a sour
cream-potato topping.*

CHICKEN CONTINENTAL

    1 can (10¾ oz.) condensed cream of
       chicken soup
    1 can (4 oz.) mushroom stems
       and pieces, drained
    ½ cup dry white wine or dry sherry
    3 cups cubed cooked chicken or turkey
    ½ cup slivered almonds
    ¼ cup sliced green onion
    2 tablespoons chopped pimiento
    ½ teaspoon salt

Potato Topping
    1 cup water
    2 tablespoons butter or margarine
    ½ teaspoon salt
    ¼ cup milk
    ½ cup sour cream
    1 egg, beaten
    1½ cups potato flakes

1. Combine all ingredients except topping in
   8-inch square glass baking dish; set aside.
2. MICROWAVE water, butter and salt in
   medium glass mixing bowl 6 to 7 minutes or
   until very hot.
3. Preheat oven to 375° F.
4. Stir milk, sour cream, egg and potato flakes
   into water mixture. Drop by tablespoonfuls
   onto chicken mixture.
5. MICROWAVE-BAKE 12 to 14 minutes or
   until chicken mixture is bubbly.

6 to 7 Servings

  TIP • With the granular-type instant potatoes,
    use 1¾ cups.

TURKEY DIVAN

    2 packages (10 ozs. each) frozen broccoli
       spears
    2 tablespoons butter or margarine
    ½ cup dry bread crumbs
    6 large slices cooked turkey or chicken
    1 can (10¾ oz.) condensed cream of
       chicken soup
    ½ cup milk
    1 tablespoon lemon juice
    1 tablespoon chopped pimiento
    ¼ teaspoon curry powder
    ¾ cup shredded Cheddar cheese

1. MICROWAVE broccoli in packages 5 to
   6 minutes or until partially thawed. Separate
   spears and drain water. Arrange in 2-quart
   (12x7) glass baking dish.
2. MICROWAVE butter in small glass bowl
   about 2 minutes or until melted. Stir in
   bread crumbs.
3. Preheat oven to 350° F.
4. Arrange sliced turkey over broccoli. Combine
   remaining ingredients in medium mixing
   bowl; pour over turkey. Sprinkle with bread
   crumb mixture.
5. MICROWAVE-BAKE 15 to 16 minutes or
   until broccoli is tender and sauce bubbly.

About 6 Servings

*A quick, last minute casserole to serve over
chow mein noodles.*

CHICKEN CHOW MEIN CASSEROLE

    2 cups cubed cooked chicken or turkey
    1 can (10¾ oz.) condensed cream of
       mushroom soup
    1 can (11 oz.) mandarin oranges, drained
    1 can (4 oz.) mushroom stems and
       pieces, undrained
    1 medium onion, finely chopped
    1 stalk celery, sliced
    ¼ cup salted cashews
Chow mein noodles

1. Combine all ingredients except cashews and
   noodles in 1½-quart glass casserole; mix
   well. Sprinkle with cashews.
2. MICROWAVE-BAKE at 350° F. for 12 to
   15 minutes or until hot. Serve over chow
   mein noodles.   4 to 6 Servings

CHICKEN LASAGNA

    6 lasagna noodles
    1 can (10¾ oz.) condensed cream of chicken soup
    1 can (10¾ oz.) condensed cream of mushroom soup
    1 cup finely chopped onion
    1 cup chopped ripe olives
    ½ cup Parmesan cheese
    ½ cup sour cream
    ¼ cup mayonnaise or salad dressing
    2 tablespoons chopped pimiento
    ½ teaspoon garlic salt
    4 cups cubed cooked chicken or turkey
    4 cups shredded processed cheese

1. Cook noodles as directed on package; drain. Combine remaining ingredients except cheese in large mixing bowl.
2. Spread about ⅓ chicken mixture over bottom of 3-quart (13x9) glass baking dish. Top with 2 alternate layers of noodles, chicken mixture and cheese, ending with cheese.
3. MICROWAVE-BAKE at 375° F. for 12 to 14 minutes or until bubbly.
4. MICROWAVE-BROIL 2½ to 3 minutes or until top is golden brown.   8 to 10 Servings

ORIENTAL CHICKEN CASSEROLE

    ¼ cup butter or margarine
    2 cups sliced celery
    1 medium carrot, sliced
    1 large onion, sliced
    1 cup water
    1 teaspoon instant chicken bouillon
    3 tablespoons cornstarch
    1 tablespoon soy sauce
    ½ teaspoon salt
    1 package (10 oz.) frozen peas
    1 can (4 oz.) mushroom stems and pieces, drained
    3 cups cubed cooked chicken or turkey

1. Combine butter, celery, carrot and onion in 2-quart glass casserole.
2. MICROWAVE, covered, 8 to 10 minutes or until vegetables are just about tender. Stir in remaining ingredients; mix well.
3. MICROWAVE, covered, 12 to 15 minutes or until done, stirring once during last half of cooking time. If desired, serve over hot cooked rice.   6 to 8 Servings

CHICKEN TETRAZZINI CASSEROLE

    ¼ cup butter or margarine
    3 tablespoons all-purpose flour
    1 teaspoon salt
    ¼ teaspoon pepper
    2 cups milk
    4 cups cubed cooked chicken or turkey
    1 can (4 oz.) mushroom stems and pieces, drained
    ½ cup chopped green pepper
    1 egg, beaten
    3 cups noodles, cooked
    ½ cup Parmesan cheese

1. MICROWAVE butter in 2-quart glass casserole 2 to 2½ minutes or until butter is melted. Blend in flour, salt, pepper and milk.
2. MICROWAVE 8 to 10 minutes, stirring once during last half of cooking time. Stir in remaining ingredients except ¼ cup Parmesan cheese. Sprinkle cheese over top of casserole.
3. MICROWAVE-BAKE at 375° F. for 10 to 12 minutes or until hot.
4. MICROWAVE-BROIL 2½ to 3 minutes or until topping is lightly browned.
    About 8 Servings

TURKEY AND BISCUIT CASSEROLE

    4 cups cubed cooked turkey or chicken
    2 cups gravy
    1 package (10 oz.) frozen peas
    2 green onions, chopped
    ½ teaspoon salt
    ½ cup sour cream
    2 cups biscuit mix
    ½ cup water

1. Combine turkey, gravy, peas, onions, salt and sour cream in 2-quart (12x7) glass baking dish.
2. MICROWAVE-BAKE, uncovered, at 400° F. for 10 minutes while preparing biscuits as directed on biscuit mix package.
3. Stir mixture in casserole. Arrange biscuits over top.
4. MICROWAVE-BAKE 8 to 10 minutes or until biscuits are cooked.   5 to 6 Servings

TIP • Substitute for gravy: 1 can condensed cream of chicken or mushroom soup plus milk to make 2 cups.

Beef

GROUND BEEF: Ground beef cooks quickly and the grinding process makes it tender, whatever the cooking method used.

When used in casseroles, the ground beef is usually partially cooked so the fat can be drained off before other ingredients are added. This partial cooking also helps the meat cook together into small chunks. The casserole recipes in this chapter can be cooked with just microwave cooking or combined with bake or broil heat to give a browned or crisp crust or topping.

For patties and meatloaves, the seasoned meat is formed into patties or a loaf and then cooked with combination microwave and bake cooking. The addition of the microwave cooking reduces the cooking time by about half.

HAMBURGER PATTIES

1 lb. ground beef
Salt and pepper

1. Preheat oven to 450° F.
2. Season ground beef with salt and pepper. Shape into 4 patties. Arrange in 8-inch square glass baking dish or on rack in 2-quart (12x7) glass baking dish.
3. MICROWAVE-BAKE 6 to 7 minutes or until desired doneness. 4 Patties

TIPS • For additional seasoning, mix one or several of the following into ground beef:

    1 tablespoon Worcestershire sauce
    2 to 4 tablespoons chopped onion
    ½ teaspoon garlic salt
    1 tablespoon barbecue sauce or catsup
    1 teaspoon prepared mustard
    2 to 4 tablespoons pickle relish
    ¼ cup chopped canned mushrooms

    • Patties may be topped with one of the following during last minute of cooking: cheese slices, sour cream, onion dip, cream of mushroom soup or cheese sauce.

Pictured, clockwise: Meat 'n Onion Loaf, page 55, Rump Roast, page 64 and Beef Short Ribs Dinner, page 65.

HAMBURGER PIE

    1 lb. ground beef
    ⅓ cup dry bread crumbs
    1 can (3 oz.) French-fried onion rings
    1 can (11 oz.) condensed Cheddar cheese soup
    1 egg
    ¼ teaspoon salt
    Dash pepper
    1 package (9 oz.) frozen cut green beans

1. Preheat oven to 350° F.
2. Combine ground beef, bread crumbs, half each of the onions and soup, the egg, salt and pepper in medium mixing bowl; mix well. Press over bottom and up sides just to top of 10-inch glass pie plate.
3. Mix together frozen green beans and remaining soup. Spoon into prepared meat crust. Sprinkle with remaining onions.
4. MICROWAVE-BAKE 15 to 17 minutes or until meat is done and beans are cooked.
    5 to 6 Servings

TIP • Substitute for cut green beans: 10-oz. package French-cut green beans. Microwave 2 to 3 minutes or until partially thawed before mixing with soup.

A fun way to serve hamburger — the savory stuffing makes a tasty surprise.

BIG BURGER

    2 tablespoons butter or margarine
    1 cup herb-seasoned stuffing mix
    1 cup shredded Cheddar cheese
    1 can (4 oz.) mushroom stems and pieces, undrained
    2 green onions, sliced
    1 teaspoon dried parsley flakes
    1½ lbs. ground beef
    1 teaspoon salt

1. MICROWAVE butter in large glass mixing bowl 1½ to 2 minutes or until melted. Stir in stuffing mix, cheese, mushrooms, green onions and parsley; mix well and set aside.
2. Preheat oven to 450° F.
3. Combine ground beef and salt; divide meat in half. Pat one-half to 9-inch circle in bottom of 3-quart (13x9) glass baking dish. Pat other half to 9-inch circle on wax paper. Spoon stuffing mixture over circle in baking dish to within 1 inch of edge. Top with other circle of meat; peel off wax paper. Press edges of meat together, sealing in stuffing.
4. MICROWAVE-BAKE 7 to 8 minutes or until done. Lift burger to serving plate with two slotted spatulas. Serve cut into wedges.
    6 to 8 Servings

MEATBALLS

   1 lb. ground beef
  ½ cup dry bread crumbs
   1 egg
  ¼ cup dry onion soup mix
  ½ teaspoon nutmeg, if desired
  Dash Tabasco sauce

1. Preheat oven to 400° F.
2. Combine all ingredients in medium mixing bowl.
3. Shape into 1-inch balls; place in 8-inch round or square glass baking dish.
4. MICROWAVE-BAKE 5½ to 6½ minutes or until done; drain.   About 24 Meatballs

TIP • Substitute for soup mix: 1 small onion, finely chopped, and 1 teaspoon salt.

Curry flavored Dutch meatballs, garnished with peach halves and served over rice.

INDONESIAN MEATBALLS

   1 can (28 oz.) peach halves
 1½ teaspoons curry powder
   1 lb. ground beef
  ¼ cup rolled oats
  ¼ cup finely chopped onion
  ¼ cup milk
   1 teaspoon salt
  ⅛ teaspoon pepper
   1 can (10½ oz.) beef gravy
  ¼ cup red wine
   1 teaspoon curry powder
   2 teaspoons cornstarch
  Hot cooked rice

1. Drain peaches, reserving ¼ cup syrup. Blend peach syrup with 1½ teaspoons curry powder; arrange peach halves in 8-inch round or square glass baking dish. Drizzle with curry mixture; set aside.
2. Preheat oven to 400° F.
3. Combine ground beef, rolled oats, onion, milk, salt and pepper in medium mixing bowl; mix well. Shape into 24 meatballs. Place in another 8-inch round or square glass baking dish.
4. Combine gravy, wine, 1 teaspoon curry powder and the cornstarch. Pour over meatballs. Place both dishes in oven.
5. MICROWAVE-BAKE 10 to 12 minutes or until meatballs are done and peach halves are hot. Serve over rice with peach halves as garnish.
                        4 to 5 Servings

SWEDISH MEATBALLS

  Meatballs, this page
  ¼ cup butter or margarine
  ¼ cup all-purpose flour
   2 tablespoons dry onion soup mix
  ¼ teaspoon nutmeg
 2½ cups milk

1. Prepare and cook meatballs as directed; set aside.
2. MICROWAVE butter in 4-cup glass measure 2 to 2½ minutes or until melted. Blend in flour, soup mix and nutmeg. Stir in milk.
3. MICROWAVE 6 to 7 minutes or until mixture boils and thickens, stirring once during last half of cooking time. Pour sauce over meatballs in glass baking dish.
4. MICROWAVE, uncovered, 3 to 4 minutes or until hot. If desired, serve with potatoes or rice.   4 to 5 Servings

MEATBALL-VEGETABLE STEW

   1 lb. ground beef
   1 teaspoon salt
  ¼ teaspoon pepper
   1 green pepper, sliced
   2 stalks celery, sliced
   3 carrots, sliced
   2 medium onions, quartered
   2 potatoes, peeled and quartered
   1 can (10¾ oz.) condensed tomato soup
   1 can (10½ oz.) beef gravy
   1 can (4 oz.) mushroom stems and pieces, drained

1. Combine ground beef, salt and pepper in 3-quart glass casserole. Shape into 12 to 15 meatballs; arrange in same casserole.
2. MICROWAVE 8 to 9 minutes or until meatballs are set; drain. Add remaining ingredients and stir lightly to mix.
3. MICROWAVE, covered, 25 to 30 minutes or until vegetables are done, stirring once.
                        4 to 5 Servings

SWEET-SOUR MEATBALLS

Meatballs, page 54
1 can (13¼ oz.) pineapple chunks, undrained
¼ cup packed brown sugar
¼ cup vinegar
1 tablespoon cornstarch
1 tablespoon soy sauce
½ green pepper, cut into strips

1. Prepare meatballs as directed except omit nutmeg and cook in 1½-quart shallow glass casserole. Drain.
2. Combine remaining ingredients in medium mixing bowl. Pour over meatballs.
3. MICROWAVE-BAKE, covered, at 400° F. for 6 to 7 minutes or until sauce boils and thickens, stirring once.   4 to 5 Servings

A meatloaf in just 25 minutes.

TANGY MEATLOAF

1½ lbs. ground beef
½ cup dry bread crumbs
1 egg
1 cup milk
1 small onion, chopped
1 tablespoon Worcestershire sauce
1 teaspoon salt
½ teaspoon dry mustard
¼ teaspoon pepper
⅛ teaspoon garlic salt
½ cup catsup, chili sauce, or barbecue sauce

1. Preheat oven to 350° F.
2. Combine all ingredients except catsup in medium mixing bowl. Press evenly into 1½-quart (8x4) glass loaf dish. Spread catsup over top.
3. MICROWAVE-BAKE 22 to 25 minutes or until done. Let stand 5 minutes before slicing.   5 to 6 Servings

Mashed potatoes frost this Swiss cheese-flavored meatloaf.

SWISS CHEESE MEATLOAF

Potato Topping
1 cup water
2 tablespoons butter or margarine
½ teaspoon salt
½ cup milk
1 jar (2½ oz.) sliced mushrooms, undrained
2 teaspoons chopped chives
1½ cups potato flakes

Meatloaf
1½ lbs. ground beef
1 cup shredded Swiss cheese
½ cup soda cracker crumbs
1 small onion, finely chopped
1½ teaspoons salt
1 teaspoon dried parsley flakes
⅛ teaspoon pepper
1 egg

1. MICROWAVE water in 4-cup glass measure 5½ to 6 minutes or until hot. Stir in remaining topping ingredients; mix well and set aside.
2. Combine Meatloaf ingredients; mix well. Shape into a roll about 9-inches long. Place on rack in 2-quart (12x7) glass baking dish.
3. MICROWAVE-BAKE at 450° F. for 10 minutes. Spread Potato Topping over meat roll with fork.
4. MICROWAVE-BROIL 5 to 6 minutes or until peaks of potato mixture are browned.
          6 to 8 Servings

TIP • When using the granular-type instant potatoes, increase amount to 1¾ cups.

MEAT 'N ONION LOAF

2 lbs. ground beef
1 envelope (1¼ oz.) dry onion soup mix
1 can (5 oz.) evaporated milk
1 egg
2 tablespoons brown sugar
1 tablespoon prepared mustard
2 tablespoons catsup

1. Preheat oven to 350° F.
2. Combine ground beef, soup mix, milk and egg in medium mixing bowl. Press evenly into 1½-quart (8x4) glass loaf dish. Combine brown sugar, mustard and catsup in small bowl; spoon over meatloaf.
3. MICROWAVE-BAKE 28 to 30 minutes or until done. Let stand 5 minutes before slicing.
          6 to 8 Servings

MANICOTTI

    7 or 8 manicotti shells
    ½ lb. ground beef
    ½ cup chopped onion
    ¼ cup chopped green pepper
    1 can (8 oz.) tomato sauce
    1 teaspoon sugar
    ¾ teaspoon salt
    1 teaspoon leaf oregano
    1½ cups ricotta or cottage cheese
    1½ cups shredded Mozzarella cheese
    ⅛ teaspoon pepper

1. Cook manicotti shells as directed on package; drain. Crumble ground beef into 1-quart glass casserole; add onion.

2. MICROWAVE 5 to 6 minutes or until meat is set. Stir to break meat into pieces; drain. Stir in green pepper, tomato sauce, sugar, salt and oregano.

3. Preheat oven to 375° F.

4. Fill manicotti shells with mixture of ricotta, 1 cup of Mozzarella cheese and the pepper. Place filled shells in 2-quart (12x7) glass baking dish. Spoon tomato mixture over shells. Sprinkle with remaining ½ cup Mozzarella cheese.

5. MICROWAVE-BAKE 10 to 12 minutes or until hot and cheese is melted.   4 to 5 Servings

SPAGHETTI

    1½ lbs. ground beef
    3 medium onions, chopped
    2 stalks celery, chopped
    2 green peppers, chopped
    1 clove garlic, finely chopped
    1 can (28 oz.) tomatoes, undrained
    1 can (6 oz.) tomato paste
    1 can (4 oz.) mushroom stems and pieces, drained
    1½ teaspoons salt
    ½ teaspoon leaf oregano
    ½ teaspoon dried parsley flakes
    ¼ teaspoon pepper
    1 bay leaf
    7 ozs. spaghetti, cooked

1. Crumble meat into 3-quart glass casserole; add onions and celery.

2. MICROWAVE 10 to 12 minutes or until meat is set. Stir to break meat into pieces; drain. Stir in remaining ingredients except spaghetti.

3. MICROWAVE, covered, 30 to 45 minutes or until flavors are well blended. Remove bay leaf. Serve over spaghetti.   6 to 8 Servings

TIP • If desired, omit step 3 and simmer sauce over low heat 1 to 2 hours.

ITALIAN LASAGNA

    1 package (16 oz.) lasagna noodles
    2 lbs. ground beef
    3 medium onions, chopped
    2 cloves garlic, finely chopped
    2 cans (15 ozs. each) tomato sauce
    1 can (6 oz.) tomato paste
    1 tablespoon sugar
    2½ teaspoons salt
    1 teaspoon dried parsley flakes
    1 teaspoon leaf basil
    ½ teaspoon leaf oregano
    3 cups creamed cottage cheese
    3 cups shredded Mozzarella cheese
    1 cup Parmesan cheese

1. Cook noodles as directed on package; drain and set aside. Crumble ground beef into 2-quart glass casserole; add onions.

2. MICROWAVE 11 to 12 minutes or until meat is set. Stir to break meat into pieces; drain. Stir in garlic, tomato sauce, tomato paste, sugar, salt, parsley, basil and oregano; mix well.

3. Assemble lasagna in two 2 or 3-quart (12x7 or 13x9) glass baking dishes by layering ⅓ of noodles, ⅓ of meat sauce, ½ of cottage cheese, and ⅓ of Mozzarella cheese between the 2 pans. Repeat with next layer of noodles, meat, cottage and Mozzarella cheese. Top with remaining noodles, meat mixture and Mozzarella cheese. Sprinkle with Parmesan cheese.

4. MICROWAVE-BAKE at 400° F. for 12 to 14 minutes or until bubbly in center.
                                10 to 12 Servings

TIPS • Lasagna can be prepared ahead and frozen. See page 194 for thawing and heating directions.

    • When cooking only one panful, cook minimum time.

Pictured top to bottom: Italian Lasagna, Spaghetti and Manicotti, this page.

MINI MEAT LOAVES

1½ **lbs. ground beef**
½ **cup cooked rice**
¼ **cup chopped green pepper**
2 **green onions, sliced**
1 **teaspoon salt**
1 **teaspoon dried parsley flakes**
¼ **teaspoon garlic salt**
¼ **teaspoon pepper**
1 **egg**
6 **slices bacon, halved crosswise**

1. Preheat oven to 450° F.
2. Combine all ingredients except bacon in medium mixing bowl; mix well. Shape into 6 oval-shaped loaves about 1½ inches thick. Crisscross 2 pieces bacon over each loaf, tucking ends under loaf. Place loaves on rack in 2-quart (12x7) glass baking dish.
3. MICROWAVE-BAKE 15 to 16 minutes or until meat is done and bacon is crisp.

6 Servings

TIP • Substitute for rice: ¼ cup dry bread crumbs.

SALISBURY STEAK

Mini Meat Loaves, this page
1 **can (10¾ oz.) condensed beef consommé**
1 **can (4 oz.) mushroom stems and pieces, drained**
⅓ **cup catsup**
1 **tablespoon cornstarch**
1 **teaspoon chopped chives**
1 **teaspoon Worcestershire sauce**
¼ **teaspoon leaf basil**

1. Prepare Mini Meat Loaves as directed except omit bacon. Cook as directed.
2. Combine remaining ingredients in 1½-quart (10x6) glass baking dish. Arrange cooked meat loaves in sauce.
3. MICROWAVE-BAKE 8 to 10 minutes or until bubbly. Serve sauce over meat. 6 Servings

GROUND BEEF STROGANOFF

1 **lb. ground beef**
1 **medium onion, finely chopped**
1 **can (10¾ oz.) condensed cream of mushroom soup**
1 **can (4 oz.) mushroom stems and pieces, drained**
½ **cup sour cream**

1. Crumble meat into 1½-quart glass casserole; add onion.
2. MICROWAVE 8 to 8½ minutes or until meat is set. Stir to break meat into pieces; drain. Stir in remaining ingredients.
3. MICROWAVE, covered, 10 to 12 minutes or until hot. 4 to 5 Servings

Spaghetti makes the crust for this pie.

CHEESY SPAGHETTI PIE

5 **ozs. spaghetti**
1 **cup shredded Cheddar cheese**
1 **egg**
1 **medium onion, chopped**
1 **teaspoon dried parsley flakes**
1 **lb. lean ground beef**
1 **egg**
1 **tablespoon all-purpose flour**
1 **teaspoon salt**
⅛ **teaspoon pepper**
1 **can (10¾ oz.) condensed cream of mushroom soup**
½ **cup shredded Cheddar cheese**
¼ **cup butter or margarine**
1½ **cups (5 ozs.) sliced fresh mrushooms**

1. Preheat oven to 350° F.
2. Cook spaghetti as directed on package; drain well. Combine spaghetti with 1 cup cheese, 1 egg, the onion and parsley. Arrange over bottom and up sides of 10-inch glass pie plate. Set aside.
3. Mix together ground beef, 1 egg, the flour, salt, pepper and half the can of soup in medium mixing bowl. Spoon into spaghetti-lined pie plate. Sprinkle with ½ cup cheese.
4. Combine butter and mushrooms in covered 1-quart glass casserole. Place casserole dish and pie in oven.
5. MICROWAVE-BAKE 18 to 20 minutes or until meat is done in center. Remove pie from oven. Stir remaining soup into cooked mushrooms.
6. MICROWAVE, covered, 3 to 4 minutes or until hot. Serve sauce over wedges of pie.

5 to 6 Servings

ENCHILADAS

>   1 lb. ground beef
>   1 medium onion, finely chopped
>   ½ cup sour cream
>   1 cup shredded Cheddar cheese
>   2 tablespoons snipped parsley
>   1 teaspoon salt
>   ¼ teaspoon pepper
>   2 to 4 tablespoons cooking oil
>   12 corn or flour tortillas

Enchilada Sauce

>   1 can (15 oz.) tomato sauce
>   ⅓ cup chopped green pepper
>   1 clove garlic, finely chopped
>   1½ to 2 teaspoons chili powder
>   ½ teaspoon leaf oregano
>   ¼ teaspoon ground cumin
>   ⅔ cup water

1. Crumble meat into medium glass mixing bowl; add onion.
2. MICROWAVE 8 to 8½ minutes or until meat is set. Stir to break meat into pieces; drain. Stir in sour cream, cheese, parsley, salt and pepper.
3. Heat 1 tablespoon oil in medium frying pan over medium heat. Add tortillas, one at a time, and heat a few seconds on each side until softened. Add additional oil to frying pan as necessary. Place about ¼ cup meat filling down center of each tortilla; roll up. Arrange in 3-quart (13x9) glass baking dish.
4. Combine Enchilada Sauce ingredients in medium mixing bowl. Pour over filled tortillas.
5. MICROWAVE, uncovered, 12 to 15 minutes or until hot.   5 to 6 Servings

CHILI CON CARNE

>   1 lb. ground beef
>   1 medium onion, chopped
>   ½ green pepper, chopped
>   1 teaspoon salt
>   2 teaspoons chili powder
>   ⅛ teaspoon pepper
>   1 can (28 oz.) tomatoes, undrained
>   1 can (15½ oz.) kidney beans, undrained

1. Crumble meat into 2-quart glass casserole; add onion.
2. MICROWAVE 8 to 8½ minutes or until meat is set. Stir to break meat into pieces; drain. Stir in remaining ingredients.
3. MICROWAVE, covered, 30 to 35 minutes or until flavors are blended.   5 to 6 Servings

MEXICAN CASSEROLE

>   1 lb. ground beef
>   1 medium onion, chopped
>   1 clove garlic, finely chopped
>   1 can (15 oz.) tomato sauce
>   1 teaspoon chili powder
>   ½ teaspoon salt
>   ¼ teaspoon ground cumin
>   1 can (4 oz.) green chilies, drained and chopped
>   3 cups corn chips
>   1 can (10¾ oz.) condensed cream of mushroom soup
>   1 cup shredded Cheddar cheese

1. Crumble meat into 1-quart glass casserole; add onion and garlic.
2. MICROWAVE 8 to 8½ minutes or until meat is set. Stir to break meat into pieces; drain. Stir in tomato sauce, seasonings and chilies.
3. Layer 2 cups corn chips and half each of meat mixture, soup and cheese in 8-inch square glass baking dish. Repeat with remaining meat mixture, soup and cheese; sprinkle with remaining corn chips.
4. MICROWAVE-BAKE, uncovered, at 400° F. for 12 to 15 minutes or until hot.
          About 5 Servings

CORN AND BEEF CASSEROLE

>   1 lb. ground beef
>   1 medium onion, chopped
>   1 can (8 oz.) whole kernel corn, undrained
>   1 can (8 oz.) tomato sauce
>   ¼ cup halved pitted ripe olives
>   2 cups uncooked noodles
>   1½ cups water
>   1 tablespoon all-purpose flour
>   1 teaspoon leaf oregano
>   ½ teaspoon salt
>   ¼ teaspoon pepper
>   1 cup shredded Cheddar cheese

1. Crumble meat into 2-quart glass casserole; add onion.
2. MICROWAVE 8 to 8½ minutes or until meat is set. Stir to break meat into pieces; drain. Stir in remaining ingredients except cheese.
3. MICROWAVE, covered, 20 to 22 minutes or until noodles are tender. Sprinkle cheese over top.
4. BROIL, uncovered, 3 minutes or until cheese is melted.   5 to 6 Servings

TIP • If you wish to omit the olives, increase salt to ¾ teaspoon.

CABBAGE ROLLS

12 cabbage leaves
1 lb. ground beef
1 medium onion, chopped
½ cup quick-cooking rice
1 teaspoon salt
1 teaspoon paprika
⅛ teaspoon pepper
1 can (15 oz.) tomato sauce

1. Place cabbage leaves in 2-quart glass casserole.
2. MICROWAVE, covered, 5 to 6 minutes or until partially cooked.
3. Combine ground beef, onion, rice, seasonings and ½ cup tomato sauce; mix well. Place ¼ cup meat mixture on each leaf, roll to enclose meat, securing with toothpicks. Place roll seam-side-down in 10-inch glass skillet or shallow baking dish. Pour remaining tomato sauce over rolls.
4. MICROWAVE, covered, 25 to 30 minutes or until cabbage is tender. Remove toothpicks.

4 to 6 Servings

TIPS • If desired, stir ¼ cup sour cream into sauce before serving.

• For ease in separating cabbage leaves, cut out core. Then hold head of cabbage under cold running water and gently pull apart leaves.

STUFFED GREEN PEPPERS

1. Prepare as for cabbage rolls, except substitute 4 medium or 3 large green peppers, halved, for cabbage leaves. Place pepper halves cut-side-up in 2-quart (12x7) glass baking dish. Cover with wax paper and cook as directed in step 2. Fill pepper halves with meat mixture and top with remaining sauce.
2. MICROWAVE-BAKE, uncovered, at 350° F. for 18 to 20 minutes or until meat mixture is cooked.

6 to 8 Pepper Halves

BEEF ROLLS

1 lb. ground beef
¼ cup dry bread crumbs
1 egg
½ teaspoon salt
1 cup shredded Cheddar cheese
¼ cup dry bread crumbs
¼ cup chopped green pepper

1. Combine ground beef, ¼ cup bread crumbs, the egg and salt in medium mixing bowl; mix well. Pat into 12x9-inch rectangle on wax paper.
2. Sprinkle cheese, ¼ cup bread crumbs and green pepper evenly over meat rectangle. Roll up jelly-roll fashion, starting with 9-inch side; use wax paper to lift and roll meat. For ease in slicing, refrigerate roll about 1 hour.
3. Preheat oven to 450° F.
4. Slice meat roll into 6 slices. Place cut-side-down in 2-quart (12x7) glass baking dish.
5. MICROWAVE-BAKE 5 to 6 minutes or until meat is done.

6 Servings

STEAKS: Most steaks are best broiled, barbecued or pan-fried using conventional methods of cooking. However, occasionally microwaves can be used to supplement this cooking. For example, with thicker steaks which take longer to broil, microwave cooking can be added to speed the cooking of the interior without overcooking the outside.

This same technique can be used with a thick steak from the barbecue grill. When the outside is the desired brownness, you can place it in the microwave oven and microwave a minute or two to cook the interior to the doneness desired.

Less tender steaks like round or flank normally require long, slow simmering to become tender. Microwaves can be used to more quickly bring the casserole or meat to a simmering temperature. Once a simmer temperature is reached, just bake is used to keep the mixture barely bubbling. If these mixtures boil too hard, they become tough.

See the freezer chapter for information on cooking frozen steaks.

A microwave-broil technique is good for a thick steak. Use this recipe as a cooking guide for a thick cut of sirloin, round or T-bone steak. Thin steaks do not need the addition of microwave cooking.

MARINATED CHUCK STEAK

   4-lb. beef chuck steak, cut 2 inches thick
   1 cup red wine
   ¼ cup cooking oil
   ½ teaspoon dry mustard
   ¼ teaspoon garlic salt
   1 tablespoon soy sauce

1. Marinate beef steak in mixture of wine, oil and seasonings for about 2 hours, turning once.
2. Remove steak from marinade and place on metal broiler pan.
3. MICROWAVE-BROIL 10 minutes. Turn meat over.
4. MICROWAVE-BROIL 10 to 12 minutes or until desired doneness.   About 8 Servings

BEEF STROGANOFF

   1½ lbs. sirloin steak
   ½ cup unsifted all-purpose flour
   ½ cup butter or margarine
   1 medium onion, thinly sliced
   1 can (10½ oz.) condensed beef consommé
   2 tablespoons tomato paste or catsup
   1 teaspoon salt
   ½ teaspoon dry mustard
   1 can (4 oz.) mushroom stems and pieces, drained
   3 tablespoons dry sherry, if desired
   ½ to 1 cup sour cream
   Hot buttered noodles

1. Cut sirloin into strips about ¼-inch thick and 1-inch long. Coat with flour. Heat butter in 10-inch freezer-to-range glass ceramic skillet over medium-high heat. Brown meat on all sides along with onion.
2. Stir in remaining ingredients except sour cream and noodles.
3. MICROWAVE, uncovered, 8 to 9 minutes or until sauce just comes to a boil. Stir in sour cream.
4. MICROWAVE, uncovered, about 2 minutes or until heated through. Serve with noodles.
                                                5 to 6 Servings

TIP • If a glass ceramic skillet is not available, brown meat and onion in frying pan. Then transfer to 1½-quart glass casserole.

ORIENTAL STEAK WITH PEA PODS

   1½-lb. flank steak
   2 tablespoons soy sauce
   2 tablespoons cooking oil
   8 ozs. (3 cups) fresh pea pods
   1 can (6 oz.) water chestnuts, drained and sliced
   2 tablespoons cornstarch
   2 tablespoons dry sherry
   1 teaspoon sugar
   Hot cooked rice

1. Slice flank steak across grain into thin slices (partially frozen steak slices easier). Combine soy sauce and oil in shallow 2-quart glass casserole or skillet; stir in steak strips, pea pods and chestnuts.
2. MICROWAVE, covered, 15 to 17 minutes or until meat is no longer pink. Combine cornstarch, sherry and sugar; stir into meat mixture.
3. MICROWAVE, covered, 3 to 4 minutes or until mixture boils and thickens. Serve over rice.   5 to 6 Servings

TIP • Substitute for fresh pea pods: 2 packages (6 ozs. each) frozen pea pods. Microwave 3 to 4 minutes before adding to soy mixture.

SWISS STEAK

   2 to 2½-lb. round steak, cut ½ inch thick
   ¼ cup all-purpose flour
   1 teaspoon salt
   ¼ teaspoon pepper
   2 tablespoons cooking oil
   1 large onion, sliced
   1 can (15 oz.) tomatoes, undrained
   1 teaspoon Worcestershire sauce

1. Cut steak into serving pieces; pound with meat mallet to help tenderize. Coat meat with mixture of flour, salt and pepper.
2. Heat oil in 10-inch freezer-to-range glass ceramic skillet. Add meat and onion and brown on both sides. Stir in tomatoes, Worcestershire sauce and any remaining flour mixture.
3. MICROWAVE-BAKE, covered, at 350° F. for 10 minutes.
4. BAKE 30 to 45 minutes or until meat is tender.   6 to 8 Servings

TIP • If a glass ceramic skillet is not available, brown meat and onion in frying pan. Then transfer to 1½-quart glass casserole.

Plan ahead with this recipe by purchasing a 6½ to 7-lb. roast. Slice 2 lbs. of the meat and use for the Beef Rouladens; use the remaining for this marinated pot roast.

SAUERBRATEN

  4½ to 5-lb. boneless rump roast
    1 onion, sliced
    1 stalk celery, sliced
    5 whole cloves
    1 bay leaf
    4 peppercorns
    1 tablespoon salt
  1¼ cups red wine vinegar
    2 cups water
    2 tablespoons cooking oil
    2 tablespoons all-purpose flour
    3 tablespoons packed brown sugar
    ¼ cup water
  12 gingersnaps, crushed

1. Place roast in plastic bag set in large mixing bowl. Add onion, celery, cloves, bay leaf, peppercorns, salt, vinegar and water. Close bag. Refrigerate 2 to 3 days, turning meat over occasionally.
2. Remove meat from marinade (save marinade) and pat dry with paper towels. Heat oil in freezer-to-range glass ceramic Dutch oven over medium-high heat. Add meat and brown on all sides. Strain marinade; add to meat.
3. MICROWAVE-BAKE, covered, at 325° F. for 15 minutes.
4. BAKE 2 to 2¼ hours or until meat is tender, turning roast over once. Remove meat from cooking liquid and set aside. Combine flour, brown sugar and water. Stir into cooking juices. Add gingersnaps.
5. MICROWAVE, covered, 3 to 4 minutes or until mixture boils and thickens. Serve sauce with sliced roast and boiled potatoes.
                         8 to 10 Servings

Pictured: Beef Rouladens, this page.

These bacon-flavored beef rolls are often served in German homes.

BEEF ROULADENS

    2 lbs. beef round, rump or sirloin tip, cut ½ inch thick
Salt and pepper
  12 slices bacon
    1 medium onion, thinly sliced
    ½ cup unsifted all-purpose flour
    1 can (10½ oz.) condensed beef consommé
    ½ cup water or red wine

1. Cut meat into 12 serving pieces; pound to ⅛-inch thickness. Season with salt and pepper.
2. MICROWAVE bacon in shallow glass baking dish about 8 minutes or until partially cooked; reserve bacon drippings. Arrange bacon slices on each piece of meat; place one onion slice over each slice bacon. Roll up jelly-roll fashion; secure with toothpicks. Coat each meat roll with flour.
3. Heat bacon drippings in freezer-to-range glass ceramic Dutch oven over medium heat. Add meat rolls and brown on all sides. Stir in remaining flour, the consommé and water.
4. MICROWAVE-BAKE, covered, at 350° F. for 15 minutes.
5. BAKE 35 to 40 minutes or until meat is tender.   6 to 8 Servings

CORNED BEEF DINNER

    2 to 2½-lb. corned beef brisket
    4 medium potatoes, peeled and quartered
    4 carrots, cut into 1-inch pieces
    3 small onions, halved
    1 stalk celery, sliced
    ½ medium head cabbage, cut into wedges
    2 cups water

1. Combine all ingredients including seasonings from corned beef in 4-quart glass casserole.
2. MICROWAVE-BAKE, covered, at 350° F. for 15 minutes.
3. BAKE 1 to 1½ hours or until meat is tender.
                         6 to 8 Servings

TIP • If corned beef does not contain seasonings, add ½ teaspoon peppercorns, 1 bay leaf and 3 whole cloves.

ROASTS: A tender roast like rib can be cooked with combination microwave and bake technique. The microwaves first warm the interior. Then the dry bake completes the cooking while browning and developing the rich beef flavor on the outside of the roast.

Mercury-type meat thermometers become inaccurate from microwaves, so this type thermometer should not be used when microwaves are being used in the oven. There are some special meat thermometers available that can be used with microwave cooking.

Less tender roasts like shoulder of chuck need long slow simmering to become tender. Microwaves are used to quickly heat the mixture to a simmer temperature. Then this slow cooking can be continued with just a bake setting. When raw vegetables are added to a partially cooked pot roast, microwaves can again be used to quickly heat the mixture and more quickly cook the vegetables.

Some roasts like rump or sirloin tip are cooked both like a tender roast and like a less tender roast. If cooking to a rare or medium rare doneness, cook like a rib roast. If cooking well done, cook in a covered container with liquid like a pot roast.

See the freezer chapter for information on cooking frozen roasts.

Here is an excellent way to achieve a juicy, evenly cooked roast. The microwaves quickly start the cooking, then bake evenly finishes the cooking and develops the rich brown flavors.

RIB OR RUMP ROAST

1. Select a 4 to 5-lb. rolled boneless or bone-in rib or rump roast. Place fat-side-up on rack in 2-quart (12x7) glass baking dish.
2. **MICROWAVE,** uncovered, 20 minutes. Insert meat thermometer into thickest part.
3. **BAKE,** uncovered, at 325° F. for 35 to 45 minutes (about 8 minutes per pound) or until thermometer registers 130° F. for rare doneness. For medium doneness, bake 55 to 65 minutes (about 13 minutes per pound). For well done roast, bake 75 to 85 minutes (about 17 minutes per pound).
   8 to 12 Servings

TIP • Once the microwaves are not being used, the meat thermometer can be used in the oven.

Pot roast requires slow simmering to become tender. Here we use microwave cooking to quickly start the simmering and cook the vegetables. The meat is removed from the oven while the vegetables cook. This allows the meat to stand before carving.

POT ROAST

   4 to 4½-lb. pot roast
   2 medium onions, sliced
1½ cups water
  ½ cup red wine
   2 teaspoons salt
  ¼ teaspoon pepper
   1 bay leaf
   3 tablespoons flour
  ¼ cup water
   5 medium potatoes, peeled and quartered
   6 medium carrots, quartered

1. Combine roast, onions, water, wine, salt, pepper and bay leaf in 3 or 4-quart glass casserole.
2. **MICROWAVE-BAKE,** covered, at 325° F. for 20 minutes.
3. **BAKE** 1¼ to 1½ hours or until meat is just about tender.
4. Combine flour and ¼ cup water in 2-quart glass casserole. Add potatoes and carrots. Stir in juices from meat. (Set meat aside in covered casserole.)
5. **MICROWAVE-BAKE** vegetables, covered, 20 to 25 minutes or until tender. Remove bay leaf. Slice meat and serve with vegetables and sauce. 6 to 8 Servings

TIPS • If desired, first brown roast in 2 tablespoons hot oil in a freezer-to-range glass ceramic Dutch oven. Add onions, water, wine and seasonings and continue as directed.

• If starting with a frozen roast, see page 192.

STEWS AND SHORT RIBS: These less tender cuts of beef need long slow simmering to become tender. The microwave-bake technique is used to quickly bring the mixture to a simmer temperature. Then the bake only is continued to maintain the simmer temperature. Trying to speed the cooking by using more microwave cooking will cause the meat to toughen. When additional food is added, the microwaves are again used to heat to a simmer temperature.

BEEF BOURGUIGNON

       4 slices bacon, cut into pieces
    1½ lbs. boneless beef stew meat
       ⅓ cup all-purpose flour
       3 small onions, sliced
       1 large carrot, sliced
       1 clove garlic, finely chopped
       1 teaspoon salt
       1 teaspoon dried parsley flakes
       ¼ teaspoon pepper
       1 bay leaf
       1 can (10¾ oz.) condensed beef
          consommé
       ½ cup burgundy wine
       ½ cup water

1. MICROWAVE bacon in freezer-to-range glass ceramic Dutch oven or 10-inch skillet 6 to 7 minutes or until crisp; remove bacon and set aside. Place Dutch oven containing drippings over medium-high heat.

2. Coat meat with flour; add to hot drippings and brown on all sides. Stir in onions, carrot and garlic. Continue cooking over medium-high heat 5 minutes or until onion is limp. Add remaining ingredients, including any remaining flour, and the bacon.

3. MICROWAVE-BAKE, covered, at 350° F. for 10 minutes.

4. BAKE 1 to 1½ hours or until meat is tender. Remove bay leaf. If desired, serve with noodles or boiled potatoes.   6 to 8 Servings

TIP • If a glass ceramic Dutch oven or skillet is not available, cook bacon in 3 or 4-quart glass casserole. Place drippings in frying pan and brown meat and vegetables. Transfer meat and vegetables to casserole.

HUNGARIAN GOULASH

       2 lbs. boneless beef stew meat
       ⅓ cup all-purpose flour
       3 tablespoons cooking oil
       1 green pepper, thinly sliced
       1 medium onion, thinly sliced
    1½ teaspoons salt
       1 teaspoon paprika
       1 teaspoon caraway seed
       ⅛ teaspoon pepper
       1 tablespoon Worcestershire sauce
    1½ cups water
    Hot buttered noodles

1. Coat meat with flour. Heat oil over medium-high heat in freezer-to-range glass ceramic Dutch oven. Add meat and brown on all sides. Stir in green pepper and onion; cook about 1 minute. Stir in remaining ingredients except noodles.

2. MICROWAVE-BAKE, covered, at 350° F. for 10 minutes.

3. BAKE 1 to 1½ hours or until meat is tender. Serve over noodles.   6 to 8 Servings.

TIP • If a glass ceramic Dutch oven is not available, brown meat, pepper and onion in frying pan. Then transfer to 3 or 4-quart glass casserole.

BEEF SHORT RIBS DINNER

       1 tablespoon cooking oil
    2½ to 3 lbs. beef short ribs
       1 medium onion, sliced
       1 cup water
       ¼ cup soy sauce
       ¼ cup dry sherry
       2 tablespoons sugar
       ¼ teaspoon cinnamon
       5 carrots, halved
       4 potatoes, peeled and quartered

1. Heat oil in freezer-to-range glass ceramic 10-inch skillet over medium-high heat. Add meat and brown on all sides. Add onion and brown lightly.

2. Add water, soy sauce, sherry, sugar and cinnamon.

3. MICROWAVE-BAKE, covered, 10 minutes.

4. BAKE about 1¼ hours or until meat is tender. Add carrots and potatoes.

5. MICROWAVE-BAKE 15 to 20 minutes or until vegetables are tender. About 6 Servings

TIP • If a glass ceramic skillet is not available, brown meat and onion in frying pan. Then transfer to 2-quart glass casserole.

Pork, Ham and Sausages

PORK ROASTS: When cooking pork, the primary consideration is that it be cooked until properly done. Since all cuts of pork are quite tender, several hours of simmering are unnecessary.

The addition of microwave cooking with baking speeds the cooking of pork roasts and other similar cuts. The combination microwave-bake is used until the meat is about ⅔ cooked. Then the roasting is completed using the bake setting. In this way the meat thermometer can be inserted at the time the microwaves are turned off. (Mercury-type thermometers should not be used in the oven during microwave cooking because the microwaves cause them to become inaccurate.) The slower cooking at the end helps the meat retain its juices and reduces the standing time needed before meat is carved.

We found some variation in times necessary to cook pork roasts due to varying amounts of fat and bone. Use the times given as guides, but rely on a meat thermometer for an accurate doneness test.

STUFFED PORK TENDERLOIN

   2 pork tenderloins (about 1 lb. each)
Salt and pepper
¼ cup butter or margarine
 1 small onion, finely chopped
 2 cups herb-seasoned stuffing mix
 1 can (8½ oz.) water chestnuts, drained and chopped
 1 egg
 1 teaspoon dried parsley flakes
½ cup water or white wine

1. Split each tenderloin almost through lengthwise; flatten slightly. Season cut side with salt and pepper; set aside.
2. MICROWAVE butter and onion in medium glass mixing bowl 5 to 6 minutes or until onion is partially cooked. Stir in remaining ingredients; mix well. Spoon stuffing onto cut side of one flattened tenderloin. Top with other tenderloin, placed cut-side-down. Tie with about 4 pieces of string to hold the two tenderloins together. Place on rack in 2-quart (12x7) glass baking dish.
3. MICROWAVE-BAKE at 350° F. for 15 to 18 minutes or until meat is no longer pink.
                                6 to 8 Servings

Pictured: Pork Chops with Vegetables, page 68, Pork Roast, this page and Bologna and Stuffing, page 74.

Use these times for boneless or bone-in pork roasts.

PORK ROAST

1. Place a 2½ to 3-lb. pork loin roast on rack in 2-quart (12x7) glass baking dish.
2. MICROWAVE-BAKE at 325°F. for 27 to 33 minutes (about 4 minutes per pound). Insert meat thermometer.
3. BAKE 15 to 25 minutes or until meat thermometer registers 170° F.
                              About 8 Servings

SWEET AND SOUR PORK

   1 can (13¼ oz.) pineapple chunks, undrained
½ cup packed brown sugar
¼ cup water
¼ cup vinegar
 3 tablespoons cornstarch
 2 tablespoons catsup
 1 tablespoon soy sauce
 1 teaspoon salt
 1 green pepper, chopped
 1 medium onion, thinly sliced
 4 cups cubed cooked pork
Hot cooked rice

1. Combine all ingredients except rice in 2-quart glass casserole; mix well.
2. MICROWAVE, covered, 18 to 20 minutes or until mixture boils, stirring once. Serve with rice.   6 to 8 Servings

Here is an excellent way to use leftover cooked pork — try also with cooked chicken or turkey.

PORK CHOP SUEY

   2 cups cubed cooked pork
 1 medium onion, thinly sliced
 3 stalks celery, sliced
 3 tablespoons cornstarch
¼ cup soy sauce
¼ cup water
 1 can (10¾ oz.) condensed chicken broth
 1 can (16 oz.) bean sprouts, drained

1. Combine all ingredients in 1½-quart glass casserole.
2. MICROWAVE, covered, 18 to 20 minutes or until mixture comes to a boil, stirring once. If desired, serve with hot cooked rice.
                              4 to 6 Servings

PORK CHOPS: There are numerous ways of preparing chops using microwave or combination cooking.

Some pork chops are browned before adding a sauce and simmering with microwave cooking. Others are combined directly with the sauce ingredients.

When a moist simmer is desired, microwave in a covered baking dish.

For broiling chops, microwave cooking is added to speed the cooking without drying the interior of the chops.

BROILED PORK CHOPS

1. Arrange 4 to 6 pork chops, cut ½ inch thick, on metal broiler pan.
2. Move oven rack to second position.
3. MICROWAVE-BROIL 4 minutes. Turn chops over.
4. MICROWAVE-BROIL 4 to 5 minutes or until meat is done.   4 to 6 Chops

PORK CHOPS WITH BARBECUE SAUCE

   5 to 6 loin pork chops, cut ½ inch thick
   1 medium onion, thinly sliced
   ¼ cup water
   ½ cup catsup
   2 tablespoons packed brown sugar
   2 tablespoons vinegar
   1 teaspoon Worcestershire sauce
   ½ teaspoon salt
   ⅛ teaspoon garlic powder
   ⅛ teaspoon pepper

1. Combine all ingredients in 2-quart shallow glass casserole.
2. MICROWAVE, covered, 20 to 25 minutes or until meat is done. If desired, serve with hot cooked rice.   5 to 6 Servings

SMOKED PORK CHOPS

1. Arrange 5 smoked pork chops (1 to 1½ lbs.) in 3-quart (13x9) glass baking dish. If desired, brush with honey, orange marmalade or add Orange-Mustard Glaze (below).
2. MICROWAVE 9 to 10 minutes or until edges of meat begin to sizzle.   About 5 Servings

TIP • ORANGE-MUSTARD GLAZE: Combine ¼ cup packed brown sugar, ¼ cup orange juice, 1 tablespoon prepared mustard, 1 teaspoon cornstarch and dash cloves. Pour over chops before cooking.

PORK CHOPS WITH VEGETABLES

   6 small potatoes, peeled and sliced
   6 small carrots, cut into quarters
   5 to 6 loin pork chops, cut ½ inch thick
   1 envelope (1¼ oz.) dry onion soup mix
   ½ teaspoon dried parsley flakes
   1 cup orange juice

1. Arrange potatoes, carrots and pork chops in 10-inch glass ceramic skillet or shallow casserole. Combine soup mix, parsley and orange juice; pour over chops.
2. MICROWAVE-BAKE, covered, at 350° F. for 25 to 30 minutes or until vegetables and meat are tender.   5 to 6 Servings

PORK CHOPS AND STUFFING

   3 tablespoons chopped onion
   2 tablespoons butter or margarine
   2 tablespoons water
   ¼ teaspoon poultry seasoning or thyme
   3 slices (3 cups) bread, cubed
   6 pork chops, cut ¼ inch thick
   1 envelope (1¼ oz.) dry onion soup mix
   ½ cup water
   ½ cup milk

1. Combine onion, butter, 2 tablespoons water and the poultry seasoning in medium glass mixing bowl.
2. MICROWAVE 2 to 2½ minutes or until butter is melted. Stir in bread cubes. Spoon 6 mounds of stuffing into 2-quart (12x7) glass baking dish. Place a pork chop on each mound.
3. Combine soup mix, ½ cup of water and milk. Pour over pork chops.
4. MICROWAVE-BAKE at 425° F. for 18 to 20 minutes or until pork chops are done.
               6 Servings

Pictured: Oven-Barbecued Ribs, page 70.

PORK RIBS: Small pieces of pork, like ribs, cook quickly with a microwave-bake setting. Country-style ribs are meatier than spareribs, but both cook using a similar method in the combination oven. When you wish to cook the meat without browning, the ribs are cooked with just microwaves.

OVEN-BARBECUED RIBS

2 to 2½ lbs. country-style ribs

Barbecue Sauce
- **½ cup catsup**
- **¼ cup chili sauce**
- **1 clove garlic, finely chopped**
- **1 small onion, chopped**
- **2 tablespoons brown sugar**
- **1 tablespoon lemon juice**
- **1 teaspoon dry mustard**
- **1 teaspoon Worcestershire sauce**

1. Cut ribs into serving-size pieces; place in 2-quart (12x7) glass baking dish.
2. MICROWAVE-BAKE at 400° F. for 10 minutes or until ribs are no longer pink. Rearrange ribs and drain fat.
3. Combine sauce ingredients; spoon over ribs.
4. MICROWAVE-BAKE 10 to 12 minutes or until ribs are done.   4 to 5 Servings

Use your oven to precook ribs or chicken before grilling over hot coals. Grilling is very speedy with little chance of scorching before the meat is done.

PATIO BARBECUED RIBS OR CHICKEN

1. Cut 3 to 3½ lbs. ribs or chicken into pieces and place in 2-quart (12x7) glass baking dish. Cover with wax paper.
2. MICROWAVE 25 to 30 minutes (20 to 25 minutes for chicken) or until meat is no longer pink. Drain juices. Prepare Barbecue Sauce from Oven-Barbecued Ribs recipe above, or favorite barbecue sauce. Spoon over meat.
3. Grill over hot coals 15 to 20 minutes, turning meat and brushing occasionally with sauce until meat is browned and heated through.
About 6 Servings

STUFFED PORK CUTLETS

- **¼ cup butter or margarine**
- **¼ cup sesame seed**
- **⅓ cup chopped celery**
- **2 tablespoons chopped onion**
- **1 teaspoon Worcestershire sauce**
- **½ teaspoon salt**
- **¼ teaspoon thyme**
- **3 slices (3 cups) bread, cubed**
- **2 pork cutlets (about 6 ozs. each)**

1. MICROWAVE butter, sesame seed, celery and onion in 1½-quart (10x6) glass baking dish 5 minutes or until vegetables are partially cooked. Stir in remaining ingredients except meat; set aside.
2. Pound or press each cutlet to a rectangle about ¼-inch thick. Divide stuffing in half and place on each cutlet. Roll up jelly-roll fashion, starting at narrow end. Arrange the two rolls in the 1½-quart baking dish.
3. MICROWAVE-BROIL 6 to 8 minutes or until meat is done. Cut each roll in half before serving.   4 Servings

TIP • When pork cutlets are not available, use ¾-lb. pork tenderloin, cut into ½ inch slices. Flatten to ¼-inch thickness. Divide stuffing among pieces. Continue as directed.

Microwave cooking is ideal for achieving the crisp vegetable textures in Oriental cooking.

PORK AND VEAL CHOW MEIN

- **1 lb. chow mein meat**
- **1 medium onion, sliced**
- **3 stalks celery, sliced**
- **3 medium carrots, sliced**
- **1 can (8½ oz.) water chestnuts, drained and sliced**
- **1 can (8½ oz.) bamboo shoots, drained**
- **1 can (4 oz.) mushroom stems and pieces, drained**
- **¼ cup soy sauce**
- **1 tablespoon cornstarch**
- **1 tablespoon packed brown sugar**
- **½ teaspoon salt**

1. Crumble meat into 3-quart glass casserole; add onion.
2. MICROWAVE 8 to 8½ minutes or until meat is set. Stir to break meat into pieces; drain. Stir in remaining ingredients.
3. MICROWAVE, covered, 20 to 22 minutes or until vegetables are desired doneness, stirring twice. Serve over chow mein noodles or hot cooked rice.   5 to 6 Servings

TIP • Chow mein meat is a mixture of coarsely ground pork and veal.

CUBED AND GROUND PORK: Cubed pork is cooked just until done. Since pork is already tender, a short microwave-bake setting is all that is necessary for cooking.

Ground pork is cooked in the same way as ground beef. For most dishes, it is cooked enough to drain the fat. Any further cooking time and technique is determined by the added ingredients.

A delicious French stew to serve with boiled potatoes.

RAGOUT

　½ cup unsifted all-purpose flour
　2 to 2½ lbs. pork hocks
　2 onions, quartered
　2 bay leaves
　2 teaspoons salt
　2 to 3 teaspoons allspice
　½ teaspoon pepper
　4 cups water
　1 lb. ground fresh pork
　⅓ cup dry bread crumbs
　1 egg
　½ teaspoon salt
　½ teaspoon thyme
　¼ teaspoon pepper
　½ cup water

1. MICROWAVE-BROIL flour in shallow glass baking dish 5 to 8 minutes until flour is a light golden brown, stirring occasionally. Set aside.
2. Combine pork hocks, onions, bay leaves, 2 teaspoons salt, the allspice, ½ teaspoon pepper and 4 cups water in 3-quart glass casserole.
3. MICROWAVE-BAKE, covered, at 350° F. for 20 minutes. Combine ground pork, bread crumbs, egg, ½ teaspoon salt, the thyme and ¼ teaspoon pepper in medium mixing bowl. Shape into about 18 meatballs. Drop into pork hock mixture.
4. BAKE, covered, 1 to 1¼ hours or until pork hocks are tender. Remove meat from pork hocks; return to casserole. Combine reserved browned flour and ½ cup water. Stir into meat mixture.
5. MICROWAVE-BAKE, uncovered, 5 to 8 minutes or until mixture boils. Remove bay leaves. Serve stew in soup bowls or over boiled potatoes.　　　5 to 6 Servings

A traditional French-Canadian meat pie often served during the holidays.

PORK PIE

　1 lb. ground fresh pork
　1 large onion, chopped
　⅓ cup potato flakes or granules
　1 teaspoon salt
　¼ teaspoon allspice
　⅛ teaspoon garlic powder
　Dash pepper
　Pastry for 2-crust pie

1. Crumble pork into medium glass mixing bowl; add onion.
2. MICROWAVE 5 to 5½ minutes or until meat is partially cooked; drain. Stir in remaining ingredients except pastry; set aside.
3. Preheat oven to 450° F.
4. Roll out half of pastry to fit a 9-inch glass pie plate. Line pie plate with pastry, trimming crust even with edge of pan. Fill with meat mixture. Roll out remaining pastry to circle the size of pie pan. Cut slits in center for escape of steam. Place top crust over filling. Fold edge of top crust under bottom crust. Pinch edges together to seal.
5. MICROWAVE-BAKE 10 to 11 minutes or until crust is golden brown. If desired, serve with catsup or pickled beets.　　5 to 6 Servings

PORK AND SAUERKRAUT DINNER

　2 lbs. lean boneless pork, cubed
　⅓ cup all-purpose flour
　¼ cup butter or margarine
　1 can (27 oz.) sauerkraut, drained
　1 cup chopped onion
　1 medium apple, peeled and chopped
　1 clove garlic, finely chopped
　1 cup white wine
　1 teaspoon dill weed
　1 teaspoon salt
　¼ teaspoon pepper

1. Coat meat with flour. Melt butter over medium-high heat in freezer-to-range glass ceramic Dutch oven. Add meat and brown on all sides.
2. Stir in remaining ingredients, including any remaining flour; mix well.
3. MICROWAVE-BAKE, covered, at 350° F. for 20 to 25 minutes or until meat is tender.
　　　　　　　　　About 8 Servings

TIP • Cubed cooked pork may be used in this recipe. Omit step 1. Combine 3 cups cubed cooked pork and 3 tablespoons flour with remaining ingredients in step 2.

Pictured: Asparagus and Ham Bake, page 73.

HAM: Most hams available are precooked, so are heated just until serving temperature is reached. The recipes in this section are for precooked hams. If you have a fresh ham (the same cut of meat as ham, but not cured) or an uncooked ham, it should be cooked following the method for pork roast.

Smaller pieces of ham like slices and cubes can be easily heated with just microwaves. Covering speeds the heating, and other ingredients or seasonings can be heated along with the ham.

For larger pieces, like a baked ham, the heating is started with microwave cooking. Then, the slower bake heat is used to allow the heat to reach the center without drying the outside of the ham.

Use this method for precooked canned or refrigerated hams. A bone does not change cooking times.

BAKED HAM

1. Place a 2 to 5-lb. precooked ham in 3 or 4-quart glass casserole.
2. MICROWAVE, covered, 20 minutes. Remove cover; insert meat thermometer into center of ham.
3. BAKE, uncovered, at 350° F. for 20 to 50 minutes (about 10 minutes per pound) or until meat thermometer registers 115° F.

GLAZED HAM SLICE

 ½ to 1-lb. ham slice, cut ¼ inch thick
 2 tablespoons honey
 1 teaspoon lemon juice
 ⅛ teaspoon ginger

1. Place ham slice in 2-quart (12x7) glass baking dish. Combine honey, lemon juice and ginger; pour over ham slice.
2. MICROWAVE 5 to 6 minutes or until hot.

                                     3 to 4 Servings

TIP • For 1½-lb. ham slice, cut 1 inch thick, microwave 8 to 9 minutes.

This sweet-sour pineapple sauce goes well with ham. There is plenty of sauce for serving over rice, too.

HAM SLICE IN TANGY PINEAPPLE SAUCE

1½-lb. ham slice, cut 1 inch thick
1 cup packed brown sugar
1 can (13¼ oz.) crushed pineapple, undrained
2 tablespoons cornstarch
1 tablespoon prepared mustard
1 tablespoon lemon juice

1. Place ham slice in 8-inch square glass baking dish. Combine remaining ingredients in small mixing bowl. Spoon over ham slice.
2. MICROWAVE 10 to 12 minutes or until ham is hot and sauce is thickened, stirring sauce once during last half of cooking time. Serve sauce over each serving.   5 to 6 Servings

HAM LOAF

1 lb. (about 4 cups) ground cooked ham
1½ cups (1½ slices) soft bread cubes
2 eggs, beaten
1 cup milk
¼ cup finely chopped onion
¼ cup finely chopped green pepper
1 teaspoon prepared mustard

1. Combine all ingredients in medium mixing bowl. Press mixture evenly into 1½-quart (8x4) glass loaf dish.
2. MICROWAVE-BAKE at 350° F. for 18 to 20 minutes or until meat thermometer inserted in center registers 140° F. Let stand 10 minutes before slicing.   5 to 6 Servings

HAM-STUFFED ZUCCHINI

4 medium zucchini
¼ cup butter or margarine
2 cups finely chopped cooked ham
2 slices bread, cubed
2 medium tomatoes, chopped
1 small onion, chopped
1 clove garlic, finely chopped
½ teaspoon dried parsley flakes

1. Cut off stem end of zucchini. Cut zucchini in half lengthwise; scoop out seeds and pulp leaving a ¼-inch shell. Arrange cut-side-up in 3-quart (13x9) glass baking dish; set aside.
2. MICROWAVE butter in medium glass mixing bowl 2½ to 3 minutes or until melted. Stir in remaining ingredients. Spoon into zucchini shells.
3. MICROWAVE, covered with wax paper, 18 to 20 minutes or until zucchini is tender.
                        6 to 8 Servings

ASPARAGUS AND HAM BAKE

2 packages (8 ozs. each) frozen cut asparagus
6 slices cooked ham, cut ¼ inch thick
1 can (10¾ oz.) condensed cream of mushroom soup
½ cup sour cream
4 slices processed Swiss cheese, halved
Paprika

1. Place frozen asparagus in 2-quart (12x7) glass baking dish. Place ham slices on asparagus, overlapping as needed.
2. Combine soup and sour cream in small mixing bowl. Pour over ham slices. Top with cheese slices; sprinkle with paprika.
3. MICROWAVE 18 minutes.
4. MICROWAVE-BROIL 3 to 3½ minutes or until top is golden brown.   About 6 Servings

HAM AND TOMATO CASSEROLE

1 can (28 oz.) tomatoes, undrained
1 can (4 oz.) mushroom stems and pieces, undrained
2 tablespoons all-purpose flour
1 teaspoon dried parsley flakes
½ teaspoon leaf oregano
2 cups uncooked noodles
3 cups cubed cooked ham
1 small onion, sliced
½ cup water

1. Combine all ingredients in 3-quart glass casserole.
2. MICROWAVE, covered, 20 to 22 minutes or until noodles are tender, stirring once.
                        5 to 6 Servings

HAM AND MACARONI CASSEROLE

2 cups (7-oz. pkg.) uncooked macaroni
1 package (10 oz.) frozen peas
1 medium onion, sliced
2 cups cubed cooked ham
½ cup sliced ripe olives
1½ cups milk
1½ cups water
1 can (10¾ oz.) condensed cream of celery soup
½ teaspoon salt
½ cup shredded Cheddar cheese

1. Combine all ingredients except cheese in 3-quart glass casserole.
2. MICROWAVE, covered, 25 to 30 mintues or until macaroni is tender. Remove cover and sprinkle cheese over top of casserole.
3. BROIL, uncovered, 3 to 3½ minutes or until cheese is melted. Cover and let stand 5 minutes before serving.   5 to 6 Servings

WIENERS AND LUNCHEON MEATS: Both wieners and luncheon meats are already cooked, so just need to be heated to serving temperature. Microwaves are normally adequate for the heating; covering speeds the heating.

WIENERS

1. Place desired number of wieners in covered glass dish or casserole.
2. MICROWAVE until hot:
   - 1 wiener — ¾ to 1 minute
   - 4 wieners — 2 to 3 minutes
   - 8 wieners — 3 to 4 minutes

Serve these hearty sausages with dark bread and German potato salad.

BRATWURST AND BEER

  1 lb. (about 6) bratwurst
  1 can (12 oz.) beer

1. Arrange bratwurst in 1½-quart (10x6) glass baking dish. Add beer.
2. MICROWAVE-BROIL 6 minutes. Turn bratwurst over.
3. MICROWAVE-BROIL 3 to 4 minutes or until browned. Drain beer. 6 Servings

FRANKS POLYNESIAN-STYLE

  ¼ cup butter or margarine
  1 medium onion, sliced
  1 stalk celery, sliced
  6 wieners
  1 can (13¼ oz.) pineapple chunks
  1 green pepper, cut into strips
  ¾ cup water
  2 tablespoons cornstarch
  1 tablespoon soy sauce
  1 teaspoon instant beef bouillon
  ¼ teaspoon prepared horseradish

1. MICROWAVE butter, onion and celery in 1½-quart glass casserole 6 to 8 minutes or until partially cooked.
2. Halve wieners crosswise. Then cut each half lengthwise into quarters. Add to vegetable mixture. Drain pineapple, reserving ¼ cup syrup. Add pineapple, reserved syrup and remaining ingredients to casserole.
3. MICROWAVE, covered, 18 to 20 minutes or until mixture boils and thickens, stirring once. If desired, serve with hot cooked rice.
   5 to 6 Servings

BOLOGNA AND STUFFING

  1-lb. ring bologna
  ⅓ cup butter or margarine
  ⅔ cup water
  1 green onion, chopped
  ¼ cup finely chopped celery
  2 cups herb-seasoned stuffing mix

1. Cut away metal clips from ring bologna and place uncut ring in 1½-quart glass casserole.
2. MICROWAVE butter, water, onion and celery in medium glass mixing bowl 5 minutes or until hot. Stir in stuffing mix.
3. Mound stuffing in the center of bologna.
4. MICROWAVE, covered, 7 to 9 minutes or until bologna is hot. 4 to 5 Servings

WIENER-VEGETABLE HOT DISH

  1 package (10 oz.) frozen mixed vegetables
  ¼ cup butter or margarine
  1 medium onion, thinly sliced
  1 cup sliced celery
  1 lb. wieners, cut into 2-inch pieces
  1 can (10¾ oz.) condensed tomato soup
  1 teaspoon sugar
  2 teaspoons prepared mustard
  ⅛ teaspoon pepper

1. MICROWAVE frozen vegetables in package 3 minutes or until partially thawed; set aside.
2. MICROWAVE butter, onion and celery in 2-quart glass casserole 6 to 8 minutes or until partially cooked.
3. Stir in remaining ingredients and mixed vegetables.
4. MICROWAVE, covered, 20 to 22 minutes or until vegetables are desired doneness.
   5 to 6 Servings

TIP • Substitute for frozen mixed vegetables: other favorite frozen vegetables.

Here is a quick and easy lunch idea — just serve with hot rolls and a salad.

CHILI DOG CASSEROLE

  1 can (15 oz.) chili with beans
  1 can (15 oz.) tomato sauce
  1 lb. wieners, cut crosswise into 1-inch pieces

1. Combine all ingredients in 1½-quart glass casserole.
2. MICROWAVE, covered, 15 to 18 minutes or until hot, stirring once. Serve in soup bowls or over toast. 5 to 6 Servings

A quick-to-make family-style dinner. Just add a tossed salad to complete the meal.

LUNCHEON MEAT DINNER

    1 can (12 oz.) luncheon meat
1½ cups water
    2 tablespoons butter or margarine
  ½ teaspoon salt
  ½ cup milk
1½ cups potato flakes
    1 can (12 oz.) whole kernel corn, drained
  ½ cup shredded Cheddar cheese

1. Cut luncheon meat into 6 slices. Place in 8-inch square glass baking dish; set aside.
2. MICROWAVE water, butter and salt in 4-cup glass measure 7 to 8 minutes or until hot. Stir in milk, potato flakes and corn; beat well. Spoon potato mixture onto each meat slice; sprinkle with cheese.
3. MICROWAVE, uncovered, 6 to 8 minutes or until hot and cheese is melted.   6 Servings

TIP • When using the granular-type instant potatoes, increase amount to 1¾ cups.

BACON AND SAUSAGE: Bacon cooks quickly using just microwaves. The thin slices and curing process cause it to brown and crisp very quickly. When conventional heat is not being used, the bacon can be placed on layers of paper towel so the grease is absorbed as the bacon cooks. (Paper should not be used if conventional heat is also being used. Then it is best to drain the bacon on paper towels after removing from oven.) Since the microwave cooking comes from all sides, no turning is necessary.

Sausage needs additional heat to brown the meat. Both links and patties are cooked using a microwave-broil technique. With the baking dish at the normal rack position and because of the short cooking time, broil can be used without using the metal broiler pan.

BACON

1. Separate bacon slices and arrange in shallow glass baking dish.
2. MICROWAVE until desired crispness:
    2 slices — 4 to 5 minutes
    4 slices — 6 to 7 minutes
    6 slices — 7 to 8 minutes
    8 slices — 10 to 12 minutes
  12 slices — 14 to 16 minutes

TIPS • If bacon is difficult to separate into slices, place section in baking dish and microwave about 1 minute or until slices separate easily. Reduce additional microwave time by about 1 minute.

    • Paper towels can be placed on the bottom of baking dish to absorb grease as it accumulates.

    • Bacon can be layered in dish, placing a layer of paper towels between each bacon layer.

GLAZED BACON

    1 lb. Canadian-style bacon
¼ cup grape or currant jelly
    2 tablespoons water

1. Place whole piece of bacon in 1½-quart (8x4) glass loaf dish. Brush with jelly. Add water to pan.
2. MICROWAVE 15 to 18 minutes or until meat thermometer inserted in center registers 130° F.   5 to 6 Servings

TIP • Orange marmalade or favorite jelly may be substituted for grape or currant jelly.

FRESH SAUSAGE LINKS

1. Place 1 lb. sausage links in 3-quart (13x9) glass baking dish.
2. MICROWAVE-BROIL 7 to 9 minutes or until golden brown and no longer pink.
    4 to 6 Servings

FRESH SAUSAGE PATTIES

1. Form 1 lb. fresh pork sausage into 4 patties. Place on rack in 2-quart (12x7) glass baking dish.
2. MICROWAVE-BROIL 6 to 7 minutes or until lightly browned and no longer pink.
    4 Servings

Lamb

LAMB: Lamb cuts usually are tender so cook quickly. The cooking techniques are similar to those used for beef except that long simmering times are not necessary to tenderize the meat.

With roasts, the meat is cooked almost entirely with a microwave-bake setting, then finished with bake only.

Ground lamb for casseroles is precooked just like ground beef. Patties and meatballs are also cooked similarly to ground beef.

Stew meat requires a slower bake setting to simmer and become tender. However, the time is shorter than for beef since the meat is more tender.

Chops, like shoulder chops, use a combination microwave-bake and bake. The thick-cut more tender chops, like loin, use microwave cooking to speed the broiling.

LAMB MEATBALLS WITH CUMBERLAND SAUCE

  1 lb. ground lamb
¼ cup dry bread crumbs
  1 small onion, finely chopped
  1 teaspoon salt
  1 teaspoon dried parsley flakes
Dash pepper
  1 egg
Cumberland Sauce, page 118

1. Preheat oven to 400° F.
2. Combine all ingredients except Cumberland Sauce in medium mixing bowl. Shape into 1-inch balls. Arrange in 2-quart (12x7) glass baking dish. Prepare Cumberland Sauce through step 1; pour over meatballs.
3. MICROWAVE-BAKE 9 to 10 minutes or until meatballs are done. Spoon sauce over meatballs before serving.   4 to 5 Servings

Pictured, clockwise: Lamb Roast, this page, Irish Stew, page 78 and Lamb Meatballs with Cumberland Sauce, this page.

Use these times for both boneless and bone-in roasts.

LAMB ROAST

1. Place a 3-lb. lamb roast on rack in 2-quart (12x7) glass baking dish.
2. MICROWAVE-BAKE at 325° F. for 27 to 30 minutes (9 minutes per pound) or until meat thermometer inserted in thickest part registers 130° F.
3. BAKE 10 to 15 minutes or until meat thermometer registers 170° F.
    8 to 10 Servings

CURRIED LAMB

  2 cups cubed cooked lamb
  1 medium onion, sliced
  2 tablespoons flaked coconut
  2 tablespoons catsup
  1 to 2 teaspoons curry powder
½ teaspoon garlic salt
¼ teaspoon thyme
  1 can (10¾ oz.) condensed beef consommé
¼ cup all-purpose flour
¾ cup milk or light cream

1. Combine all ingredients in 2-quart glass casserole.
2. MICROWAVE-BAKE, covered, at 350° F. for 10 minutes.
3. BAKE 30 to 35 minutes or until sauce is thickened and flavors blended. If desired, serve with hot cooked rice and curry condiments.   4 to 5 Servings

LAMB PATTIES

⅔ cup water
⅔ cup potato flakes or granules
¼ cup milk
  1 small onion, finely chopped
  1 lb. ground lamb
  1 tablespoon dried parsley flakes
  1 teaspoon salt
⅛ teaspoon pepper

1. MICROWAVE water in medium glass mixing bowl 5 to 5½ minutes or until hot.
2. Preheat oven to 450° F.
3. Stir potato flakes and milk into water; beat until fluffy. Stir in remaining ingredients; mix well. Shape into 4 patties; place on rack in 2-quart (12x7) glass baking dish.
4. MICROWAVE-BAKE 9 to 10 minutes or until done.   4 Servings

A company-type casserole of Greek origin. A delicious combination of flavors.

MOUSSAKA

    1 lb. ground lamb
    1 medium onion, chopped
    1 teaspoon salt
    1 teaspoon dried parsley flakes
    ⅛ teaspoon nutmeg
    ⅛ teaspoon pepper
    1 can (16 oz.) tomatoes, undrained
    ¼ cup dry red wine
    1 medium eggplant, peeled
    4 eggs
    ½ cup milk
    ¼ cup Parmesan cheese

1. Crumble meat into medium glass mixing bowl; add onion.
2. MICROWAVE 5 to 5½ minutes or until meat is set. Stir meat to break into pieces; drain. Stir in seasonings, tomatoes and wine; set aside.
3. Preheat oven to 375° F.
4. Slice eggplant lengthwise into ½-inch thick slices. Arrange half of slices in bottom of 2-quart (12x7) glass baking dish. Top with half of meat mixture, remaining eggplant and meat mixture.
5. MICROWAVE-BAKE 16 to 18 minutes or until eggplant is tender. Beat eggs, milk and Parmesan cheese in small mixing bowl; pour over hot casserole.
6. BAKE 5 to 6 minutes or until custard is set.
                                    5 to 6 Servings

LAMB AND CORN CASSEROLE

    ½ cup unsifted all-purpose flour
    2 cups water
    ½ teaspoon garlic salt
    ¾ teaspoon salt
    ⅛ teaspoon ground ginger
    ⅛ teaspoon pepper
    1 tablespoon dried parsley flakes
    1 tablespoon Worcestershire sauce
    1 medium onion, chopped
    1 stalk celery, chopped
    1 can (16 oz.) whole kernel corn, drained
    1 can (8 oz.) tomato sauce
    1½ lbs. lamb shanks

1. Combine all ingredients except lamb shanks in 3-quart glass casserole. Add lamb shanks.
2. MICROWAVE-BAKE, covered, at 350° F. for 20 minutes; stir.
3. BAKE 45 to 60 minutes or until meat is tender. If desired, remove meat from bones before serving.   5 to 6 Servings

Very pretty and colorful.

IRISH STEW

    1 lb. lamb stew meat, cut into 1-inch cubes
    ¼ cup all-purpose flour
    ¼ cup butter or margarine
    2 cups water
    2 teaspoons instant beef bouillon
    ½ teaspoon salt
    ⅛ teaspoon thyme
    ⅛ teaspoon pepper
    1 stalk celery, sliced
    3 carrots, cut into 1-inch pieces
    1 green pepper, sliced
    3 medium onions, quartered
    3 medium potatoes, peeled and cubed
    1 package (10 oz.) frozen peas
    1 tablespoon dried parsley flakes

1. Coat meat with flour. Melt better in freezer-to-range glass ceramic Dutch oven over medium-high heat. Add meat and brown on all sides. Add remaining ingredients except peas and parsley.
2. MICROWAVE-BAKE, covered, at 350° F. for 15 minutes.
3. BAKE 45 minutes; stir in peas.
4. BAKE 8 to 10 minutes or until peas are cooked and meat is tender. Sprinkle with parsley before serving.   4 to 6 Servings

BROILED LAMB CHOPS

1. Arrange 5 loin lamp chops (1½ lbs.), cut 1 inch thick, on metal broiler pan.
2. MICROWAVE-BROIL 4 minutes; turn chops over.
3. MICROWAVE-BROIL 4 to 5 minutes or until desired doneness.   5 Servings

CRANBERRY-ORANGE LAMB CHOPS

    1 tablespoon butter or margarine
    4 lamb shoulder chops (about 2 lbs.)
    1 cup (8-oz. can) whole cranberry sauce
    ½ cup raisins
    ¼ cup water
    ½ teaspoon salt
    1 can (11 oz.) mandarin oranges, drained

1. Melt butter in 10-inch freezer-to-range glass ceramic skillet over medium heat. Add chops and brown on both sides. Top with cranberry sauce, raisins, water and salt.
2. MICROWAVE-BAKE, covered, at 350° F. for 10 minutes.
3. BAKE 30 to 40 minutes or until meat is tender. Stir in mandarin oranges.
4. MICROWAVE-BAKE 1 to 1½ minutes or until hot.   4 Servings

TIP • If using a homemade cranberry sauce that is quite thin, omit water.

Peaches and cinnamon add a refreshing flavor to lamb chops.

SPICY CHOPS AND PEACHES

    1 tablespoon butter or margarine
    6 lamb shoulder chops
    1 can (16 oz.) sliced peaches
    ¼ cup peach syrup
    1 tablespoon grated orange peel
    2 tablespoons packed brown sugar
    2 teaspoons cornstarch
    ½ teaspoon salt
    ¼ teaspoon cinnamon
    ¼ cup dry sherry

1. Melt butter in 10-inch freezer-to-range glass ceramic skillet over medium heat. Add chops and brown on both sides.
2. Drain peaches, reserving ¼ cup syrup. Combine syrup and remaining ingredients; add to chops along with peaches.
3. MICROWAVE, covered, 15 to 18 minutes or until done.   6 Servings

MINTED LAMB CHOPS

    ½ cup red wine
    1 clove garlic, finely chopped
    4 sprigs fresh mint, finely snipped
    5 to 6 rib or loin lamb chops

1. Combine wine, garlic and mint in shallow glass baking dish. Add chops, turning to coat with wine mixture. Let marinate for 1 hour, turning chops over once.
2. Arrange chops on metal broiler pan.
3. MICROWAVE-BROIL 4 minutes; turn chops over.
4. MICROWAVE-BROIL 4 to 5 minutes or until desired doneness.   5 to 6 Servings

LAMB CHOPS WITH GREEN GRAPES

    1 tablespoon butter or margarine
    6 lamb shoulder chops
    3 green onions, sliced
    ½ cup water
    1 tablespoon cornstarch
    1 teaspoon instant chicken bouillon
    1 teaspoon sugar
    ½ teaspoon salt
    1 cup green grapes

1. Melt butter in 10-inch freezer-to-range glass ceramic skillet over medium heat. Add chops and brown on both sides. Add onions.
2. Combine remaining ingredients except grapes; add to lamb chops.
3. MICROWAVE, covered, 15 to 18 minutes or until done. Add grapes.
4. MICROWAVE, covered, 1 to 2 minutes or until hot.   6 Servings

LAMB CHOPS WITH CURRIED RICE

    1½ cups quick-cooking rice
    1 small onion, chopped
    1 medium apple, chopped
    1 teaspoon salt
    1 teaspoon sugar
    ½ teaspoon garlic salt
    1½ to 2 teaspoons curry powder
    2 cups water
    4 to 5 rib or loin lamb chops

1. Combine all ingredients except chops in 8-inch square glass baking dish. Arrange chops on top. Season lightly with salt and pepper .
2. MICROWAVE-BAKE at 375° F. for 20 to 25 minutes or until done.   4 to 5 Servings

Veal

VEAL: Most cuts of veal are tender. Since veal is very young beef and the flavor is mild, it is often simmered in a flavorful sauce to enhance the flavor.

Cuts requiring short cooking times, like cutlets and round steak, can be cooked more quickly with the microwave-bake setting.

Larger pieces like roasts and cuts like stew meat where flavor needs to develop, start cooking with a microwave-bake technique and are then completed by simmering with a bake setting.

VEAL PARMIGIANA

  1½ lbs. veal cutlet or round steak
   ⅓ cup Parmesan cheese
   2 tablespoons dry bread crumbs
   1 egg, beaten
   3 tablespoons cooking oil
   1 medium onion, chopped
   1 can (8 oz.) tomato sauce
   ½ teaspoon salt
   ⅛ teaspoon pepper
   ⅛ teaspoon leaf oregano
   1 cup shredded Mozzarella cheese
   ¼ cup Parmesan cheese

1. Cut meat into 6 pieces. Pound to ¼-inch thickness. Combine ⅓ cup Parmesan cheese and the bread crumbs in shallow dish. Dip meat in egg, then coat with crumb mixture. Heat oil in frying pan over medium heat. Add meat one layer at a time and brown on both sides. Arrange in shallow 8-inch glass baking dish.
2. Add onion to frying pan and cook until tender. Stir in tomato sauce and seasonings. Sprinkle meat with Mozzarella cheese. Top with sauce, then sprinkle with ¼ cup Parmesan cheese.
3. MICROWAVE-BAKE at 350° F. for 14 to 15 minutes or until hot.   About 6 Servings

Pictured, top to bottom: Company Veal Stew and Veal Parmigiana, this page.

VEAL ROAST

  4 to 5-lb. veal rump roast
  1 medium onion, sliced
  1 cup sliced fresh mushrooms
  2 teaspoons salt
 ⅛ teaspoon pepper
 ½ cup dry white wine
  1 cup water
 ¼ cup all-purpose flour
 ¼ cup milk or light cream
  1 tablespoon soy sauce

1. Place roast fat-side-up in 3 or 4-quart glass casserole. Add onion, mushrooms, salt, pepper, wine and water.
2. MICROWAVE-BAKE, covered at 350° F. for 20 minutes.
3. BAKE 1¼ to 1½ hours or until meat thermometer inserted in center registers 170° F. Turn meat over once during cooking.
4. Remove roast to serving plate; set aside. Combine flour, milk and soy sauce; stir into pan juices.
5. MICROWAVE-BAKE 3 to 3½ minutes or until mixture boils. Slice roast and serve with sauce.   8 to 10 Servings

COMPANY VEAL STEW

  2 tablespoons butter or margarine
  1 lb. veal stew meat
 ½ green pepper, sliced
  1 stalk celery, chopped
  1 can (4 oz.) mushroom stems and pieces, drained
  1 cup water
 ¼ cup light cream
  1 tablespoon cornstarch
  1 teaspoon instant chicken bouillon
  1 teaspoon dried parsley flakes
 ½ teaspoon salt
 ½ teaspoon onion salt
Dash pepper

1. Melt butter in freezer-to-range glass ceramic skillet over medium-high heat. Add meat and brown on all sides. Stir in remaining ingredients.
2. MICROWAVE-BAKE, covered, at 350° F. for 10 minutes.
3. BAKE 50 to 60 minutes or until meat is tender. If desired, serve with buttered noodles.   4 to 5 Servings

TIP • If a glass ceramic skillet is not available, brown the meat in a frying pan. Then transfer to 2-quart glass casserole.

Variety Meats

VARIETY MEATS: Included here are recipes for the more tender variety meats which cook relatively quickly — liver, brains and kidneys. The larger organ meats like heart and tongue need long, slow simmering to become tender. This is best achieved on a burner over low heat.

The slow baking and the addition of vinegar help tenderize these beef kidneys.

BEEF KIDNEYS AND ONIONS

    1 lb. beef kidneys
    2 cups water
    ¼ cup butter or margarine
    2 medium onions, sliced
    1 cup water
    ½ teaspoon salt
    ½ teaspoon sugar
    2 tablespoons vinegar
    Dash pepper
    2 tablespoons cornstarch
    ¼ cup water

1. Slit and wash kidneys; remove and discard center membranes. Place kidneys in 1½-quart glass casserole; add 2 cups water.
2. MICROWAVE, covered, 5 minutes; let stand 30 minutes. Drain well. Cut into pieces; set aside.
3. MICROWAVE butter and onions in 1½-quart glass casserole 5 to 6 minutes or until onion is limp. Stir in kidneys, 1 cup water, the salt, sugar, vinegar and pepper.
4. MICROWAVE-BAKE, covered, at 350° F. for 10 minutes.
5. BAKE 45 to 50 minutes or until kidneys are tender.
6. Stir in a mixture of cornstarch and ¼ cup water.
7. MICROWAVE-BAKE, covered, 2½ to 3 minutes or until mixture boils and thickens.
                      4 to 5 Servings

Pictured: Liver Casserole and Brains in Browned Butter, this page.

Microwave cooking is used to precook the brains. Then they are browned until crispy in a conventional frying pan.

BRAINS IN BROWNED BUTTER

    ¾ lb. frozen brains
    4 cups water
    1 tablespoon vinegar
    ¼ cup butter or margarine
    Salt and pepper
    1 teaspoon dried parsley flakes

1. DEFROST brains about 5 minutes or just enough to loosen from container. Place in 1½-quart glass casserole; add water and vinegar.
2. MICROWAVE, covered, 16 to 18 minutes or until set and no longer pink. Drain and cool under cold water. Remove membranes and veins; pat dry with paper towels.
3. Melt butter in frying pan over medium heat until lightly browned. Add brains and brown on all sides; season with salt, pepper and parsley.
                      3 to 4 Servings

TIPS • Brains may be sliced and coated with flour before frying.

    • Sliced or chopped onion may be added when frying brains.

    • Frozen brains may also be loosened from container by placing under cold running water or microwaved 2½ to 3 minutes or until they just loosen.

LIVER CASSEROLE

    1 lb. beef liver
    ⅓ cup all-purpose flour
    ¼ cup butter or margarine
    4 medium onions, sliced
    1 cup sliced fresh mushrooms
    1 stalk celery, chopped
    ½ teaspoon salt
    Dash pepper
    1 can (12 oz.) mixed vegetable juice

1. Cut liver into serving pieces; coat with flour. Set aside. Melt butter in frying pan over medium heat; add liver and brown on both sides. Place in 2-quart glass casserole.
2. Add onions, mushrooms and celery to same frying pan; brown lightly. Spoon over liver. Stir in remaining ingredients including any remaining flour.
3. MICROWAVE-BAKE, uncovered, at 350° F. for 20 to 22 minutes or until tender.
                      5 to 6 Servings

TIPS • Substitute for mixed vegetable juice: 1½ cups tomato juice.

    • Substitute for fresh mushrooms: 4-oz. can mushroom stems and pieces, drained.

Eggs and Cheese

FRIED OR BAKED EGGS: Eggs cooked alone, like fried or baked eggs are difficult to cook with microwaves because the yolk and white cook at different speeds. The yolk can become very hard, while the white remains watery.

For fried eggs, we recommend using a frying pan on top of the range.

For baked eggs, microwave cooking is combined with a baking temperature to supplement and even the cooking.

Individual baked eggs in a sauce, topped with golden crumbs.

SHIRRED EGGS

  2 tablespoons butter or margarine
  ½ cup dry bread crumbs
  2 tablespoons Parmesan cheese
  1 can (10¾ oz.) condensed Cheddar cheese soup
  ¼ cup milk
  ⅛ teaspoon bouquet garni
  6 eggs
  Salt and pepper

1. MICROWAVE butter in small glass mixing bowl 1½ to 2 minutes or until melted. Stir in bread crumbs and Parmesan cheese; set aside.
2. Preheat oven to 300° F.
3. Combine soup, milk and bouquet garni in medium mixing bowl. Divide among six 5-oz. glass custard cups. Break an egg into sauce in each cup. Season with salt and pepper; sprinkle with reserved bread crumbs.
4. MICROWAVE-BAKE 5 to 6 minutes or until eggs are set. 6 Servings

TIP • Substitute for bouquet garni: leaf oregano.

Pictured: Quiche Lorraine, page 88.

SOUFFLES AND OMELETS: We have not included recipes for soufflés or omelets using combination cooking. In our testing we did not feel the addition of microwave cooking contributed to either the cooking speed or the end product. Soufflés are best cooked with the slower conventional bake setting and omelets are best cooked in a frying pan on top of the range.

HARD-COOKED EGGS: Microwave cooking should not be used for preparing hard-cooked eggs. The quick cooking of the egg and buildup of steam inside the shell may cause the egg to burst. These eggs require slow simmering water, best achieved on a conventional burner.

POACHED AND SCRAMBLED EGGS: The hot water used in poaching eggs helps even the cooking of the egg yolk and white and supplements the microwave cooking. The microwaves are used by both the water and the eggs.

For scrambled eggs, the yolk and white are combined, minimizing differences in cooking speed of the two parts. It is necessary to stir the eggs once during cooking since the edges cook faster than the center.

POACHED EGGS

1. MICROWAVE 1 cup warm tap water in 1-quart covered glass casserole 5 to 6 minutes or until steaming hot.
2. Break 1 to 4 eggs into hot water.
3. MICROWAVE, covered, 1½ to 3 minutes or until eggs are desired doneness.

As with conventional cooking, egg dishes may be difficult to wash after standing. We found that a vegetable spray-on coating applied to the dish before cooking made cleaning easier. If you wish to omit melting butter, just cut it into pieces and add along with milk.

SCRAMBLED EGGS

1. MICROWAVE butter or margarine (1 teaspoon per egg) in glass casserole until melted. Add eggs and milk (1 tablespoon milk per egg); mix with fork to scramble.
2. MICROWAVE, covered, just until set and moistened, stirring once during last half of cooking time:
      1 to 2 eggs — 2 to 3 minutes
      3 to 4 eggs — 5 to 6 minutes
      5 to 6 eggs — 7 to 8 minutes
3. Stir after cooking; season to taste.

EGG CASSEROLES: Many egg dishes adapt well to microwave cooking. Often a bake or broil heat is also added for browning a topping, crisping a crust or melting cheese. This additional source of heat helps even the cooking of egg dishes that need not be stirred during cooking.

Casseroles containing eggs are much easier to cook than eggs by themselves. The additional ingredients help even the cooking. Also, with most of these dishes, the yolk and white are combined so that the difference in cooking time of the two parts is eliminated.

The flavor and elegance of Eggs Benedict, but without the last minute fuss.

PARTY EGGS BENEDICT

4 English muffins, split
1 tablespoon butter or margarine
¼ cup dry bread crumbs
1 teaspoon dried parsley flakes
2 cups water
8 eggs
8 thin slices Canadian-style bacon or ham
8 slices tomato
½ cup mayonnaise or salad dressing
⅓ cup sour cream
1 teaspoon prepared mustard
1 tablespoon milk

1. Toast muffin halves under broiler until lightly browned. Arrange cut-side-up in 3-quart (13x9) glass baking dish; set aside.
2. MICROWAVE butter in small glass dish 1½ to 2 minutes or until melted. Stir in bread crumbs and parsley; set aside.
3. MICROWAVE water in shallow 8-inch square glass baking dish 6 to 7 minutes or until hot. Break eggs into water.
4. MICROWAVE, uncovered, 4 to 4½ minutes or until yolks are just about set.
5. Arrange bacon and tomato slices on muffins. Remove eggs from water with slotted spatula or spoon; place an egg on each tomato slice. Combine mayonnaise, sour cream, mustard and milk; spoon over eggs. Sprinkle with bread crumb mixture. (If desired, let eggs stand at room temperature up to an hour.)
6. MICROWAVE-BROIL 2 to 3 minutes or until hot and topping is lightly browned.

6 to 8 Servings

TIP • To double the amount, use 2 baking dishes, cook eggs in two batches and microwave-broil in step 6 for 3 to 4 minutes.

This recipe is especially appealing for a brunch or luncheon. Serve with broccoli or asparagus spears and fruit in season.

EGG AND SHRIMP BAKE

1 cup uncooked rice
2 tablespoons chopped chives
½ teaspoon salt
2 cups water
6 hard-cooked eggs
¼ cup mayonnaise or salad dressing
¼ teaspoon curry powder
¼ teaspoon paprika
¼ teaspoon salt
Dash pepper
2 tablespoons butter or margarine
2 tablespoons all-purpose flour
1 cup milk
½ cup shredded Cheddar cheese
1 can (10¾ oz.) condensed cream of shrimp soup
1 can (4½ oz.) shrimp, drained
1 tablespoon chopped chives

1. MICROWAVE rice, 2 tablespoons chives, ½ teaspoon salt and the water in covered 2-quart glass casserole 14 to 15 minutes or until rice is just about tender. Set aside.
2. Cut eggs in half lengthwise; remove yolks to small mixing bowl. Mash yolks along with mayonnaise, curry powder, paprika, ¼ teaspoon salt and pepper. Fill egg whites with yolk mixture. Fluff rice with fork; arrange eggs over rice and set aside.
3. MICROWAVE butter in 4-cup glass measure 1 to 1½ minutes or until melted. Stir in flour and milk.
4. MICROWAVE 6 to 8 minutes or until mixture boils, stirring once during last half of cooking time. Stir in remaining ingredients.
5. MICROWAVE 5 to 6 minutes or until hot. Pour over eggs and rice.
6. MICROWAVE, covered, 4 to 5 minutes or until hot. About 6 Servings

TIP • If desired, transfer cooked rice to shallow 2-quart (12x7) glass baking dish. Top with eggs and continue with step 3. Microwave uncovered in step 6.

Pictured: Party Eggs Benedict, this page.

BACON AND EGG BRUNCH

    1 package (12 oz.) frozen hash brown potatoes
    ½ teaspoon salt
    2 tablespoons chopped chives
    ⅓ cup sour cream
    ⅓ cup milk
    4 ozs. Canadian-style bacon, cut into 4 slices
    4 eggs
    Salt and pepper

1. Place frozen potatoes in 8-inch square glass baking dish.
2. MICROWAVE, covered with wax paper, 5 to 6 minutes or until completely thawed; drain off water if necessary. Stir in salt, chives, sour cream and milk.
3. Preheat oven to 400° F.
4. Arrange slices of bacon in a row down center of dish, overlapping slightly. Make four depressions on each side of bacon. Break egg into each. Season with salt and pepper.
5. BAKE 5 minutes. ✤
6. MICROWAVE-BAKE 5 to 6 minutes or until eggs are desired doneness.   **4 Servings**

    TIP • For 8 servings, double recipe using a 3-quart (13x9) glass baking dish. Microwave in step 1 for 8 to 9 minutes, bake in step 5 for 8 minutes, turn dish one-quarter turn and microwave-bake in step 6 for 7 to 8 minutes.

Serve this classic dish for lunch or supper.

QUICHE LORRAINE

    12 slices bacon
    9-inch unbaked pastry shell
    1½ cups shredded Swiss cheese
    2 green onions, chopped
    3 eggs, beaten
    1 cup whipping cream
    ½ cup milk
    ⅛ teaspoon pepper
    Dash cayenne pepper

1. MICROWAVE bacon in shallow glass baking dish 14 to 16 minutes or until crisp.
2. Preheat oven to 450° F.
3. Sprinkle cheese into pastry shell. Crumble bacon; add bacon and onions to pastry shell. Combine remaining ingredients in medium mixing bowl; pour over cheese mixture.
4. MICROWAVE-BAKE 7 minutes.
5. BAKE 6 to 7 minutes or until knife inserted near center comes out clean. Let stand 10 minutes before cutting.   **About 6 Servings**

DENVER BRUNCH CASSEROLE

    8 slices bacon, cut into pieces
    6 eggs
    ⅓ cup milk
    ½ cup mayonnaise or salad dressing
    1 medium tomato, chopped
    ¼ cup chopped pimiento
    ¼ cup chopped green pepper
    ¼ teaspoon salt

1. MICROWAVE bacon in 1½-quart (10x6) glass baking dish 10 to 12 minutes or until crisp; drain.
2. Preheat oven to 450° F.
3. Beat together eggs, milk and mayonnaise in medium mixing bowl; stir in remaining ingredients and pour over bacon.
4. MICROWAVE-BAKE 6 minutes.
5. BAKE 8 to 10 minutes or until knife inserted near center comes out clean. Let stand 10 minutes before cutting into squares.   **5 to 6 Servings**

Scrambled eggs rolled in tortillas and topped with colorful tomato sauce.

RANCH-STYLE EGGS

    2 to 3 tablespoons cooking oil
    8 flour or corn tortillas
    8 eggs
    ½ cup milk
    ½ teaspoon salt
    ⅛ teaspoon pepper
    ½ green pepper, finely chopped
    1 tablespoon butter or margarine
    1 can (15 oz.) tomato sauce
    ½ teaspoon chili powder
    ¼ teaspoon salt
    ⅛ teaspoon pepper
    1 cup shredded Cheddar cheese

1. Heat 1 tablespoon oil in medium frying pan over medium heat. Add tortillas, one at a time, and heat a few seconds on each side until softened. Add additional oil to frying pan as necessary.
2. Combine eggs, milk, salt and pepper in 1-quart glass casserole; beat well. Stir in green pepper and butter.
3. MICROWAVE, covered, 10 to 11 minutes or until set, stirring once during last half of cooking time. Stir after cooking. Fill tortillas with egg mixture and roll up. Place in 2-quart (12x7) glass baking dish. Combine tomato sauce, chili powder, salt and pepper; pour over filled tortillas. Sprinkle with cheese.
4. MICROWAVE-BROIL 4 to 5 minutes or until cheese is melted and mixture is hot.   **6 to 8 Servings**

CHEESE DISHES: Cheese dishes make good use of microwave cooking. The even heating from all sides melts the cheese with little chance of scorching or sticking. Some cheese dishes are combined with bake or broil heat when browning is desired.

Since there is little chance of sticking and scorching with microwave cooking, macaroni for macaroni and cheese can be added without precooking. The starches which cook from the macaroni help to thicken the sauce. This type of dish requires ample liquid and needs to be cooked covered to allow the macaroni to rehydrate. When the dish is cooked uncovered or when there is little additional liquid, the macaroni is first precooked.

Cheese curdles and separates if overcooked. When a mixture boils several minutes, it is best to add the cheese toward the end of the cooking time.

A welcome change for a meatless main course. Noodles and cheese — served like a pie and topped with a pretty tomato sauce.

NOODLE-OMELET PIE

    2 cups uncooked noodles
    1 cup creamed cottage cheese
    2 eggs
    1 cup shredded Cheddar cheese
    1 teaspoon salt
    ⅛ teaspoon pepper
    ¼ cup Parmesan cheese
    1 egg

1. Preheat oven to 350° F.
2. Cook noodles as directed on package; drain well. Stir in cottage cheese, 2 eggs, Cheddar cheese, salt and pepper. Turn into ungreased 9-inch glass pie plate. Beat together Parmesan cheese and 1 egg. Spoon over top of pie, spreading to cover.
3. BAKE 5 minutes. ✿
4. MICROWAVE-BAKE 5 to 7 minutes or until center is set. Let stand 10 minutes before cutting. Serve with Tomato-Mushroom or other favorite sauce. 5 to 6 Servings

TOMATO-MUSHROOM SAUCE

Combine 1 can (8 oz.) tomato sauce, 1 can (4 oz.) mushroom stems and pieces, drained, and ½ teaspoon dill weed in 2-cup glass measure. Microwave-bake at 350° F. for 5 to 6 minutes or until hot.

TIP • The heat is not necessary for cooking this sauce. It is only used because the oven is on for the noodle pie.

MACARONI AND CHEESE

    1 cup uncooked macaroni
    1 small onion, finely chopped
    2 tablespoons all-purpose flour
    1 teaspoon salt
    Dash Tabasco sauce
    1 cup milk
    1 cup water
    2 tablespoons butter or margarine
    1 cup shredded Cheddar cheese

1. Combine all ingredients except cheese in 2½-quart glass casserole.
2. MICROWAVE, covered, 17 to 18 minutes or until macaroni is tender. Stir in cheese until melted. 3 to 4 Servings

TOMATO AND CHEESE MACARONI

    5 slices bacon, cut into pieces
    1 small onion, finely chopped
    1 cup macaroni, cooked
    1 can (16 oz.) tomatoes, undrained
    1 teaspoon leaf basil
    ½ teaspoon salt
    Dash Tabasco sauce
    2 cups shredded processed cheese

1. MICROWAVE bacon and onion in 1½-quart glass casserole 6 to 7 minutes or until onion is limp. Stir in remaining ingredients except cheese. Sprinkle with cheese.
2. MICROWAVE-BAKE, uncovered, at 350° F. for 10 to 12 minutes or until hot and bubbly. 5 to 6 Servings

An American version of Swiss cheese fondue. Mildly flavored and creamy.

AMERICAN CHEESE FONDUE

    ¼ cup butter or margarine
    ¼ cup all-purpose flour
    1 cup milk
    1 lb. processed American cheese, cubed
    1 teaspoon onion salt
    ¼ cup dry white wine
    French bread, cubed

1. MICROWAVE butter in glass ceramic fondue pot or 1-quart glass casserole 2 to 2½ minutes or until melted. Stir in flour and milk.
2. MICROWAVE 5 to 6 minutes or until thickened, stirring once during last half of cooking time. Stir in cheese, onion salt and wine.
3. MICROWAVE 3½ to 4½ minutes or until cheese is melted. Serve by dipping French bread cubes into fondue. 6 to 8 Servings

TIP • Cherry tomatoes, ham cubes, apple wedges or vegetable sticks may also be used for dipping in the fondue.

Soups

HEATED SOUPS: Cooked soups are easily reheated using microwave cooking. Canned or leftover soup can be simply heated right in the bowl in which it will be served. Covering with a plate or similar cover helps retain the heat and speed the heating process. A larger amount of soup is best heated in a covered casserole.

CANNED SOUP

1. Divide contents of 10¾-oz. can condensed soup between 2 or 3 glass soup bowls. Add equal amounts of water to each. Cover with small glass plate.
2. MICROWAVE 6 to 7 minutes or until hot.

2 to 3 Servings

TIPS • For 4 to 6 servings, use 2 cans of soup and microwave 7 to 9 minutes.

• For one bowl of soup, microwave 3 to 3½ minutes.

Dry soup mixes need time to rehydrate after coming to a boil. We do not suggest using individual soup bowls because the soup may boil over.

DEHYDRATED SOUP MIX

1. Prepare 1 envelope of soup mix in 4-cup glass measure or 1 or 2-quart glass casserole, using amount of liquid called for on package.
2. MICROWAVE, covered, about 10 minutes or until mixture comes to a boil. Let stand, covered, at least 5 minutes to allow food pieces to rehydrate.   3 to 4 Servings

Pictured, clockwise: Ground Beef-Vegetable Soup, page 92, Leek Soup, page 93 and French Onion Soup, page 93.

SOUP-FOR-A-CUP MIX

1. Combine ¾ cup water and 1 envelope soup-for-a-cup mix in glass cup.
2. MICROWAVE 5 to 5½ minutes or until hot. Stir before serving.

TIP • For 2 cups of soup, microwave about 6 to 7 minutes.

ASPARAGUS SOUP WITH CROUTONS

1 can (10¾ oz.) condensed cream of asparagus soup
1 can (15 oz.) cut asparagus, undrained
1 cup light cream

Croutons
2 slices white bread
2 teaspoons anchovy paste
Garlic powder
2 tablespoons butter or margarine

1. Combine soup, asparagus and cream in 2-quart glass casserole; mix well.
2. MICROWAVE, covered, 12 to 15 minutes or until hot; set aside.
3. Remove crust from bread. Spread bread slices with anchovy paste; sprinkle with garlic powder. Cut into strips or cubes.
4. MICROWAVE butter in shallow glass casserole or pie plate about 2 minutes or until melted. Stir in bread pieces and toss to coat with butter.
5. MICROWAVE 8 to 10 minutes or until golden brown. Serve croutons with soup.

5 to 6 Servings

BEANIE-WIENIE SOUP

¼ cup butter or margarine
¼ cup all-purpose flour
1 can (15½ oz.) kidney beans, undrained
1 can (15½ oz.) cut green beans, undrained
1 can (10¾ oz.) condensed tomato soup
1 can (6 oz.) tomato paste
1 lb. wieners, sliced
1 teaspoon salt
½ to 1 teaspoon chili powder
4 cups water

1. MICROWAVE butter in 3-quart glass casserole 2½ to 3 minutes or until melted. Stir in flour and remaining ingredients.
2. MICROWAVE, covered, 20 to 22 minutes or until mixture boils.   8 to 10 Servings

SIMMERED SOUPS: Most simmered soups included here require fairly short simmering times to cook the various ingredients. A cover speeds the heating and cooking of these soups and microwave cooking is the only heat necessary. A soup that begins with a soup bone requires several hours of simmering and is most easily cooked on a burner.

OYSTER STEW

  ¼ **cup butter or margarine**
  1 **small onion, finely chopped**
  ¼ **cup all-purpose flour**
  2 **cups milk**
  1 **cup whipping cream**
  1 **cup or a half-pint oysters with liquid**
  2 **teaspoons salt**
  2 **teaspoons Worcestershire sauce**

1. MICROWAVE butter and onion in covered 2-quart glass casserole 4 minutes; stir in flour and remaining ingredients.
2. MICROWAVE, covered, 12 to 14 minutes or until mixture boils and thickens, stirring once during last half of cooking time.

                                       4 to 6 Servings

CLAM CHOWDER

  5 **slices bacon, cut into pieces**
  2 **cups (4 med.) peeled, cubed potato**
  1 **medium onion, sliced**
  ¼ **cup all-purpose flour**
  ½ **teaspoon salt**
  ⅛ **teaspoon leaf thyme**
  ⅛ **teaspoon paprika**
  ⅛ **teaspoon pepper**
  2 **cans (6½ ozs. each) minced clams, undrained**
  3 **cups milk**

1. MICROWAVE bacon in 3-quart glass casserole 6 to 7 minutes or until crisp; stir in potato and onion.
2. MICROWAVE, covered, about 15 minutes or until potatoes are just tender. Stir in flour and remaining ingredients.
3. MICROWAVE, covered, 13 to 15 minutes or until hot.   5 to 6 Servings

SPLIT PEA SOUP WITH HAM

  1½-**lb. ham hock**
  1 **medium onion, sliced**
  1 **carrot, sliced**
  1 **tablespoon Worcestershire sauce**
  4 **cups water**
  1 **cup (8 ozs.) dried split peas**
  1 **cup water or milk**
Salt and pepper

1. Combine ham hock, onion, carrot, Worcestershire sauce and 4 cups water in 3-quart glass casserole.
2. MICROWAVE, covered, 20 minutes. Stir in peas.
3. MICROWAVE, covered, 40 to 45 minutes or until peas and meat are tender. Remove ham hock and cut meat from bone; return meat to soup. Stir in 1 cup water or milk and season to taste with salt and pepper.
4. MICROWAVE, covered, 5 minutes or until hot.

                                       6 to 8 Servings

GROUND BEEF-VEGETABLE SOUP

  1 **lb. ground beef**
  1 **large onion, finely chopped**
  1½ **cups (5 ozs.) sliced fresh mushrooms**
  1 **can (16 oz.) tomatoes, undrained**
  1 **can (10¾ oz.) condensed Minestrone soup**
  1 **can (10¾ oz.) condensed tomato soup**
  4 **cups water**
  1 **teaspoon Worcestershire sauce**
  ½ **teaspoon salt**
  ½ **teaspoon chili powder**
  ¼ **teaspoon pepper**
  ⅛ **teaspoon garlic salt**

1. Crumble meat into 4-quart glass casserole. Add onion and mushrooms.
2. MICROWAVE 8 to 10 minutes or until meat is set. Stir to break meat into pieces; drain. Stir in remaining ingredients.
3. MICROWAVE, covered, 20 to 22 minutes or until soup is hot.   8 to 10 Servings

TIPS • Substitute for fresh mushrooms: 4-oz. can mushroom stems and pieces, drained.

    • If desired, add 1 cup cooked noodles or macaroni.

POTATO SOUP

2 cups (4 med.) peeled, cubed potato
1 medium onion, chopped
2 cups water
1 cup milk
¼ cup all-purpose flour
1 teaspoon salt
2 teaspoons instant chicken bouillon
1 teaspoon dried parsley flakes
⅛ teaspoon pepper
2 tablespoons butter or margarine

1. MICROWAVE potato, onion and water in covered 2-quart glass casserole 16 to 18 minutes or until potato is just tender. Combine milk and flour; stir into vegetable mixture along with remaining ingredients.

2. MICROWAVE, covered, 8 to 10 minutes or until soup boils. If desired, thin with additional milk.   5 to 6 Servings

LEEK SOUP

2 large leeks
½ cup butter or margarine
¼ cup all-purpose flour
1 teaspoon salt
¼ teaspoon nutmeg
⅛ teaspoon pepper
3 cups milk
1 cup chicken broth

1. Slice leeks thinly (including green portion). Place in 3-quart glass casserole; add butter.

2. MICROWAVE, covered, 9 to 10 minutes or until leeks are soft. Stir in flour and remaining ingredients.

3. MICROWAVE, covered, 20 to 22 minutes or until soup is steaming hot, stirring occasionally during last 5 minutes of cooking time.   5 to 6 Servings

TIP • Leeks are a difficult vegetable to clean as dirt tends to collect inside the layers. To ease cleaning, cut down through the green part to the bulb and open up. Place under cold running water to easily remove the dirt.

FRENCH ONION SOUP

¼ cup butter or margarine
3 medium onions, chopped
2 tablespoons soy sauce
1 tablespoon Worcestershire sauce
½ teaspoon paprika
Dash pepper
Dash Tabasco sauce
4 cups beef bouillon

1. MICROWAVE butter and onions in 4-quart glass casserole 10 to 12 minutes or until onions are tender. Stir in remaining ingredients.

2. MICROWAVE, covered, 10 to 12 minutes or until piping hot.   4 to 6 Servings

TIPS • If more browning is desired, cook onions in butter in glass ceramic casserole over medium-high heat. Then add remaining ingredients and continue with step 2.

• If desired, broil slices of French bread on each side until golden brown. Sprinkle with shredded Swiss cheese; broil until cheese is melted. Top each bowl of soup with a slice.

• For beef bouillon, use canned bouillon or combine 4 teaspoons instant beef bouillon and 4 cups water.

SPINACH SOUP

10 ozs. (8 cups) fresh spinach
¼ cup butter or margarine
1 small onion, chopped
1 can (10¾ oz.) condensed chicken broth
¼ cup all-purpose flour
½ teaspoon salt
⅛ teaspoon nutmeg
⅛ teaspoon pepper
4 cups water
1 cup light cream

1. MICROWAVE spinach, butter and onion in covered 3-quart glass casserole 10 to 12 minutes or until spinach is limp. Transfer mixture to blender container; add chicken broth and process at high speed until smooth. Return to casserole. Stir in flour and remaining ingredients.

2. MICROWAVE, covered, 20 to 22 minutes or until mixture boils.   6 to 8 Servings

TIP • Substitute for fresh spinach: 10-oz. package frozen chopped spinach.

Sandwiches

HOT SANDWICHES: The quick heating of this type of sandwich is easiest using just microwave cooking. The filling will determine the time needed for heating. Thinly-sliced meats heat more quickly and the bread is less likely to be overcooked than with thicker-sliced meats. The buns are placed directly on the oven racks. If they are placed on a plate or pan, the moisture from the roll will condense on the plate and make the bottom of the bun soggy. If conventional heat is used along with the microwave cooking, the buns can be placed on a baking pan or dish. Be careful not to overheat sandwiches. Even when the filling is very hot, the bun may not feel especially warm.

HOT DOGS

1. Place a wiener in each hot dog bun. Arrange buns on oven rack.
2. MICROWAVE until the wiener feels warm:
   - 1 hot dog — ¾ to 1 minute
   - 3 hot dogs — 2 to 2½ minutes
   - 6 hot dogs — 2½ to 3 minutes

TACOS

- 1 lb. ground beef
- ½ cup chopped onion
- ½ cup catsup
- 1 teaspoon salt
- 1 teaspoon leaf oregano
- 1 to 2 teaspoons chili powder
- Dash Tabasco sauce
- 8 to 10 taco shells
- 1 cup shredded Cheddar cheese
- 1 cup shredded lettuce
- 1 tomato, chopped

1. Crumble meat into 1-quart casserole; add onion.
2. MICROWAVE 8 to 8½ minutes or until meat is set. Stir to break meat into pieces; drain. Stir in catsup and seasonings.
3. MICROWAVE 3 to 3½ minutes or until flavors are blended. Spoon meat filling into taco shells. Top with cheese, lettuce and tomato.   8 to 10 Tacos

Pictured, top to bottom: Oven-Grilled Reuben Sandwich, page 96, Wieners in a Wrap, page 99, Sliced Meat Sandwich and Poor Boy Sandwich, this page.

Sliced, cooked meat sandwiches can be quickly heated using microwave cooking. The amount of filling and the thickness of the meat slices determine the time necessary to heat.

SLICED MEAT SANDWICHES

1. Place 3 to 4 thin slices cooked meat or poultry in a split hamburger or sandwich bun. Arrange buns directly on oven rack.
2. MICROWAVE 1 or 2 buns about 1 minute; 3 or 4 buns about 2 minutes or until filling steams when top of bun is lifted.

FISHWICHES

- **8 hot dog buns, split**
- **Tartar sauce**
- **8 frozen, breaded precooked fish sticks**

1. Spread buns with tartar sauce. Place 1 fish stick in each bun. Arrange buns on oven rack.
2. MICROWAVE 4 to 4½ minutes or until hot.
                                           8 Sandwiches

Foil is used as the baking pan for this sandwich.

POOR BOY SANDWICH

- 1 loaf French bread, unsliced
- 1½ cups shredded Swiss cheese
- ⅓ cup salad dressing or mayonnaise
- ¼ cup pickle relish, drained
- 1 teaspoon prepared mustard
- 4 ozs. sliced salami
- 4 ozs. sliced turkey
- 3 medium tomatoes, sliced
- **Pitted olives**

1. Preheat oven to 450° F.
2. Cut French bread horizontally into 3 slices. Spread bottom and middle slices with mixture of Swiss cheese, salad dressing, relish and mustard.
3. Arrange salami on bottom slice; top with second slice. Arrange turkey and tomato slices on second slice; cover with top slice of bread. Secure layers with long wooden skewers; garnish with olives.
4. Cut a strip of 12-inch wide foil the length of the French loaf. Fold the strip of foil in half lengthwise. Place sandwich on foil and set on oven rack.
5. MICROWAVE-BAKE 4 to 5 minutes or until hot. Cut into serving pieces.   6 to 8 Servings

TIP • Soaking wooden skewers in water will prevent them from browning during baking.

GRILLED SANDWICHES: The metal broiler pan works best for most oven-grilled sandwiches. The openness of the rack on the broiler pan helps prevent the bottom side of the sandwich from becoming soggy. Although the metal pan does change the microwave cooking pattern, the cooking from microwaves is still very adequate to help heat the filling while the broiler is toasting the bread. This microwave-broil technique assures a hot filling by the time the bread is toasted.

Often the recipe will indicate that the rack should be raised to the second position. However, if the recipe does not indicate a change, use the normal third rack position.

Use this timetable as a guide for grilling sandwiches using your favorite fillings. The number of sandwiches does not affect the time needed.

GRILLED SANDWICHES

1. Place oven rack in second position. Place sandwiches on metal broiler pan.
2. BROIL 3 to 4 minutes or until toasted; turn over.
3. MICROWAVE-BROIL 1 to 1½ minutes or until golden brown.

An all-time favorite, quickly grilled with the broiler.

OVEN-GRILLED REUBEN SANDWICHES

  8 slices pumpernickel or other dark bread
  8 ozs. thinly sliced corned beef
  1 can (8 oz.) sauerkraut, well drained
  ¼ cup Thousand Island salad dressing
  4 slices Swiss cheese
  2 tablespoons butter or margarine

1. Top 4 slices bread with corned beef, sauerkraut, salad dressing and cheese. Top with remaining bread slices.
2. MICROWAVE butter in small glass dish about 2 minutes or until melted. Brush both sides of sandwiches with butter; arrange on metal broiler pan.
3. Move oven rack to second position.
4. BROIL 2½ to 3 minutes or until toasted; turn sandwiches over.
5. MICROWAVE-BROIL 1 to 1½ minutes or until toasted and filling is hot.   4 Sandwiches

OPEN-FACED SANDWICHES: Toasting the bread helps prevent the base of open-faced sandwiches from becoming soggy. Since these are microwave-broiled on one side only, they are often placed further from the heat than grilled sandwiches. This way the topping will not become too brown before the sandwich is heated. The use of microwave cooking along with the broiler helps with the heating.

TANGY TURKEY COMBOS

  6 slices rye bread, toasted
  2 tablespoons salad dressing or mayonnaise
  6 slices boiled ham
  6 slices Swiss cheese
  6 slices cooked turkey or chicken
  3 tomatoes, sliced

Bleu 'n Swiss Dressing
  ½ cup shredded Swiss cheese
  ½ cup salad dressing or mayonnaise
  ¼ cup crumbled bleu cheese
  ¼ cup whipping cream
  ½ teaspoon dried parsley flakes

1. Spread salad dressing on toasted bread slices and arrange on metal broiler pan. Top with ham, cheese, turkey and tomato slices.
2. Mix together dressing ingredients in small mixing bowl; spoon onto sandwiches.
3. MICROWAVE-BROIL 3½ to 4 minutes or until hot and lightly browned.   6 Sandwiches

Apple and curry are the delicious tasting surprises in these sandwiches.

TURKEY SANDWICH SURPRISES

  1 tart apple, peeled and shredded
  ½ cup salad dressing or mayonnaise
  ¼ teaspoon curry powder
  6 slices bread, toasted and buttered
Sliced cooked turkey or chicken
Green pepper strips
Sliced ripe olives, if desired

1. Combine apple, salad dressing and curry powder in small mixing bowl.
2. Arrange toast on metal broiler pan. Top with turkey slices and apple mixture, spreading apple mixture to cover turkey. Garnish with green pepper and olives.
3. MICROWAVE-BROIL 3½ to 4 minutes or until hot.   6 Sandwiches

Pictured: Hamburger on a Bun, this page.

An unusual, but super easy way to make hamburgers. Sure to be a favorite with kids of any age.

HAMBURGER ON A BUN

   6 slices bread, toasted, or 6 small
      hamburger buns, split
   Prepared mustard or catsup
   1 lb. lean ground beef
   1 small onion, finely chopped
   ½ cup shredded Cheddar cheese
   1 teaspoon salt
   1 teaspoon dried parsley flakes
   ¼ teaspoon pepper

1. Spread one side of toasted bread or cut side of hamburger buns with mustard or catsup.
2. Mix remaining ingredients; spread over bread, covering to edge. Arrange meat-side-up on metal broiler pan.
3. MICROWAVE-BROIL 5 to 6 minutes or until meat is done.   6 Servings

SLOPPY JOES

   1 lb. ground beef
   1 small onion, chopped
   ⅔ cup barbecue sauce
   2 tablespoons dried parsley flakes
   1 tablespoon soy sauce
   1 teaspoon sugar
   1 teaspoon salt
   ½ teaspoon ginger, if desired
   Dash pepper

1. Crumble meat into 1-quart glass casserole; add onion.
2. MICROWAVE 8 to 8½ minutes or until meat is set. Stir to break meat into pieces; drain. Stir in remaining ingredients.
3. MICROWAVE, covered, 5 to 6 minutes or until flavors are blended. Serve over cornbread or spoon between split and toasted hamburger buns.   4 to 6 Servings

BAKED SANDWICHES: Combination cooking is most common with this type of sandwich. The heat browns and toasts the outside while the microwaves speed the heating and cooking of the interior.

With small individual sandwiches, the bake step sometimes precedes the combination cooking. This allows the dough to brown without over-cooking the inside of the sandwich.

Chicken and dressing — the makings for a sandwich, served like a casserole.

SOUPER BAKED SANDWICH

   1 small onion, finely chopped
  ¼ cup chopped celery
1½ cups milk
   1 can (10¾ oz.) condensed cream of
     mushroom soup
   2 eggs
   1 teaspoon dry mustard
  ¾ teaspoon salt
  ¼ teaspoon pepper
   3 cups diced cooked chicken or turkey
   3 cups herb-seasoned stuffing mix
   1 cup shredded Cheddar cheese

1. MICROWAVE onion and celery in covered medium glass mixing bowl 4 to 5 minutes or until just about tender.
2. Preheat oven to 450° F.
3. Blend milk, soup, eggs and seasonings into onion mixture; stir in chicken.
4. Arrange stuffing mix in greased 8-inch square glass baking dish; top with chicken mixture. Stir lightly to combine with stuffing. Sprinkle with cheese.
5. MICROWAVE-BAKE 10 to 12 minutes or until knife inserted near center comes out clean.   6 to 8 Servings

A meal in a crust. Serve like a sandwich or top with favorite cream sauce and serve with a fork.

TUNA PASTIES

   1 package (11 oz.) pie crust mix
   1 package (9 oz.) frozen cut green beans
   1 can (6½ oz.) tuna, drained
   1 medium potato, peeled and shredded
   1 cup shredded Cheddar cheese

  ¼ cup chopped onion
  ¼ cup tartar sauce
  ½ teaspoon garlic salt
  ¼ teaspoon pepper

1. Prepare pastry as directed on package; divide into 8 portions.
2. MICROWAVE green beans in covered 1½-quart glass casserole 3 minutes or until thawed; drain. Stir in remaining ingredients; set aside.
3. Preheat oven to 450° F.
4. Roll out each pastry portion to form a 7-inch circle. Spread about ½ cup tuna mixture to within ½-inch of edge of each circle. Moisten edge with water. Fold pastry circles in half, sealing edges with fork. Arrange on ungreased metal baking sheet. Prick tops with fork.
5. MICROWAVE-BAKE 12 to 14 minutes or until golden brown.   8 Pasties

A complete meal-in-a-dish. Good served with fruit salad.

TUNA SANDWICH BAKE

  ⅓ cup butter or margarine
  12 slices bread
   1 package (10 oz.) frozen peas
   1 can (6½ oz.) tuna, drained
   1 small onion, finely chopped
  ½ cup shredded Swiss cheese
  ½ teaspoon salt
   1 can (10¾ oz.) condensed cream of
     mushroom soup
   4 eggs
   2 cups milk

1. MICROWAVE butter in 3-quart (13x9) glass baking dish 2½ to 3 minutes or until melted.
2. Preheat oven to 450° F.
3. Brush melted butter on one side of each bread slice; arrange 6 slices, buttered-side-up, in baking dish.
4. Combine peas, tuna, onion, cheese and salt. Spread over bread in baking dish. Cover with remaining bread slices, buttered-side-up. Beat together soup, eggs and milk; pour over sandwiches.
5. MICROWAVE-BAKE 10 minutes.
6. BAKE 10 to 12 minutes or until knife inserted near center comes out clean.   6 Sandwiches

TIP • If frozen peas are in a solid block, microwave 2 to 3 minutes or until they can be separated.

Familiar flavors in a special shape.

HAM AND CHEESE WHEELS

> 1 package (8 oz.) refrigerated crescent rolls
> 4 slices processed American cheese, cut into quarters
> 8 slices boiled ham (4x4-inch size)
> Catsup or mustard
> Melted butter or margarine
> Poppy seed

1. Preheat oven to 450° F.
2. Divide dough for rolls into 8 squares. Top each with a piece of cheese, slice of ham and another piece of cheese. Spread with catsup or mustard.
3. Cut diagonally through layers from each corner to within ½ inch of center. Fold every other point to center, overlapping and pinching edges to seal; secure center with toothpick. Arrange on ungreased metal baking sheet. Brush with butter; sprinkle with poppy seed.
4. BAKE 6 minutes. ✿
5. MICROWAVE-BAKE 2 to 3 minutes or until lightly browned.　　8 Sandwiches

So gooey and good you must eat it with a fork.

DEEP-DISH PIZZA SANDWICH

> 1 lb. ground beef
> 1 can (15 oz.) tomato sauce
> 1 teaspoon leaf oregano
> 2 cups biscuit mix
> 1 egg
> ⅔ cup milk
> 2 cups shredded Mozzarella cheese
> 1 can (4 oz.) mushroom stems and pieces, drained
> ¼ cup Parmesan cheese

1. Crumble meat into 1½-quart glass casserole.
2. MICROWAVE, uncovered, 8 to 8½ minutes or until meat is set. Stir to break meat into pieces, drain. Stir in half the tomato sauce and the oregano; set aside.
3. Preheat oven to 400° F.
4. Mix together biscuit mix, egg and milk to form a soft dough. Spread in greased 3-quart (13x9) glass baking dish.
5. Pour remaining tomato sauce over dough. Layer with half of Mozzarella cheese, the meat mixture, mushrooms and remaining Mozzarella cheese; sprinkle with Parmesan cheese.
6. MICROWAVE-BAKE 10 to 12 minutes or until done. Serve cut into squares.　6 to 8 Servings

WIENERS IN A WRAP

> 8 wieners
> 8 strips Cheddar cheese
> 1 package (8 oz.) refrigerated crescent rolls

1. Preheat oven to 450° F.
2. Slit wieners lengthwise, but do not cut all the way through. Fit strips of cheese into slits in wieners. Separate crescent roll dough into individual rolls. Place a wiener at wide end of each piece of dough; roll up toward narrow end. Arrange on ungreased metal baking sheet.
3. BAKE 7 minutes. ✿
4. MICROWAVE-BAKE 2 to 2½ minutes or until lightly browned.　　8 Sandwiches

A metal pizza pan can be used for baking this recipe.

PIZZA

> ½ cup hot water
> 1 tablespoon butter or margarine
> 1½ to 1¾ cups unsifted all-purpose flour
> 1 tablespoon sugar
> ½ teaspoon salt
> 1 package active dry yeast
> 1 egg

Topping
> 1 can (8 oz.) tomato sauce
> ½ teaspoon leaf oregano or Italian seasoning
> Sliced salami or pepperoni
> Sliced ripe or green olives
> Sliced mushrooms
> Green pepper strips
> 2 cups shredded Mozzarella cheese

1. Combine water, butter, ¾ cup flour, the sugar, salt, dry yeast and egg in medium mixing bowl. Beat well. Stir in remaining ¾ to 1 cup flour to form a stiff dough. Knead on floured surface until smooth, about 5 minutes.
2. Preheat oven to 475° F.
3. Press dough with buttered fingers into 14-inch metal pizza pan. Spread tomato sauce over dough; sprinkle with oregano. Add favorite cooked meat, olives, and vegetables. Sprinkle with cheese.
4. MICROWAVE-BAKE 8 to 9 minutes or until crust is well browned.　　14-inch Pizza

TIP • Substitute for pizza pan: a 15x10x1-inch metal baking pan.

Vegetables

FRESH VEGETABLES: A small amount of water is usually necessary to provide steam for cooking vegetables. Covering them retains the steam and speeds cooking.

Microwave cooking is usually the only cooking necessary unless a drying effect is desired, such as with baked potatoes.

The larger, stem end of some vegetables needs longer cooking than the flower end. Placing the stem end in water and toward the outside of the dish will help to properly distribute the cooking of these two parts.

Vegetables continue to cook for a few minutes after being removed from the oven. For the best finished vegetable, remove just before it reaches the doneness desired. Then allow it to finish cooking during the standing time.

For fresh vegetable cooking times, see directions given with each vegetable.

FROZEN VEGETABLES: There is usually enough moisture on frozen vegetables so that no additional liquid is necessary. Covering retains the heat and speeds cooking.

Plastic cooking pouches can be used with microwave cooking. The pouch is slit on the top so that steam can escape as the vegetable heats. If combination cooking is being used, the pouch should be emptied into a covered casserole. When the oven is hot but microwave cooking only is being used, the pouch should be placed in another baking dish so that it does not rest directly on the hot oven rack.

Sometimes it is convenient to cook frozen vegetables right in the cardboard package. This is especially true when you want to thaw or cook the vegetable before adding it to another mixture. Only microwave cooking should be used when cooking in the packages.

Cooking Times for Frozen Vegetables:
1 package or pouch — microwave 10 to 12 minutes in 1-quart covered glass casserole
2 packages or pouches — microwave 14 to 16 minutes in 2-quart covered glass casserole

CANNED VEGETABLES: Since these vegetables are already cooked, they just need to be heated before serving. When using microwave cooking, you can do this heating right in the dish that will be used for serving. Covering will speed the heating and eliminate the need to stir.

The canning liquid may be left on for heating or drained. Seasonings are added after draining the excess liquid.

Pictured, clockwise: Crunchy Potato Salad Boats, page 110, Corn-in-the Husk, page 108, Zucchini Combo, page 115 and Mustard-Glazed Broccoli, page 104.

ARTICHOKES

PREPARATION: Wash thoroughly. Cut off 1 inch straight across top; remove any loose leaves around bottom. Remove thorns on each leaf by clipping about ½ inch off leaf tips. Dip cut edges in lemon juice to prevent darkening.

COOKING METHOD: Place upright in covered glass casserole. After cooking, remove prickly area in center with a spoon.

TIME: 1 or 2 artichokes — microwave 8 to 10 minutes
3 or 4 artichokes — microwave 15 to 19 minutes

SEASONINGS: Cream, Hollandaise or Mornay sauce; butter, lemon juice or nutmeg.

ASPARAGUS

PREPARATION: Wash thoroughly to remove dirt and sand. Snap off base of stalks, discarding base. Leave spears whole or cut or break into 1 to 2-inch pieces.

COOKING METHOD: Use a shallow glass casserole covered with lid or plastic wrap for spears, a covered casserole for pieces. Add 3 to 4 tablespoons water.

TIME: 1 lb. (about 25 stalks) — microwave 9 to 11 minutes
1½ lbs. (about 36 stalks) — microwave 12 to 14 minutes

SEASONINGS: Cheese, cream, Hollandaise or mustard sauce; butter, chives, bacon, nutmeg, toasted almonds or water chestnuts.

BUTTER-GLAZED ASPARAGUS

2 tablespoons butter or margarine
3 tablespoons slivered almonds
1 lb. fresh asparagus, cut into 1-inch pieces
¼ teaspoon salt
⅛ teaspoon lemon pepper seasoning

1. MICROWAVE butter and almonds in 1-quart glass casserole 12 to 14 minutes or until almonds are lightly toasted.

2. Add asparagus; toss lightly to coat with butter.

3. MICROWAVE, covered, 7 to 8 minutes or until desired doneness. Season with salt and seasoning.   3 to 4 Servings

TIP • Substitute for fresh asparagus: 8 or 10-oz. package frozen cut asparagus or asparagus spears. Cook uncovered in step 3, stirring once.

DRIED BEANS, PEAS AND LENTILS: Most dried beans and peas need long slow simmering to rehydrate and become tender. This can be done by simmering on a burner or by using microwave cooking and an uncovered casserole. Because of the amount of water necessary to cook the beans, care should be taken to use a casserole dish large enough to avoid boiling over.

Since lentils cook more quickly than other dried beans and peas, they require less special care.

Microwaves are used to precook the beans in this recipe. Then they are used to supplement the long, slow baking that is necessary to develop the flavor of baked beans.

OVEN BAKED BEANS

1 lb. (2 cups) dried navy beans
6 cups water
¼ cup packed brown sugar
¼ cup chopped onion
¼ cup chili sauce
¼ cup molasses
1½ teaspoons salt
3 slices bacon, cut into pieces
1 cup water

1. Rinse beans. Combine beans and 6 cups water in 3-quart glass casserole. Cover and let stand 12 hours or overnight.
2. MICROWAVE, uncovered, 45 minutes.
3. Stir in remaining ingredients.
4. MICROWAVE-BAKE, covered, at 300° F. for 10 minutes.
5. BAKE, covered, 3 to 4 hours or until beans are tender and flavorful, stirring once or twice. If necessary, add ½ to 1 cup additional water.   About 8 Servings

TIP • To eliminate overnight presoaking, combine beans and water in 3-quart casserole. Microwave, covered, 15 minutes. Let stand 1 hour. Continue with step 2.

A new look and taste to an old-time standby, pork and beans.

SOUTHERN BAKED BEANS

3 slices bacon, cut into pieces
1 can (31 oz.) pork and beans
1 can (15½ oz.) cut green beans, drained
1 tablespoon honey or molasses
1 tablespoon prepared mustard
1 teaspoon dried parsley flakes
1 can (3 oz.) French-fried onion rings

1. MICROWAVE bacon in 1½ or 2-quart glass casserole 6 to 7 minutes or until crisp. Stir in remaining ingredients except onion rings; arrange onion rings on top.
2. MICROWAVE 10 to 12 minutes or until hot and bubbly.   5 to 6 Servings

Lentils are similar to dried beans, but require no presoaking. This hearty casserole is ready to serve in less than an hour. Just serve with pickles and a crisp salad.

LENTIL AND SAUSAGE CASSEROLE

1 cup (½ lb.) dried lentils
2½ cups water
1 lb. fresh pork sausage
1 medium onion, chopped
1 can (12 oz.) whole kernel corn, drained
¼ cup chili sauce
2 tablespoons sliced pimiento
1 tablespoon Worcestershire sauce
½ teaspoon salt
⅛ teaspoon pepper
1 clove garlic, finely chopped

1. Combine lentils and water in 2-quart glass casserole; cover. Crumble sausage into 1½-quart glass baking dish; add onion.
2. MICROWAVE both dishes 14 to 15 minutes, stirring once. Drain sausage; set aside.
3. MICROWAVE lentil mixture 15 minutes more or until the lentils are tender. Stir sausage and remaining ingredients into lentils.
4. MICROWAVE, covered, 10 to 12 minutes or until flavors are blended.   6 to 8 Servings

BEANS — Green, Wax and Lima

PREPARATION: Wash green and wax beans thoroughly; remove stem and tip ends. Leave whole, cut lengthwise into strips or break or cut into 1 to 2-inch pieces. With lima beans, remove beans from shell and wash thoroughly.

COOKING METHOD: Place in covered glass casserole. Add ¼ cup water.

TIME: 1 lb. (4 cups) — microwave 16 to 18 minutes
2 lbs. (8 cups) — microwave 20 to 22 minutes

SEASONINGS: Cheese, cream or mustard sauce; butter, bacon, nutmeg, onions, toasted almonds or water chestnuts.

SUNNY GREEN BEANS

1 package (10 oz.) frozen French-cut green beans
¼ cup sunflower seeds
¼ cup butter or margarine
½ teaspoon leaf oregano
¼ teaspoon garlic salt
½ tablespoon cornstarch
2 tablespoons Parmesan cheese

1. MICROWAVE green beans in package 3 minutes or until thawed; drain.
2. MICROWAVE sunflower seeds, butter and seasonings in 1-quart glass casserole 3 to 3½ minutes. Stir in green beans and cornstarch.
3. MICROWAVE, covered, 7 to 8 minutes or until beans are desired doneness. Sprinkle with cheese before serving. About 4 Servings

GREEN BEANS 'n BACON

6 slices bacon, cut into pieces
1 package (9 oz.) frozen cut green beans
1 medium onion, finely chopped
½ teaspoon seasoned salt

1. MICROWAVE bacon in 1½-quart glass casserole 7 to 8 minutes or until just about crisp.
2. MICROWAVE beans in package 3 to 4 minutes or until thawed; drain.
3. Stir beans and remaining ingredients into bacon.
4. MICROWAVE, uncovered, 8 to 10 minutes, stirring once. 4 to 5 Servings

HERBED GREEN BEANS

2 packages (10 oz. each) frozen French-cut green beans

Herb-Butter Sauce
1 small onion, sliced
¼ cup butter or margarine
1 teaspoon lemon juice
½ teaspoon dried parsley flakes
⅛ teaspoon leaf thyme
¼ teaspoon paprika
⅛ teaspoon salt
⅛ teaspoon pepper

1. Cook green beans in covered 2-quart glass casserole 14 to 16 minutes or until done; drain and set aside.
2. Combine all sauce ingredients in 2-cup glass measure.
3. MICROWAVE 4 to 5 minutes or until onion is tender-crisp. Serve sauce over beans.
6 to 8 Servings

BEETS

PREPARATION: Scrub beet with brush to remove dirt. Leave 1 inch of top attached to beet. (For beet greens, prepare as spinach.)

COOKING METHOD: Place in covered 2-quart glass casserole. Cover with water.

TIME: 9 small — microwave 20 to 22 minutes

SEASONINGS: Butter, orange juice, marmalade, sweet-sour sauce or sour cream.

A classic French way of preparing beets.

BEETS FERMIERE

1 can (16 oz.) sliced beets, drained
1 medium onion, coarsely chopped
¼ cup butter or margarine
2 tablespoons packed brown sugar
½ tablespoon cornstarch
1 clove garlic, finely chopped
1 teaspoon dried parsley flakes
¼ teaspoon salt
⅛ teaspoon pepper

1. Combine all ingredients in 1 or 1½-quart glass casserole.
2. MICROWAVE, covered, 10 to 11 minutes or until sauce boils and thickens, stirring once during last half of cooking time.
5 to 6 Servings

BROCCOLI

PREPARATION: Wash carefully, removing large outer leaves and tough portion of stalk. Slit stem ends to speed cooking.

COOKING METHOD: Place in covered glass casserole. Add ¼ cup water.

TIME: 2 lbs. — microwave 12 to 14 minutes

SEASONINGS: Cheese, egg, mustard, Hollandaise or shrimp sauce; butter, bacon, sour cream or toasted almonds.

MUSTARD-GLAZED VEGETABLES

2 lbs. fresh broccoli or 1 medium head cauliflower

Sour Cream Mustard Sauce
1 cup sour cream
1 tablespoon finely chopped onion
1 tablespoon prepared mustard
1 teaspoon dried parsley flakes
¼ teaspoon salt
Dash pepper

1. Cook broccoli as directed this page; drain.
2. Combine sauce ingredients; spoon over vegetable.
3. MICROWAVE, uncovered, 1½ to 2 minutes or until hot.   About 6 Servings

Serve this recipe as a vegetable or salad. Here we suggest broccoli, but try the marinade with asparagus spears or Brussels sprouts, too.

BROCCOLI A LA VINAIGRETTE

2 lbs. fresh broccoli

Vinaigrette
¼ cup cooking oil
3 tablespoons lemon juice
2 tablespoons cider vinegar
2 teaspoons dried parsley flakes
1 teaspoon grated lemon peel
½ teaspoon sugar
¼ teaspoon garlic powder
¼ teaspoon salt
⅛ teaspoon pepper

1. Cook broccoli as directed this page; drain and set aside.
2. Combine Vinaigrette ingredients in 1-cup glass measure.
3. MICROWAVE 1½ to 2 minutes or until hot. Pour Vinaigrette over broccoli and marinate at least 1 hour. Serve warm or cold.
                              5 to 6 Servings

BRUSSELS SPROUTS

PREPARATION: Discard wilted outer leaves, wash thoroughly. Cut off stem.

COOKING METHOD: Place in 1 to 1½-quart covered glass casserole. Add 2 tablespoons water.

TIME: ½ lb. (2 cups) — microwave 7 to 9 minutes
1 lb. (4 cups) — microwave 9 to 11 minutes

SEASONINGS: Cream, mustard or Hollandaise sauce; butter, bacon or cream cheese.

An exquisite sauce for Brussels sprouts, broccoli or cauliflower. For an extra special touch, garnish serving plate with several cooked shrimp.

BRUSSELS SPROUTS WITH SHRIMP SAUCE

1 lb. fresh Brussels sprouts

Shrimp sauce
1 package (3 oz.) cream cheese with chives
1 can (10¾ oz.) condensed cream of shrimp soup
¼ cup milk
2 tablespoons lemon juice

1. Cook Brussels sprouts as directed this page; drain and set aside.
2. MICROWAVE cream cheese in 2-cup glass measure 1½ to 2 minutes or until soft. Stir until creamy. Blend in soup, milk and lemon juice.
3. MICROWAVE 4 to 5 minutes or until hot. If necessary, beat until smooth with rotary beater. Serve over Brussels sprouts.
                              5 to 6 Servings

CABBAGE

PREPARATION: Wash and remove any wilted outside leaves. With red cabbage add a little vinegar or lemon juice to retain color. Shred or cut into wedges.

COOKING METHOD: Place in covered 1½-quart glass casserole. Add 2 tablespoons water.

TIME: ½ head, shredded or wedges — microwave 10 to 12 minutes

SEASONINGS: Butter, cream cheese, cheese, mustard, bacon or nutmeg.

Try this sour cream and dill sauce with green beans, too.

SOUR 'n DILL CABBAGE

4 cups (½ med. head) shredded cabbage

Sour 'n Dill Sauce
  ½ cup sour cream
  ½ teaspoon dill weed
  ¼ teaspoon salt
  ¼ teaspoon dried parsley flakes
  Dash pepper

1. Cook cabbage as directed this page; drain. Stir in sauce ingredients.
2. MICROWAVE, covered, 1½ to 2 minutes or until hot.   4 to 5 Servings

STIR-FRY VEGETABLES: With microwave cooking you do not actually fry, but you can achieve much of the effect of stir-fry cooking by cooking the vegetables with the butter-seasonings.

  Normally vegetables are cooked covered so that they steam and cook quickly. With the stir-fry technique, some vegetables can be cooked uncovered to allow the excess moisture on the vegetable to evaporate. Cooking uncovered usually increases the cooking time a few minutes.

  Frozen vegetables are usually partially cooked so that the liquid can be drained before adding the seasonings. If this step means an additional dirty dish, you can thaw the vegetable right in the paper packaging.

  With fresh vegetables, seasonings are added at the beginning and the vegetable cooked covered to speed cooking.

  Occasional stirring helps to season the vegetables as they cook.

CARROTS

PREPARATION: Scrape or peel with vegetable peeler to remove thin layer of outer skin. Cut off tops and tips. Leave whole, slice, dice or cut into strips.

COOKING METHOD: Place in covered 1 to 1½-quart glass casserole. Add 2 tablespoons water.

TIME: 2 carrots — microwave 7 to 9 minutes
      4 carrots — microwave 10 to 12 minutes
      6 carrots — microwave 12 to 14 minutes

SEASONINGS: Butter, cinnamon, cream, cream cheese, bacon, brown sugar, nutmeg, parsley or dill weed.

This sweet-tangy fruit sauce adds a special touch to carrots. Try it too, over cooked, quartered acorn squash or cooked sweet potatoes.

HONEYED CARROTS HAWAIIAN

3 to 4 medium carrots, sliced

Fruit Glaze
  1 can (13¼ oz.) pineapple chunks, drained
  ¼ cup walnut halves
  4 orange slices, cut into quarters
  4 lemon slices, cut into quarters
  ¼ cup honey
  2 teaspoons cornstarch
  ⅛ teaspoon salt

1. Cook carrots as directed this page; drain and set aside.
2. Combine glaze ingredients in 4-cup glass measure.
3. MICROWAVE 6 to 7 minutes or until mixture boils, stirring once during last half of cooking time. Combine carrots and glaze in glass serving dish.
4. MICROWAVE 1 to 2 minutes or until hot.
                    5 to 6 Servings

DUTCH CARROTS

  ¼ cup butter or margarine
  4 medium carrots, cut into strips
  1 medium onion, sliced
  ¼ teaspoon salt
  ⅛ teaspoon nutmeg
  ⅛ teaspoon pepper

1. Combine all ingredients in 1½-quart glass casserole.
2. MICROWAVE, covered, 10 to 12 minutes or until tender, stirring once.   4 to 5 Servings

CAULIFLOWER

PREPARATION: Remove outer leaves and excess part of stem. Wash thoroughly. Leave whole or cut into flowerettes.

COOKING METHOD: Place whole cauliflower in large covered glass casserole (if necessary, use another overturned casserole for cover). For flowerettes, place in covered 1½-quart glass casserole. Add 2 tablespoons water.

TIME: 1 med. head — microwave 12 to 16 minutes
Flowerettes — microwave 10 to 12 minutes

SEASONINGS: Cheese, cream, Hollandaise or shrimp sauce; butter, chives, mustard, nutmeg or Parmesan cheese.

For this recipe, use a whole head of cauliflower or cut the head into flowerettes.

CHEESY CAULIFLOWER

1 medium head cauliflower

Cheese Sauce
   2 tablespoons butter or margarine
   2 tablespoons all-purpose flour
   ½ teaspoon salt
   ½ teaspoon Worcestershire sauce
   1 cup milk
   1 cup shredded Cheddar cheese
   1 tomato, cut into wedges
   Parsley

1. Cook cauliflower as directed this page; drain and set aside.
2. MICROWAVE butter in 2-cup glass measure 2 minutes or until melted. Blend in flour, salt, Worcestershire sauce and milk.
3. MICROWAVE 6 to 7 minutes or until sauce boils and thickens, stirring once during last half of cooking time. Stir in cheese until melted.
4. Arrange cauliflower on serving plate. Pour cheese sauce over; garnish with tomato wedges and parsley.
5. MICROWAVE 1 to 2 minutes or until heated through.   About 6 Servings

TIP • Try this sauce with brococli or asparagus spears.

Pictured: Cheesy Cauliflower, page 107.

ORANGE-MUSTARD CAULIFLOWER

1 medium head cauliflower

Orange-Mustard Sauce
   ½ cup orange juice
   1 tablespoon dried parsley flakes
   2 teaspoons cornstarch
   1 teaspoon dry mustard
   1 teaspoon grated orange peel
   6 tablespoons butter or margarine

1. Cook cauliflower as directed this page; drain and set aside.
2. Combine sauce ingredients in 2-cup glass measure.
3. MICROWAVE 5 to 6 minutes or until mixture boils, stirring once during last half of cooking time. Serve over cauliflower. If desired, garnish with orange slices.   About 6 Servings

CELERY

PREPARATION: Separate stalks and wash thoroughly. Cut off base and any blemishes. Cut stalks into slices or strips.

COOKING METHOD: Place in covered 1½-quart glass casserole. Add 2 tablespoons water.

TIME: 4 cups — microwave 10 to 12 minutes

SEASONINGS: Beef or chicken bouillon, butter, cheese sauce or cream cheese.

CELERY CASSEROLE

   4 cups thinly sliced celery
   ¼ cup chopped green pepper
   1 tablespoon water

Cheese Sauce
   2 tablespoons butter or margarine
   2 tablespoons all-purpose flour
   ½ teaspoon salt
   ½ teaspoon Worcestershire sauce
   1 cup milk
   1 cup shredded Cheddar cheese

1. MICROWAVE celery, green pepper and water in covered 1½-quart glass casserole 10 to 12 minutes or until tender; drain.
2. Stir in butter until melted; blend in flour. Stir in remaining ingredients.
3. MICROWAVE, covered, 7 to 8 minutes or until sauce thickens and boils, stirring once during last half of cooking time.
   About 6 Servings

CORN

PREPARATION: Remove husk and silk; trim ends. Wash thoroughly. Leave on cob or cut off using sharp knife.

COOKING METHOD: Place corn on cob in shallow glass baking dish. Not necessary to add water. Cover dish with plastic wrap. Place corn cut from cob in 1-quart covered glass casserole. Add 2 tablespoons water or cream.

TIME: 1½ cups — microwave 6 to 7 minutes
3 cups — microwave 7 to 8 minutes
2 ears — microwave 8 to 10 minutes
4 ears — microwave 12 to 14 minutes
6 ears — microwave 14 to 16 minutes
4 frozen ears — microwave 16 to 18 minutes

SEASONINGS: Butter, cream cheese, chives, bacon, green pepper, onion or pimiento.

CORN RELISH

  1 can (16 oz.) whole kernel corn
  ¼ cup sugar
  ¼ cup chopped green pepper
  ¼ cup pickle relish
  1 tablespoon cornstarch
  2 tablespoons chopped pimiento
  2 tablespoons finely chopped onion
  2 tablespoons vinegar
  ½ teaspoon celery seed

1. Drain corn, reserving ¼ cup liquid (if necessary, add water to make ¼ cup). Combine corn, reserved liquid and remaining ingredients in 1-quart glass casserole.
2. MICROWAVE, covered, 5 to 7 minutes or until mixture boils and thickens, stirring once during last half of cooking time.

                   2½ Cups Relish

Corn and beans with a spicy Mexican flavor. For a less spicy flavor, reduce the amount of green chilies added.

CORN AND BEANS MEXICALI

  2 tablespoons cooking oil
  1 medium onion, sliced
  1 can (16 oz.) kidney beans, drained
  1 can (16 oz.) whole kernel corn, drained
  1 can (4 oz.) chopped green chilies, drained
  ¼ cup chopped pimiento
  ¼ teaspoon salt

1. MICROWAVE oil and onion in 1½-quart glass casserole 4 to 5 minutes or until onion is limp. Stir in remaining ingredients.
2. MICROWAVE, covered, 4 to 5 minutes or until heated through.   5 to 6 Servings

Serve this vegetable dish with poultry or pork.

COLORFUL CORN MEDLEY

  1 package (10 oz.) frozen chopped spinach
  2 tablespoons butter or margarine
  2 tablespoons finely chopped onion
  ⅛ teaspoon instant minced garlic
  2 tablespoons all-purpose flour
  ½ teaspoon salt
  ⅛ teaspoon pepper
  1 cup milk
  1 can (16 oz.) whole kernel corn, drained
  1 cup shredded Swiss cheese

1. MICROWAVE spinach in package 7 to 8 minutes or until thawed. Drain well and set aside.
2. MICROWAVE butter, onion and garlic in 1-quart glass casserole 4 to 5 minutes. Blend in flour, salt and pepper. Stir in milk.
3. MICROWAVE 4 to 5 minutes or until mixture boils, stirring once during last half of cooking time. Stir in drained spinach and corn. Sprinkle with cheese.
4. MICROWAVE-BROIL 4 to 5 minutes or until cheese is bubbly.   5 to 6 Servings

CORN SCALLOP

  2 eggs
  1 cup milk
  1 can (17 oz.) cream-style corn
  1 can (4 oz.) mushroom stems and pieces, drained
  ¾ cup coarse soda cracker crumbs
  6 green onions, chopped
  ½ teaspoon salt
  ⅓ cup coarse soda cracker crumbs
  2 tablespoons butter or margarine

1. Beat eggs in medium mixing bowl. Mix in milk, corn, mushrooms, ¾ cup cracker crumbs, the onions and salt. Pour into greased 1½-quart (10x6) glass baking dish. Sprinkle with ⅓ cup cracker crumbs; dot with butter.
2. MICROWAVE-BAKE at 375° F. for 15 to 17 minutes or until knife inserted near center comes out clean.   About 6 Servings

CORN-IN-THE-HUSK

1. Pull husk back enough to remove silk from corn; wash corn thoroughly. Bring husk back around corn.
2. MICROWAVE as directed for corn on the cob in chart above. Remove husk and season corn to taste.

PEAS

PREPARATION: Shell peas, removing peas from pod. Wash thoroughly.

COOKING METHOD: Place in covered glass casserole. Add 2 tablespoons water.

TIME: 1 cup shelled — microwave 10 to 12 minutes
2 cups shelled — microwave 14 to 16 minutes

SEASONINGS: Butter, chives, cream, cream cheese, dill weed, green onion, mint, mushrooms or orange marmalade.

Peas, onions and mandarin oranges — a delightful, colorful combination.

PEAS MANDARIN

1 package (10 oz.) frozen peas
1 can (16 oz.) small whole onions, drained
¼ cup butter or margarine
1 tablespoon cornstarch
1 tablespoon honey
½ teaspoon salt
¼ teaspoon leaf rosemary, if desired
Dash pepper
1 can (11 oz.) mandarin oranges, drained

1. MICROWAVE peas in 1½-quart covered shallow glass casserole 3 to 4 minutes or until thawed; drain.
2. Stir in remaining ingredients except mandarin oranges.
3. MICROWAVE, uncovered, 6 to 7 minutes or until peas are tender. Stir in oranges.
4. MICROWAVE about 1 minute or until hot.
5 to 6 Servings

PEAS AND MUSHROOMS

1 package (10 oz.) frozen peas
1 small onion, thinly sliced
1 jar (2½ oz.) whole mushrooms, drained
¼ cup butter or margarine
2 tablespoons chopped pimiento
½ teaspoon salt
½ teaspoon dill weed

1. MICROWAVE peas in 1 or 1½-quart covered shallow glass casserole 3 to 4 minutes or until thawed; drain. Add remaining ingredients.
2. MICROWAVE, uncovered, 10 to 11 minutes or until done, stirring once. 5 to 6 Servings

VEGETABLE MEDLEY

1 package (10 oz.) frozen peas
1 package (9 oz.) frozen cut green beans
1 medium onion, sliced
½ cup chopped celery
¼ cup chopped pimiento
1 clove garlic, finely chopped
2 tablespoons butter or margarine
1 teaspoon bouquet garni
½ teaspoon salt
1 package (3 oz.) cream cheese with chives

1. MICROWAVE peas and green beans in 1½-quart covered glass casserole 5 to 6 minutes or until thawed; drain.
2. Stir in remaining ingredients except cream cheese.
3. MICROWAVE, uncovered, 6 minutes; stir and add cream cheese.
4. MICROWAVE 6 to 7 minutes or until vegetables are tender. Stir to blend cheese with vegetables. About 8 Servings

TIP • Substitute for bouquet garni: ¼ teaspoon leaf oregano, ¼ teaspoon leaf basil, ¼ teaspoon leaf thyme and ¼ teaspoon dill weed.

Serve this attractive, flavorful vegetable with pork or poultry.

CHINESE PEA PODS

1 package (6 oz.) frozen pea pods
1 can (6 oz.) water chestnuts, drained and sliced
3 green onions, sliced
¼ cup butter or margarine
1 tablespoon soy sauce
1 teaspoon cornstarch
¼ teaspoon salt
⅛ teaspoon ground ginger

1. MICROWAVE pea pods in 1-quart covered glass casserole 3 minutes or until thawed; drain.
2. Stir in remaining ingredients.
3. MICROWAVE, uncovered, 8 to 9 minutes or until pea pods are tender-crisp, stirring once.
3 to 4 Servings

TIP • For a double recipe, use a 2-quart casserole. Increase cooking time in step 1 to 5 minutes and the time in step 3 to 10 to 12 minutes.

POTATOES AND SQUASH: The outer peel or skin of both potatoes and squash holds in the steam and helps speed cooking. Pricking this skin is normally not necessary. These vegetables are cooked directly on the oven rack.

For baked potatoes, one can use just microwaves or combination cooking. The combination cooking technique gives a drier, more mealy potato and helps even the cooking, even with potatoes of unlike size. With microwave cooking only, turning the potatoes over about half way through the cooking time helps assure even cooking. Microwave cooking is especially convenient on warm days and when you just want cooked potatoes to use in a salad or casserole.

The acorn and butternut squash are larger than potatoes and cook faster and more evenly with combination cooking.

Both potatoes and squash are best removed from the oven when just tender. With about 5 minutes of standing time, they should be the proper doneness without any danger of overcooking.

Peeled and cut up potatoes or squash, are cooked in a casserole until tender. Covering is normal unless a browning effect is desired during cooking.

STUFFED BAKED POTATOES

  6 medium potatoes
¼ cup butter or margarine
  6 green onions, sliced
½ to 1 cup light cream or milk
  1 teaspoon salt
  1 cup shredded Cheddar cheese
  2 tablespoons sesame seed

1. Cook potatoes as directed, next page. Turn oven off.
2. Cut potatoes in half lengthwise; scoop out potato into medium mixing bowl; mash. Set aside shells.
3. MICROWAVE butter and onions in small glass bowl 5 minutes or until limp. Add to potatoes along with cream and salt; beat until fluffy. Pile into potato shells; top with mixture of cheese and sesame seed. Place in 3-quart (13x9) glass baking dish.
4. MICROWAVE-BAKE at 450° F. for 5 to 6 minutes or until cheese is bubbly and potatoes heated through.

12 Stuffed Potatoes

TIPS • To Make Ahead, prepare through step 3 and let stand at room temperature up to 4 hours. Heat when ready to serve.

• Stuffed Baked Potatoes can be kept in the freezer for easy last minute preparation. See page 197 for freezer directions.

POTATOES AU GRATIN

¼ cup butter or margarine
¼ cup all-purpose flour
  2 cups milk
½ teaspoon salt
¾ cup shredded Cheddar cheese
¼ cup Parmesan cheese
  4 cups sliced cooked potatoes
  1 tablespoon butter or margarine
¼ cup dry bread crumbs

1. MICROWAVE butter in 1½-quart glass casserole 2½ to 3 minutes or until melted. Blend in flour, milk and salt.
2. MICROWAVE 6 to 7 minutes or until mixture boils and thickens, stirring once during last half of cooking time. Stir in cheeses and potatoes.
3. MICROWAVE butter in small glass dish 1½ minutes or until melted; mix in bread crumbs. Sprinkle over potatoes.
4. MICROWAVE-BROIL 4½ to 5 minutes or until heated through and topping is golden brown. 5 to 6 Servings

TIP • 5 medium potatoes will give the 4 cups sliced potatoes needed for this recipe.

Hot potato salad in the shell — a unique finish to an old-time favorite.

CRUNCHY POTATO SALAD BOATS

  4 large potatoes
  1 teaspoon salt
  1 teaspoon sugar
⅛ teaspoon pepper
  2 tablespoons vinegar
  1 tablespoon chopped onion
½ cup chopped celery
½ cup mayonnaise or salad dressing
  6 stuffed green olives, sliced
½ cup crushed potato chips
½ cup shredded Cheddar or American cheese

1. Cook potatoes as directed, next page. Leave oven turned on or preheat to 450° F.
2. Cut potatoes in half lengthwise. Scoop out potatoes into large mixing bowl, leaving potato in fairly large pieces; set aside shells.
3. Combine potato pieces with salt, sugar, pepper, vinegar, onion, celery, mayonnaise and olives. Pile into potato shells and place in 2-quart (12x7) glass baking dish. Top with mixture of potato chips and cheese.
4. MICROWAVE-BAKE 5 to 7 minutes or until lightly browned. 8 Stuffed Potatoes

POTATOES — White and Sweet

PREPARATION: Wash and scrub thoroughly. Peel or leave skins on. With peeled potatoes cut into quarters or halves.

COOKING METHOD: Place whole unpeeled potatoes directly on oven rack. Microwave, turning over half way through cooking. Or microwave-bake at 450° F. without turning over. Place peeled potatoes in covered 1½ or 2-quart glass casserole. Add ¼ cup water.

TIME: 1 whole — microwave 11 to 14 minutes, turn over once
1 whole — microwave-bake 450° 8 to 10 minutes
4 whole — microwave 16 to 18 minutes, turn over once
4 whole — microwave-bake 450° 14 to 16 minutes
8 whole — microwave 22 to 25 minutes, turn over once
8 whole — microwave-bake 450° 18 to 20 minutes
2 peeled and quartered — microwave 12 to 15 minutes

SEASONINGS: White — butter, cheese, chives, cream cheese, bacon, green onion or sour cream.
Sweet — butter, brown sugar, bacon, orange or maple syrup.

Use this recipe as a guide for brown sugar-glazed sweet potatoes. If you prefer, start with canned yams or sweet potatoes.

PEACHY YAMS

  6 medium yams or sweet potatoes
  1 can (16 oz.) sliced peaches
⅓ cup packed brown sugar
⅓ cup butter or margarine
¼ teaspoon nutmeg
⅓ cup chopped nuts

1. Cook potatoes as directed, this page. Cool enough to handle; peel and slice into 2-quart glass casserole.
2. Drain peaches, reserving ¼ cup syrup. Add peaches to sweet potatoes. Mix brown sugar, butter and nutmeg with reserved liquid in 1-cup glass measure.
3. MICROWAVE butter mixture 2½ to 3 minutes or until melted. Pour mixture over potatoes; sprinkle with nuts.
4. MICROWAVE-BAKE at 450° F. for 6 to 8 minutes or until heated through. Spoon sauce from bottom of dish over potatoes before serving.   6 to 8 Servings

Mashed sweet potatoes with a golden marshmallow topping.

YAM-MARSHMALLOW BAKE

  6 medium yams or sweet potatoes
⅓ cup butter or margarine
½ cup orange juice
½ cup flaked or shredded coconut
½ cup chopped nuts
½ teaspoon salt
36 marshmallows

1. Cook potatoes as directed, this page. Cool enough to handle; peel and mash in 2-quart glass casserole. Stir in butter, orange juice, coconut, nuts and salt.
2. MICROWAVE-BAKE, covered, at 450° F. for 5 to 7 minutes or until heated through. Arrange marshmallows on top.
3. MICROWAVE-BAKE, uncovered, 2 to 3 minutes or until marshmallows are browned.
    About 6 Servings

TIP • To Make Ahead, prepare through step 1 and refrigerate. Increase cooking time in step 2 to 8 to 10 minutes.

Here is a way to dress up instant potatoes. Or, use the same additions to glamorize your own mashed potatoes.

FLUFFY HERBED POTATOES

1½ cups water
  2 tablespoons butter or margarine
½ cup milk
1½ cups instant potato flakes
  1 cup shredded Cheddar cheese
  1 green onion, sliced
½ teaspoon salt
½ teaspoon dry mustard
½ teaspoon dried parsley flakes
¼ teaspoon onion salt
  2 eggs, separated
  2 tablespoons dry bread crumbs

1. MICROWAVE water and butter in 1-quart glass casserole about 8 minutes or until hot. Add milk; stir in potato flakes, ½ cup cheese, the onion and seasonings. Beat well.
2. Beat egg whites just until stiff peaks form. Beat egg yolks until light and lemon colored. Fold egg whites and yolks into potato mixture. Sprinkle top of mixture with remaining cheese and the bread crumbs.
3. MICROWAVE-BROIL 6 to 7 minutes or until top is golden brown.   4 to 5 Servings

TIP • For the granular-type instant potatoes, use the water, butter and milk additions as directed on the package for 4 servings.

Partially covering Scalloped Potatoes speeds cooking and keeps them from boiling over.

SCALLOPED POTATOES

  1½ cups milk
  4 medium potatoes, peeled and thinly sliced
  2 tablespoons all-purpose flour
  1 teaspoon salt
  ⅛ teaspoon pepper
  2 tablespoons butter or margarine

1. MICROWAVE milk in 2-cup glass measure 5 to 5½ minutes or until hot.
2. Place ⅓ of potatoes in greased 2-quart glass casserole. Sprinkle with 1 tablespoon flour, ½ teaspoon salt and dash pepper. Repeat layering ending with potatoes. Pour hot milk over potatoes to barely cover. Dot with butter.
4. MICROWAVE, partially covered, 15 to 17 minutes or until potatoes are tender. Remove cover.
5. BROIL 6 to 7 minutes or until lightly browned.

                                    4 to 5 Servings

DILL 'n CHIVE POTATOES

  1 lb. new red potatoes (about 8)
  2 tablespoons butter or margarine
  1 tablespoon lemon juice
  1 tablespoon chopped chives
  ½ teaspoon dill weed

1. Place scrubbed potatoes in 1-quart glass casserole.
2. MICROWAVE, covered, 10 to 11 minutes or until just tender. Add remaining ingredients.
3. MICROWAVE, uncovered, 2 to 3 minutes or until butter is melted. Stir to coat potatoes with butter.   About 4 Servings

  TIP • Potatoes can be left unpeeled or peeled. For an attractive unpeeled potato, remove just a thin strip of peel around center, leaving the peeling at both ends.

HERB-BUTTER FRIES

  2 tablespoons butter or margarine
  ½ teaspoon dried parsley flakes
  1 teaspoon chopped chives
  ½ teaspoon dill weed
  ½ teaspoon salt
  16 ozs. frozen French fries

1. MICROWAVE butter and seasonings in 2-quart (12x7) glass baking dish 2 to 2½ minutes or until melted. Add French fries and toss to coat with butter.
2. MICROWAVE-BAKE at 450° F. for 13 to 15 minutes or until lightly browned.

                                    3 to 4 Servings

OVEN-BROWNED POTATOES

  3 tablespoons butter or margarine
  5 to 6 medium potatoes, peeled
  1 medium onion, sliced
  Salt and pepper
  Snipped Parsley

1. MICROWAVE butter in 8-inch square glass baking dish about 2 minutes or until melted. Slice potatoes into ½-inch slices; add potatoes and onion to butter. Season with salt and pepper. Stir lightly to coat potatoes with butter.
2. MICROWAVE-BAKE, uncovered, at 425° F. for 20 to 22 minutes or until potatoes are tender, stirring once. Sprinkle with parsley.

                                    5 to 6 Servings

CHEESY HASH BROWNS

  1 package (12 oz.) frozen hash brown potatoes
  2 tablespoons chopped onion
  ½ teaspoon salt
  ⅛ teaspoon pepper
  ½ cup milk or cream
  ½ cup shredded Cheddar or American cheese

1. MICROWAVE potatoes in covered 1-quart glass casserole 4 to 5 minutes or until thawed. Stir in remaining ingredients except cheese. Sprinkle with cheese.
2. MICROWAVE-BROIL 4 to 5 minutes or until lightly browned.   About 4 Servings

ONION AND POTATO BAKE

  1 package (12 oz.) frozen hash brown potatoes
  3 medium onions, finely chopped
  1 tablespoon honey
  1 teaspoon salt
  1 teaspoon dried parsley flakes
  ¼ teaspoon pepper
  2 tablespoons dry bread crumbs
  ¼ cup butter or margarine

1. MICROWAVE potatoes in covered 1-quart glass casserole 4 to 5 minutes or until thawed; drain.
2. Stir in remaining ingredients except bread crumbs and butter; sprinkle top with bread crumbs.
3. MICROWAVE butter in small glass dish about 1½ minutes or until melted. Drizzle over bread crumbs.
4. MICROWAVE-BAKE at 375° F. for 10 to 12 minutes or until potatoes and onions are tender.   5 to 6 Servings

Pictured: Onion-Filled Squash, page 114.

SPINACH

PREPARATION: Wash leaves, removing any wilted leaves or tough stems.

COOKING METHOD: Place in covered 2-quart glass casserole. Not necessary to add additional water.

TIME: 10 ozs. (8 cups) — microwave 8 to 10 minutes

SEASONINGS: Butter, egg sauce, bacon, lemon, nutmeg or onion.

Creamed spinach makes an unusual filling for these easy onion cups.

SPINACH-STUFFED ONIONS

1 package (10 oz.) frozen chopped spinach
1 package (3 oz.) cream cheese
1 egg
¼ cup dry bread crumbs
½ cup Parmesan cheese
¼ cup milk
¼ teaspoon salt
Dash pepper
1 large onion

1. MICROWAVE spinach in covered 1-quart glass casserole 10 to 12 minutes; drain well.
2. MICROWAVE cream cheese in medium glass mixing bowl about 2 minutes or until softened. Beat in egg; stir in crumbs, cheese, milk, salt, pepper and drained spinach.
3. Peel onion and cut in half crosswise; separate each layer to form an onion cup. Place the 6 larger cups (save the others for chopping) in 8-inch square glass baking dish. Fill with spinach mixture.
4. MICROWAVE, uncovered, 8 to 10 minutes or until hot.   6 Servings

VEGETABLE CASSEROLES: Vegetable casseroles usually combine a cooked vegetable with a sauce or seasoning and sometimes have a crumb or cheese topping.

When the casserole has a topping that needs browning, combination cooking is often used. It can be microwave-bake where there is dry heat surrounding the dish, or microwave-broil when the dry heat is concentrated on the topping. In both cases, the heat browns the topping while microwaves heat the main part of the casserole.

Other scooped out vegetables can serve as dishes for individual casseroles. The Stuffed Tomatoes and Spinach-Stuffed Onions recipes are examples.

SQUASH

PREPARATION: Acorn — leave whole until cooked. Hubbard or other winter varieties — wash and cut into serving pieces. Peel either before or after cooking.
Zucchini — wash and slice thinly. Do not peel.

COOKING METHOD: Place whole squash on oven rack and microwave-bake at 400°. Place cut or sliced squash in covered casserole. Add 2 tablespoons water.

TIME: 1 Acorn — microwave-bake 400° 15 to 17 minutes
2 Acorn — microwave-bake 400° 17 to 19 minutes
4 cups cubed Hubbard — microwave 12 to 15 minutes
3 cups sliced Zucchini — microwave 10 to 12 minutes

SEASONINGS: Butter, brown sugar, bacon, orange peel or maple syrup.

Acorn squash halves filled with creamy pearl onions. A pretty and tasty serving.

ONION-FILLED SQUASH

2 acorn squash
1 package (10 oz.) frozen onions in cream sauce
¼ cup butter or margarine
½ cup dry bread crumbs
1 teaspoon dried parsley flakes
¼ cup chopped nuts
Salt
Nutmeg

1. Cook squash as directed, this page. Turn oven off.
2. MICROWAVE pouch of onions in shallow glass baking dish 5 to 6 minutes or until thawed.
3. MICROWAVE butter in small glass mixing bowl 2 to 2½ minutes or until melted. Stir in bread crumbs, parsley and nuts.
4. Cut squash in half; scoop out seeds. Arrange halves, cut-side-up, in shallow glass baking dish; sprinkle with salt. Divide onion mixture among squash halves. Sprinkle with nutmeg; top with crumb mixture.
5. MICROWAVE-BAKE at 400° F. for 8 to 10 minutes or until topping is browned and filling bubbly.   4 Squash Halves

BRANDIED SQUASH HALVES

2 acorn squash
4 tablespoons butter or margarine
4 tablespoons packed brown sugar
2 tablespoons brandy

1. Cook squash as directed, opposite page. Let stand 5 minutes. Cut in half and scoop out seeds. Place cut-side-up in shallow glass baking dish.
2. Place 1 tablespoon butter, 1 tablespoon brown sugar and ½ tablespoon brandy in each squash half.
3. MICROWAVE-BAKE at 400° F. for 6 to 8 minutes or until butter mixture boils and glazes squash.　　　　4 Squash Halves

ZUCCHINI COMBO

3 medium zucchini or summer squash
2 cups (8 ozs.) sliced fresh mushrooms
¼ teaspoon garlic powder
½ teaspoon salt
¼ cup butter or margarine
2 medium tomatoes, cut into wedges
¼ cup Parmesan cheese

1. Slice zucchini and combine with mushrooms in 1½-quart glass casserole. Sprinkle with garlic powder and salt; dot with butter.
2. MICROWAVE, covered, 7 to 8 minutes or until zucchini is tender. Stir in tomatoes and cheese.
3. MICROWAVE, covered, 2 to 3 minutes or until hot.　　　　4 to 5 Servings

ZUCCHINI 'n CORN COMBO

3 cups sliced zucchini
1 can (16 oz.) whole kernel corn, drained
2 tablespoons chopped pimiento
¼ cup butter or margarine
½ teaspoon salt
½ teaspoon dill weed
⅛ teaspoon pepper

1. Combine all ingredients in 1½-quart glass casserole; mix well.
2. MICROWAVE, uncovered, 10 to 12 minutes or until zucchini is tender, stirring once.
　　　　5 to 6 Servings

TIP • Substitute for canned corn: about 2½ cups fresh corn; increase cooking time to 15 to 17 minutes.

Hollowed out tomatoes make colorful and attractive "servers" for your favorite vegetable. Here we have used creamed peas and onions, but other favorite vegetable combinations can be used.

STUFFED TOMATOES

6 medium tomatoes
1 package (10 oz.) frozen peas and onions
1 package (3 oz.) cream cheese
2 tablespoons butter or margarine
¼ cup dry bread crumbs

1. Cut off tops of tomatoes and hollow out insides (save pulp for use in salads). Place tomatoes, hollow-side-up, in 8-inch square glass baking dish.
2. MICROWAVE frozen peas and onions in medium glass mixing bowl 3 to 4 minutes or until thawed; drain. Add cream cheese.
3. MICROWAVE about 1½ minutes or until cheese is soft. Stir to combine peas with cheese; spoon mixture into tomatoes. Sprinkle with mixture of melted butter and bread crumbs.
4. MICROWAVE 5 to 6 minutes or until heated through.　　　　6 Servings

VEGETABLES WITH SAUCES: Sauces can be mixed and matched with a variety of vegetables. Many of the recipes with sauces have the sauce ingredients set apart so that they may be prepared with ease for use with other vegetables.

Often the sauce and vegetable are cooked separately and then combined on the serving plate or dish. If the vegetable cools while the sauce is being prepared, the finished dish can be brought to piping hot serving temperature with a minute or two of microwave cooking.

Both fresh and frozen vegetables adapt readily to sauces. Just cook the vegetable as directed, then prepare the sauce as directed and combine. When using canned vegetables, you just need to heat them either before adding the sauce or along with the sauce.

When there is more than enough sauce for a vegetable, refrigerate the extra and reheat it another day for a different vegetable.

For additional sauces, see the Sauce Chapter, page 116.

Sauces

SAUCES: Sauces cook easily with microwaves because the cooking comes from all sides, eliminating the possibility of scorching.

Glass measuring cups make it easy to measure, cook, and pour with just one container. Just be sure that the capacity of the cup is about double the amount of sauce to allow ample room for boiling.

When sauces are thickened with flour or cornstarch, they need to come to a boil. This cooks the flour or starch and causes the sauce to thicken. Most of these sauces are stirred once, during the last half of cooking, to disperse the thickening that tends to settle at the bottom of the cup. If this step is omitted, the thickened portion tends to remain in the bottom of the cup and the sauce has a lumpy appearance when stirred after cooking.

WHITE SAUCE

    2 tablespoons butter or margarine
    2 tablespoons all-purpose flour
  ½ teaspoon salt
    1 cup milk

1. MICROWAVE butter in 2-cup glass measure 2 to 2½ minutes or until melted. Stir in flour and salt. Add milk all at once; mix well.
2. MICROWAVE 6 to 7 minutes or until mixture boils and thickens, stirring once during last half of cooking time.   1 Cup Sauce

TIPS • Thick White Sauce: increase butter and flour to 3 tablespoons each.

    • Thin White Sauce: decrease butter and flour to 1 tablespoon each.

    • BECHAMEL SAUCE: add 1 teaspoon instant minced onion and a dash each of nutmeg and thyme with flour.

    • CHEESE SAUCE: add ¼ teaspoon dry mustard with flour. After cooking, stir in ½ cup shredded cheese.

    • CREAMED EGG SAUCE: add ¼ teaspoon dry mustard with flour. After cooking, stir in 2 to 3 chopped or sliced hard-cooked eggs.

    • Double Recipe: use 4-cup glass measure and increase cooking time to 10 to 12 minutes.

BROWN SAUCE

    3 tablespoons butter or margarine
    3 tablespoons all-purpose flour
    2 teaspoons instant beef bouillon
    2 cups water
  ¼ teaspoon salt
  ⅛ teaspoon pepper

1. MICROWAVE butter in 4-cup glass measure about 2 minutes or until melted. Stir in remaining ingredients.
2. MICROWAVE 9 to 11 minutes or until mixture boils and thickens, stirring once during last half of cooking time.
    2 Cups Sauce

TIPS • One can (10½ oz.) condensed beef bouillon or consommé may be used with water to make 2 cups liquid; omit instant beef bouillon.

    • Meat drippings from a roast may be used with water to make the 2 cups liquid. If desired, omit instant beef bouillon.

    • BORDELAISE SAUCE: Add 2 tablespoons finely chopped green onion, 1 clove garlic, finely chopped, 1 bay leaf and 4 peppercorns to butter and use ½ cup Burgundy wine for part of the water. Remove bay leaf and peppercorns before serving.

GRAVY

  ½ cup pan drippings
  ¼ cup all-purpose flour
  ½ teaspoon salt
  Dash pepper
1½ cups water or milk

1. Combine all ingredients in 4-cup glass measure.
2. MICROWAVE 8 to 10 minutes or until mixture boils, stirring once during last half of cooking time.   About 2 Cups

Pictured, top to bottom: Mornay Sauce, page 118, Fudge Sauce, page 119 and Cranberry Sauce, page 118.

A tangy, sweet sauce to serve with lamb, duck or poultry.

CUMBERLAND SAUCE

¼ **cup currant jelly**
¼ **teaspoon cornstarch**
¼ **teaspoon dry mustard**
⅛ **teaspoon ground ginger**
1 **teaspoon grated orange peel**
1 **teaspoon grated lemon peel**
3 **tablespoons orange juice**
2 **tablespoons lemon juice**

1. Combine all ingredients in 1-cup glass measure.
2. MICROWAVE 3 to 4 minutes or until bubbly. Serve as a sauce with cooked meat or brush over meat during last ½ hour of cooking.   ½ Cup Sauce

The flavors of this sauce are especially good with fish, vegetables and pastas.

MORNAY SAUCE

3 **tablespoons butter or margarine**
3 **tablespoons all-purpose flour**
1 **teaspoon instant chicken bouillon**
¾ **cup light cream or milk**
¾ **cup water**
½ **cup Parmesan cheese**
½ **cup shredded Swiss cheese**

1. MICROWAVE butter in 4-cup glass measure about 2 minutes or until melted. Blend in flour, bouillon, cream and water.
2. MICROWAVE 6 to 7 minutes or until mixture boils and thickens, stirring once during last half of cooking time.
3. Blend in cheeses; stir until smooth.
                    2 Cups Sauce

Serve this sauce with game, ham or pork.

RAISIN SAUCE

½ **cup packed brown sugar**
1 **tablespoon cornstarch**
2 **tablespoons lemon juice**
1 **teaspoon dry mustard**
1 **cup water**
¼ **cup raisins**
1 **tablespoon butter or margarine**

1. Combine all ingredients in 2-cup glass measure.
2. MICROWAVE 6 to 7 minutes or until bubbly, stirring once during last half of cooking time.
                    1½ Cups Sauce

Hollandaise sauce needs special attention during cooking to keep it smooth and creamy.

HOLLANDAISE SAUCE

¼ **cup butter or margarine**
¼ **cup light cream or evaporated milk**
2 **egg yolks, beaten**
1 **tablespoon lemon juice or vinegar**
½ **teaspoon dry mustard**
¼ **teaspoon salt**

1. MICROWAVE butter in 2-cup glass measure 2 to 2½ minutes or until melted. Blend in remaining ingredients.
2. MICROWAVE 2½ to 3 minutes or until mixture thickens, stirring several times during cooking.   ⅔ Cup Sauce

TIP • BEARNAISE SAUCE: Add 1 tablespoon finely chopped onion, 1 teaspoon leaf tarragon and ½ teaspoon chervil to butter and add 2 tablespoons white wine with lemon juice.

CRANBERRY SAUCE

2 **cups fresh cranberries**
2 **cups sugar**
¾ **cup water**

1. Combine all ingredients in 1-quart glass casserole.
2. MICROWAVE, covered, about 18 minutes or until the berries are popped open. Cool before serving.   About 2½ Cups Sauce

Use this sauce to baste poultry while roasting or barbecuing, or serve over slices of cooked poultry.

ORANGE-LEMON SAUCE

2 **tablespoons cornstarch**
2 **tablespoons honey**
2 **tablespoons lemon juice**
2 **tablespoons butter or margarine**
2 **teaspoons grated orange peel**
⅛ **teaspoon cinnamon**
Dash cloves
1 **cup orange juice**
1 **tablespoon dry sherry, if desired**
1 **lemon, sliced**

1. Combine all ingredients except sherry and lemon in 4-cup glass measure.
2. MICROWAVE 6 to 7 minutes or until mixture boils and thickens, stirring once during last half of cooking time. Stir in sherry and lemon.
                    1½ Cups Sauce

DESSERT SAUCES: The cooking method for sauces is similar to puddings. Microwave cooking is used until the mixture boils and thickens. Stirring during the last half of cooking time disperses the starches throughout and keeps the sauce smooth.

BUTTERSCOTCH SAUCE

½ cup packed brown sugar
1 tablespoon cornstarch
1 cup milk
Dash salt
2 tablespoons butter or margarine
1 tablespoon brandy, if desired
½ teaspoon vanilla

1. Combine all ingredients except brandy and vanilla in 2-cup glass measure.
2. MICROWAVE 4 to 5 minutes or until mixture boils and thickens, stirring occasionally during last half of cooking time.
3. Stir in brandy and vanilla.   1⅓ Cups Sauce

LEMON SAUCE

1 cup sugar
2 tablespoons cornstarch
½ cup water
¼ cup lemon juice
½ cup butter or margarine

1. Combine all ingredients in 4-cup glass measure.
2. MICROWAVE 6 to 8 minutes or until mixture boils, stirring occasionally during last half of cooking time.   1½ Cups Sauce

HOT BUTTER SAUCE

½ cup butter or margarine
¾ cup sugar
½ cup evaporated milk
½ teaspoon vanilla

1. Combine butter, sugar and milk in 4-cup glass measure.
2. MICROWAVE 4 to 6 minutes or until mixture boils. Stir in vanilla. Serve warm.
     1½ Cups Sauce

FUDGE SAUCE

1 can (5 oz.) evaporated milk
1 cup (6-oz. pkg.) semi-sweet chocolate pieces
1 cup sugar
⅓ cup butter or margarine
1 teaspoon vanilla

1. Combine all ingredients except vanilla in 4-cup glass measure.
2. MICROWAVE 9 to 10 minutes or until mixture boils, stirring occasionally during last half of cooking time. Beat until smooth; stir in vanilla. Serve warm or cold.   2 Cups Sauce

TIP • For an easy butterscotch sauce, substitute butterscotch pieces for chocolate pieces.

CARAMEL SAUCE

1 bag (14 oz.) caramels
½ cup milk

1. Combine unwrapped caramels with milk in 4-cup glass measure.
2. MICROWAVE 6 to 7 minutes, or until caramels are melted and mixture begins to boil, stirring occasionally during last half of cooking time. Serve warm or cold.
     1⅔ Cups Sauce

ORANGE SAUCE

¼ cup sugar
1 tablespoon cornstarch
1 tablespoon grated orange peel
2 tablespoons butter or margarine
¾ cup orange juice
1 to 2 tablespoons Grand Marnier or other orange-flavored liqueur

1. Combine all ingredients except Grand Marnier in 4-cup glass measure.
2. MICROWAVE 6 to 7 minutes or until mixture boils and thickens, stirring occasionally during last half of cooking time. Stir in Grand Marnier.   1⅓ Cups Sauce

Rice and Noodles

RICE: Microwave cooking works well for cooking rice. The water and rice are combined in a casserole with a tight fitting lid, and then cooked, allowing the water to heat the rice to absorb the water and become moist. The time saved is minimal since rice needs time to absorb the hot liquid.

With quick-cooking rice, the rice is added after the water and butter are heated. Just as with conventional preparation, no additional cooking is needed.

Long-grain varieties of rice are cooked in about twice the amount of liquid. The rice is removed from the oven when it is almost tender since it continues to cook for about 5 minutes. Casserole size and shape are important in cooking rice. If a large size or shallow dish is used, the water or liquid will evaporate faster and there may not be enough for the rice to become tender. If the rice becomes dry before the cooking time is completed, an additional ½ to ¾ cup water should be added. When there is not enough moisture, longer cooking will not make the rice tender.

A small amount of butter or other fat added to the rice during cooking helps prevent boiling over.

Converted rice can be substituted for long-grain rice, but allow about 5 minutes additional cooking time.

Leftover rice reheats very nicely in the oven. Just place in a covered casserole and heat with microwaves until steaming hot.

RICE YIELDS:
1 cup quick-cooking rice = 2 cups cooked rice
1 cup long-grain rice = 3 cups cooked rice
1 cup wild rice = 3½ cups cooked rice
1 cup brown rice = 4 cups cooked rice

Pictured: Wild Rice Casserole, page 122, Mostaccioli Romanoff, page 123 and Orange-Raisin Rice, this page.

FLUFFY WHITE RICE

1 cup uncooked long-grain rice
2 cups water
1 tablespoon butter or margarine
½ teaspoon salt
Dash pepper, if desired

1. Combine all ingredients in 2-quart glass casserole.
2. **MICROWAVE,** covered, 13 to 15 minutes or until rice is just about tender. Fluff with fork. Cover and let stand 5 minutes before serving.   **5 to 6 Servings**

TIPS • For color and flavor, add some snipped parsley, dill weed, leaf oregano or basil, chopped pimiento or green pepper.

    • When using converted rice, increase cooking time to 18 to 20 minutes.

QUICK-COOKING RICE

1½ cups water
  2 teaspoons butter or margarine,
    if desired
1½ cups quick-cooking rice
1 teaspoon salt

1. **MICROWAVE** water and butter in 1-quart glass casserole 5 to 6 minutes or until mixture boils.
2. Stir in rice and salt; cover. Let stand 5 minutes. Fluff with fork before serving.   **About 4 Servings**

Try this rice dish with chicken, duck, or pork.

ORANGE-RAISIN RICE

1 cup uncooked long-grain rice
1 cup water
1 cup orange juice
½ cup raisins
¼ cup chopped green pepper
¼ cup butter or margarine
1 to 2 tablespoons grated orange peel
2 tablespoons honey
½ teaspoon salt

1. Combine all ingredients in 1½-quart glass casserole; mix well.
2. **MICROWAVE,** covered, 18 to 20 minutes or until rice is just about tender. Fluff with fork; cover and let stand 5 minutes before serving.   **5 to 6 Servings**

RICE PILAF

- ⅓ cup butter or margarine
- 1½ cups uncooked long-grain rice
- 2½ cups water
- ½ cup chopped onion
- ½ cup chopped celery
- 1 can (4 oz.) mushroom stems and pieces, drained
- 2 tablespoons dried parsley flakes
- 2 teaspoons instant chicken bouillon
- ½ teaspoon salt
- ¼ teaspoon leaf thyme
- Dash pepper

1. Combine all ingredients in 2-quart glass casserole.
2. MICROWAVE, covered, 18 to 20 minutes or until rice is just about tender. Fluff with fork; cover and let stand 5 minutes before serving.

6 to 8 Servings

SPANISH RICE

- 3 slices bacon, cut into pieces
- 1 cup uncooked long-grain rice
- 1¼ cups water
- ⅓ cup chopped green pepper
- 1 small onion, chopped
- 1 can (16 oz.) tomatoes, undrained
- 1 teaspoon salt
- 1 teaspoon dried parsley flakes
- ½ teaspoon leaf oregano
- ⅛ teaspoon pepper

1. MICROWAVE bacon in 1½-quart glass casserole 5 to 6 minutes or until bacon is crisp. Stir in remaining ingredients.
2. MICROWAVE, covered, 18 to 20 minutes or until rice is just about tender. Fluff with fork; cover and let stand 5 minutes before serving.

5 to 6 Servings

WHITE AND WILD RICE CASSEROLE

- 5 slices bacon, cut into pieces
- 1 package (6 oz.) seasoned white and wild rice mix
- 1 cup chopped celery
- 1 medium onion, sliced
- 2 cups water

1. MICROWAVE bacon in 2-quart glass casserole 7 to 8 minutes or until crisp. Stir in remaining ingredients, including packet of seasoning from rice mix.
2. MICROWAVE, covered, 25 to 30 minutes or until rice is tender. Fluff with fork; cover and let stand 5 minutes before serving.

5 to 6 Servings

Wild rice is always a favorite served with game or poultry. The texture is more chewy than either white or brown rice.

WILD RICE CASSEROLE

- ½ cup uncooked wild rice
- 1¾ cups water
- ½ cup chopped celery
- 1 medium onion, sliced
- 1 can (4 oz.) mushroom stems and pieces, drained
- 2 tablespoons butter or margarine
- ¼ teaspoon salt
- ¼ teaspoon garlic salt
- ¼ teaspoon leaf thyme
- ⅛ teaspoon pepper

1. Combine all ingredients in 1½-quart glass casserole; mix well.
2. MICROWAVE, covered, 35 to 40 minutes or until rice is cooked. Fluff with fork; cover and let stand 5 minutes before serving.

4 to 6 Servings

TIPS • If you prefer a milder flavor, use a combination of white or brown rice and wild rice.

• The wild rice can be soaked overnight or washed in boiling water before using. Just drain well before combining with other ingredients.

BROWN RICE CASSEROLE

- 1 cup uncooked brown rice
- 1 medium onion, finely chopped
- 1 tablespoon dried parsley flakes
- 1 tablespoon chopped pimiento
- 1 tablespoon soy sauce
- 2 teaspoons instant beef bouillon
- 2½ cups water
- ½ cup chopped nuts, if desired

1. Combine all ingredients except nuts in 1½-quart glass casserole.
2. MICROWAVE-BAKE, covered, at 350° F. for 12 minutes.
3. BAKE 30 to 35 minutes or until rice is tender. Fluff with fork; cover and let stand 5 minutes before serving. Sprinkle with nuts.

5 to 6 Servings

NOODLES: Noodles and other pasta require a large quantity of water to remove excess starch during cooking. We found it easier to work with this amount of water on a burner rather than in the oven. It is possible to heat the water and cook the noodles in the oven, but it does not save time. Also, the noodles tend to be more pasty because the container holds less water than normal.

In some casseroles, uncooked noodles or macaroni are added to the uncooked sauce and cooked together. This method works well with the microwave oven. (There are several recipes using it in other parts of the book. Some examples are: Ham and Tomato Casserole, page 73, and Corn and Beef Casserole, page 59.

A sour cream and noodle casserole that uses the large mostaccioli macaroni or regular noodles.

MOSTACCIOLI ROMANOFF

    8 ozs. (4 cups) mostaccioli macaroni
    2 tablespoons butter or margarine
    2 tablespoons flour
    1 teaspoon salt
    3 green onions, sliced
    1 clove garlic, finely chopped
    1 cup milk
    ½ cup sour cream
    ½ cup Parmesan cheese

1. Cook macaroni as directed on package; drain.
2. MICROWAVE butter in 1½-quart glass casserole 2 to 2½ minutes or until melted. Stir in flour, salt, onions, garlic and milk.
3. MICROWAVE 5 to 6 minutes or until sauce boils and thickens, stirring once during last half of cooking time. Stir in cooked macaroni, sour cream and half of cheese. Sprinkle remaining cheese over top.
4. MICROWAVE-BROIL 5 to 6 minutes or until lightly browned.   5 to 6 Servings

    TIP • Substitute for mostaccioli macaroni: 8 ozs. (4 cups) rigatoni or regular noodles.

NOODLES ROMANOFF MIX

    1 package (5.5 oz.) Noodles Romanoff mix
    1½ cups water
    ½ cup milk
    1 tablespoon chopped chives
    1 can (4 oz.) mushroom stems and pieces, drained

1. Combine noodles, including sauce mix and remaining ingredients, in 1½-quart glass casserole.
2. MICROWAVE, covered, 14 to 16 minutes or until noodles are just about tender. Let stand 5 minutes before serving.   About 4 Servings

POPPY SEED-NOODLE BAKE

    8 ozs. (4 cups) uncooked noodles
    1 package (8 oz.) cream cheese
    ½ teaspoon salt
    2 teaspoons poppy seed
    Dash Tabasco sauce
    ½ cup shredded Swiss cheese

1. Cook noodles as directed on package; drain and place in 2-quart glass casserole.
2. Cut cream cheese into cubes; add to noodles along with salt, poppy seed and Tabasco sauce. Mix well. Sprinkle with Swiss cheese.
3. MICROWAVE-BROIL 9 to 10 minutes or until lightly browned.   5 to 6 Servings

SPINACH-NOODLE BAKE

    4 cups uncooked noodles
    1 package (10 oz.) chopped spinach
    1 cup milk
    2 eggs, beaten
    3 green onions, chopped
    1 teaspoon salt
    ⅛ teaspoon pepper
    1½ cups shredded Swiss cheese

1. Cook noodles as directed on package; drain and set aside.
2. MICROWAVE spinach in 2-quart glass casserole 7 to 8 minutes or until thawed.
3. Stir in milk, eggs, onions, salt, pepper, ¾ cup of cheese and the noodles.
4. MICROWAVE-BAKE, covered, at 350° F. for 7 minutes. Stir mixture and sprinkle top with remaining cheese.
5. MICROWAVE-BAKE 4 to 5 minutes or until knife inserted near center comes out clean.
                                5 to 6 Servings

Salads

SALADS: With salad preparation, some of the basic microwave cooking techniques used with other foods are applied to heat various salad ingredients. For example, a dressing may be heated with microwaves to make a wilted salad or a warm potato salad. Potatoes and rice are cooked with microwaves to make Potato Salad and Rice Salad. And, water is heated for dissolving gelatin for a chilled salad.

These same techniques can be applied to any of your own favorite salad recipes which require some type of cooking or heating.

A main dish salad with a Mexican flavor. Good for a summer supper.

MEXICAN BEEF SALAD

　½ head lettuce
　4 ozs. fresh spinach
　1 lb. ground beef
　½ teaspoon onion salt
　½ teaspoon chili powder
　¼ teaspoon salt
　¼ teaspoon garlic powder
　¼ teaspoon Tabasco sauce
　½ cup water
　1 can (15 oz.) garbanzo beans or chick peas, drained
　3 tomatoes, cut into wedges
　1 avocado, peeled and sliced
　1 cup shredded Cheddar cheese
　2 cups tortilla or corn chips
　1 small onion, finely chopped
　¼ cup salad dressing or mayonnaise
　¼ cup chili sauce

1. Wash and tear lettuce and spinach into bite-size pieces. Chill.
2. Crumble ground beef into 1½ or 2-quart glass casserole.
3. MICROWAVE 8 to 8½ minutes or until meat is set. Stir to break meat into pieces; drain fat. Stir in onion salt, chili powder, salt, garlic powder, Tabasco sauce, water and garbanzo beans.
4. MICROWAVE, covered, 3 to 3½ minutes or until hot.
5. Combine salad greens and remaining ingredients in large salad bowl; toss well to combine. Add hot meat mixture; toss lightly. Serve at once.　　5 to 6 Servings

CHILLED RICE SALAD VINAIGRETTE

　2 cups uncooked long-grain rice
　4 cups water
　1 teaspoon salt
　1 tablespoon butter or margarine
　1 can (4 oz.) mushroom stems and pieces, drained
　2 green onions, thinly sliced
　½ teaspoon salt
　½ teaspoon dried parsley flakes
Dash pepper
　1 tablespoon vinegar
　2 tablespoons cooking oil

1. Combine rice, water, 1 teaspoon salt and the butter in 3-quart glass casserole.
2. MICROWAVE, covered, 15 to 17 minutes or until rice is just about tender. Fluff with fork. Cover and let stand 5 minutes.
3. Add remaining ingredients; toss to coat well. Chill at least 2 hours before serving.
　　　　　　　　　　　　　5 to 6 Servings

CURRIED RICE SALAD

　2 cups uncooked long-grain rice
　4 cups water
　1 teaspoon salt
　1 tablespoon butter or margarine
　1 carrot, grated
　2 green onions, thinly sliced
　½ cup sliced celery
　½ cup sour cream
　½ cup mayonnaise or salad dressing
　1 teaspoon curry powder
　½ teaspoon seasoned salt

1. Combine rice, water, salt and butter in 3-quart glass casserole.
2. MICROWAVE, covered, 15 to 17 minutes or until rice is just about tender. Fluff with fork. Cover and let stand 5 minutes.
3. Add remaining ingredients; mix well. Chill at least 2 hours before serving.　6 to 8 Servings

TIP • For a main course salad, add cooked shrimp or cubed cooked chicken or turkey.

Pictured: Lime-Cheese Mold, page 127 and Mexican Beef Salad, this page.

CLASSIC POTATO SALAD

6 medium potatoes
**3 green onions, thinly sliced or 1 small
onion, finely chopped**
2 stalks celery, chopped
3 hard-cooked eggs, chopped
1 cup mayonnaise or salad dressing
1 teaspoon prepared mustard
½ teaspoon salt
⅛ teaspoon pepper

1. Cook potatoes as directed on page 111. Peel potatoes and coarsely chop into serving bowl.
2. Add remaining ingredients; mix well. Chill at least 1 hour before serving.   5 to 6 Servings

TIPS • ¼ cup drained pickle relish may be added to recipe if desired.

  • For best blend of flavors, mix potato salad while potatoes are still warm. If potatoes are cold, chop and microwave about 3 minutes to heat them before adding dressing.

  • Cooked Salad Dressing, this page, may be substituted for mayonnaise and mustard.

Microwaves cook the potatoes and dressing for this recipe. And, if the salad cools before serving, they can also be used to reheat it.

GERMAN POTATO SALAD

4 medium potatoes
4 slices bacon, cut into pieces
**1 medium onion, finely chopped, or
6 green onions, sliced**
2 tablespoons sugar
1 tablespoon all-purpose flour
1 teaspoon instant beef bouillon
1 teaspoon salt
¼ teaspoon allspice, if desired
Dash pepper
¼ cup vinegar
½ cup water

1. Cook potatoes as directed on page 111.
2. MICROWAVE bacon in glass bowl or serving dish 4 minutes; stir in onion.
3. MICROWAVE 6 to 6½ minutes or until bacon is crisp and onion is tender. Stir in remaining ingredients, except potatoes.
4. MICROWAVE 4½ to 5 minutes or until thickened. Peel potatoes and slice into dressing. Toss lightly to coat. Serve warm.
5 to 6 Servings

COOKED SALAD DRESSING

2 tablespoons all-purpose flour
2 tablespoons sugar
1¼ teaspoons salt
½ teaspoon dry mustard
Dash Tabasco sauce
2 eggs
¾ cup milk
¼ cup vinegar
3 tablespoons cooking oil

1. Combine all ingredients except vinegar and oil in 2-cup glass measure; beat smooth with rotary beater.
2. MICROWAVE 5 to 6 minutes or until mixture thickens, stirring occasionally during last half of cooking time. Stir in vinegar and oil; beat with rotary beater until smooth. 1¾ Cups

WILTED LETTUCE SALAD

5 slices bacon, cut into pieces
¼ cup vinegar
1 tablespoon sugar
½ teaspoon salt
¼ teaspoon dry mustard
¼ teaspoon pepper
**1 head leaf lettuce, torn into bite-size
pieces**
2 green onions, sliced
2 hard-cooked eggs, sliced
1 tomato, cut into wedges
6 radishes, sliced

1. MICROWAVE bacon in 3-quart glass casserole or serving dish 9 to 11 minutes or until bacon is crisp.
2. Drain bacon drippings except for 2 tablespoons; stir vinegar, sugar and seasonings into the 2 tablespoons drippings.
3. MICROWAVE 2 to 2½ minutes or until hot.
4. Add remaining ingredients; toss lightly to coat greens with dressing.   About 8 Servings

TIP • Substitute for leaf lettuce: 10 ozs. fresh spinach. Or, use half spinach and half lettuce.

HOT CABBAGE SALAD

> **3 slices bacon, cut into pieces**
> **1 tablespoon packed brown sugar**
> **1 teaspoon salt**
> **¼ cup vinegar**
> **4 cups (½ med. head) shredded cabbage**
> **1 medium cucumber, sliced**
> **1 green onion, sliced**
> **5 to 6 radishes, sliced**

1. MICROWAVE bacon in 1½-quart glass casserole 7 to 8 minutes or until crisp. Add remaining ingredients; toss lightly.
2. MICROWAVE 3 to 4 minutes or until warm.
    About 8 Servings

TOMATO ASPIC

> **½ cup water**
> **1 package (3 oz.) lemon-flavored gelatin**
> **1 can (12 oz.) tomato juice**
> **1 small onion, finely grated or chopped**
> **1 cup chopped celery**
> **¼ cup pickle relish**
> **1½ tablespoons lemon juice**
> **½ teaspoon salt**
> **⅛ teaspoon Tabasco sauce**

1. MICROWAVE water in 1-quart glass casserole 4 to 5 minutes or until hot. Stir in gelatin until dissolved.
2. Stir in remaining ingredients. Chill until thickened. Stir mixture; pour into 4 or 5-cup mold. Chill 4 hours or until set. Unmold.
    5 to 6 Servings

TIP • Tomato sauce or canned tomatoes may be substituted for tomato juice. Use about 1½ cups.

CREAMY ASPARAGUS MOLD

> **1 envelope unflavored gelatin**
> **¼ cup cold water**
> **1 can (15 oz.) cut asparagus**
> **1 cup sour cream**
> **⅓ cup salad dressing or mayonnaise**
> **1 stalk celery, finely chopped**
> **1 green onion, finely chopped**
> **½ tablespoon prepared mustard**
> **1 teaspoon salt**

1. Soften gelatin in cold water in medium glass mixing bowl.
2. MICROWAVE 1 minute or until gelatin is dissolved. Drain asparagus; add water to liquid to make ¾ cup. Add asparagus and liquid to gelatin mixture. Stir in remaining ingredients. Pour into 4-cup mold; chill at least 4 hours or until set. Unmold before serving.
    About 6 Servings

Use this recipe as a guide for preparing gelatin salads with the microwave oven. With layered gelatin salads such as this one, the gelatin sometimes sets before it is ready to be used. Microwave cooking can be used to warm and melt gelatin again.

LIME-CHEESE MOLD

> **1 cup water**
> **1 package (3 oz.) lime-flavored gelatin**
> **1 can (8 oz.) sliced peaches, undrained**
> **10 Maraschino cherries**
> **1 package (8 oz.) cream cheese**
> **24 large marshmallows**
> **½ cup flaked coconut**

1. MICROWAVE water in 4-cup glass measure 5 to 6 minutes or until hot. Stir in gelatin until dissolved. Drain peach syrup into same measuring cup; add water to make 2¼ cups. Pour half of mixture into 5 or 6-cup mold; garnish with cherries. Chill to set while preparing next layer. (Leave remaining gelatin at room temperature.)
2. MICROWAVE cream chese and marshmallows in small glass mixing bowl 2½ to 3 minutes or until marshmallows and cream cheese are soft. Beat until smooth. Stir in peaches and ½ cup of remaining lime gelatin mixture. Chill until consistency of unbeaten egg whites; pour over set layer of gelatin. Chill until set. Stir coconut into remaining liquid gelatin mixture. Spoon over set layers. Chill until set. Unmold.
    6 to 8 Servings

Breads

QUICK BREADS: Quick breads usually require a short baking time. Therefore, the addition of microwave cooking decreases the time less for these breads than for many other foods. Conventional heat is necessary to achieve attractive browning and crusting, so the breads begin cooking with normal bake temperatures or sometimes 25° higher. Once the bread has started to set and brown, microwave cooking is added to quickly set and cook the interior. The finished bread has a light to golden brown crust with a light, moist interior.

Breads become tough and dry if overcooked. For this reason, if additional cooking time is necessary, it is best to continue with just the bake setting rather than the faster microwave-bake. This reduces chances of overcooking.

Since microwave cooking results in a time reduction and produces some "steam leavening" in the bread, leavening agents such as baking powder and soda can be reduced by about one-half. When they are not reduced, the finished bread may have a leavening-like taste.

Because microwave cooking is used for these breads, glass baking dishes are required except for muffins where a good substitute glass pan is not available. With metal pans, cooking techniques and times are very similar to those used for glass baking dishes.

HEATING ROOM TEMPERATURE ROLLS

Place rolls directly on oven rack or place on napkin on oven rack. Microwave until rolls feel warm:

    1 Roll — ½ to 1 minute
    4 Rolls — 1 to 2 minutes
    6 Rolls — 1½ to 2 minutes

HERB-BUTTERED GARLIC BREAD

  1 loaf French bread
½ cup butter or margarine
  1 tablespoon dried parsley flakes
  1 clove garlic, finely chopped

1. Cut bread diagonally into ½-inch slices, but do not slice all the way through loaf.
2. MICROWAVE butter, parsley and garlic in small glass bowl 2½ to 3 minutes or until melted.
3. Brush butter mixture on each slice of bread. Cut a strip of 12-inch foil the length of French loaf; fold the strip of foil in half lengthwise. Place loaf on foil and set on oven rack.
4. MICROWAVE 1 to 1¼ minutes or until hot.

                          1 Loaf

TIP • Substitute for clove of garlic: ⅛ teaspoon garlic powder.

BREAD MIXES

MIX	PAN	COOKING METHOD (preheated oven)
Corn Bread	8-inch square glass baking dish	BAKE 425° F for 8 min. ✤ MICROWAVE-BAKE 2 to 2½ min.
Muffin Mix	Metal muffin pans (12 cups)	BAKE 425° F for 5 min. ✤ MICROWAVE-BAKE 2½ to 3 min.
Nut Bread Mix	1½-quart (8x4) glass baking dish	BAKE 350° F for 15 min. ✤ MICROWAVE-BAKE 7 to 8 min.
Coffee Cake Mix	8-inch square glass baking dish	BAKE 400° F for 12 min. ✤ MICROWAVE-BAKE 3 to 4 min.

Pictured, clockwise: Cream Coffee Cake, page 132, Swiss Egg Braid, page 134 and Cheese Muffins, page 131.

QUICK CASSEROLE BREAD

⅓ cup butter or margarine
½ cup chopped onion
3 cups biscuit mix
½ teaspoon dill weed
½ teaspoon celery seed
1 egg, beaten
1 cup milk

1. MICROWAVE butter and onion in large glass mixing bowl 3 to 4 minutes or until butter is melted.
2. Preheat oven to 425° F.
3. Add remaining ingredients to butter mixture; stir just until moistened. Spread in greased 1½-quart glass casserole.
4. BAKE 12 minutes. ✿
5. MICROWAVE-BAKE 5 to 6 minutes or until toothpick inserted in center comes out clean. Cool 5 minutes; loosen edges and turn out of dish.   1 Loaf

A moist cornmeal-type bread to serve with a spoon and top with butter. Try with baked ham.

OLD SOUTH SPOON BREAD

2 cups milk
½ cup cornmeal
½ teaspoon salt
2 tablespoons butter or margarine
2 eggs

1. Combine milk, cornmeal and salt in 1-quart glass casserole.
2. MICROWAVE 8 minutes or until mixture is bubbly, stirring once.
3. Preheat oven to 425° F.
4. Stir butter into cornmeal mixture until melted. Beat in eggs, one at a time, beating well after each addition.
5. BAKE 10 minutes. ✿
6. MICROWAVE-BAKE 5 to 6 minutes or until toothpick inserted in center comes out clean.
                                         4 to 5 Servings

Cheese lovers will agree that these rolls are delicious.

INDIVIDUAL CHEESE ROLLS

3 tablespoons butter or margarine
2¾ cups biscuit mix
1 cup shredded Cheddar cheese
¼ cup Parmesan cheese
½ teaspoon leaf oregano
1½ cups buttermilk or sour milk
2 tablespoons Parmesan cheese

1. MICROWAVE butter in small glass dish about 2½ minutes or until melted; set aside.
2. Preheat oven to 450° F.
3. Combine biscuit mix, Cheddar cheese, ¼ cup Parmesan cheese, the oregano and buttermilk in medium mixing bowl; mix well. Spoon into 8 greased 6-oz. glass custard cups. Brush tops with melted butter; sprinkle with 2 tablespoons Parmesan cheese.
4. BAKE 5 minutes. ✿
5. MICROWAVE-BAKE 5 to 6 minutes or until toothpick inserted in center comes out clean.
                                              8 Rolls

CORNBREAD

1 cup unsifted all-purpose flour
1 cup cornmeal
2 tablespoons sugar
3 teaspoons baking powder
1 teaspoon salt
2 eggs, slightly beaten
¼ cup cooking oil or melted shortening
1 cup milk

1. Preheat oven to 425° F.
2. Combine flour, cornmeal, sugar, baking powder and salt in medium mixing bowl. Combine remaining ingredients; add to dry ingredients and stir until smooth. Pour into greased 8-inch square glass baking dish.
3. BAKE 8 minutes. ✿
4. MICROWAVE-BAKE 2½ to 3 minutes or until toothpick inserted in center comes out clean.
                                         8 to 9 Servings

SCOTTISH SCONES

   2 cups unsifted all-purpose flour
   2 tablespoons sugar
   2 teaspoons baking powder
   1 teaspoon salt
   ¼ teaspoon soda
   ½ cup raisins
   ¼ cup cooking oil
   ½ cup sour cream
   3 tablespoons milk
   1 egg
Milk and sugar

1. Preheat oven to 450° F.
2. Combine flour, sugar, baking powder, salt, soda and raisins in medium mixing bowl; stir in oil, sour cream, milk and egg just until a dough forms. Turn onto floured surface and knead 12 to 15 times. Divide dough into 2 balls.
3. Pat out on floured surface to form slightly mounded 5-inch circles. Brush with some milk and sprinkle with sugar. Cut each circle into 6 wedges; place 1 inch apart on greased metal baking sheet.
4. BAKE 6 minutes. ✿
5. MICROWAVE-BAKE 1½ to 2 minutes or until no longer doughy.   12 Scones

BANANA BREAD

   2 cups unsifted all-purpose flour
   1 cup sugar
   ½ cup chopped nuts
   ½ teaspoon baking powder
   ½ teaspoon soda
   ½ teaspoon salt
   1 cup (2 med.) mashed ripe banana
   ½ cup cooking oil
   ¼ cup milk
   2 eggs

1. Preheat oven to 375° F.
2. Combine flour, sugar, nuts, baking powder, soda and salt in large mixing bowl. Combine remaining ingredients. Add to dry ingredients; stir until just moistened. Pour into 1½ or 2-quart (8x4 or 9x5) glass loaf dish, greased on bottom only.
3. BAKE 15 minutes. ✿
4. MICROWAVE-BAKE 7 to 9 minutes or until toothpick inserted in center comes out clean. Remove from pan; cool.   1 Loaf

Home recipe muffins require a higher oven temperature for browning than do muffin mixes.

CHEESE MUFFINS

   2 cups unsifted all-purpose flour
   3 tablespoons sugar
   2 teaspoons baking powder
   ½ teaspoon salt
   1 cup shredded Cheddar cheese
   1 cup milk
   1 egg
   ¼ cup cooking oil
Poppy seed

1. Preheat oven to 450° F.
2. Combine flour, sugar, baking powder, salt and cheese in large mixing bowl.
3. Beat together milk, egg and oil; add to dry ingredients. Mix just until combined. Spoon into 12 greased metal muffin cups; sprinkle with poppy seed.
4. BAKE 7 minutes. ✿
5. MICROWAVE-BAKE 3 to 3½ minutes or until toothpick inserted in center comes out clean.   12 Muffins

These light muffins contain no leavening. For ease in baking and a more desirable size, we have used the metal muffin pans.

COFFEE TIME GEMS

   ½ cup butter or margarine
   ¾ cup sugar
   3 eggs
   1 teaspoon vanilla
   1 cup unsifted all-purpose flour
   ¼ teaspoon salt
   3 tablespoons butter or margarine
   ¼ cup sugar
   ½ teaspoon cinnamon

1. MICROWAVE ½ cup butter in large glass mixing bowl about 1½ minutes or until softened.
2. Preheat oven to 425° F.
3. Add ¾ cup sugar to butter and beat until light and fluffy; beat in eggs and vanilla. Stir in flour and salt. Spoon into 12 greased metal muffin cups.
4. BAKE 5 minutes. ✿
5. MICROWAVE-BAKE 3 to 3½ minutes or until toothpick inserted in center comes out clean. Remove from oven and turn oven off. Remove muffins from pans; cool 5 minutes.
6. MICROWAVE 3 tablespoons butter in medium glass bowl 2 to 2½ minutes or until melted. Dip tops of muffins into butter, then into mixture of sugar and cinnamon.
    12 Muffins

Here is a convenient way to cook several pieces of French Toast at one time.

FRENCH TOAST

¼ **cup butter or margarine**
2 **eggs, beaten**
½ **cup milk**
1 **tablespoon sugar**
6 **slices bread**

1. Move oven rack to second position. Turn on broiler.
2. MICROWAVE-BROIL (while broiler preheats) butter in 15x10x1-inch metal jelly roll pan 3 to 3½ minutes or until melted.
3. Combine eggs, milk and sugar in shallow dish. Dip bread slices into egg mixture; place in butter in baking pan.
4. MICROWAVE-BROIL 3 to 3½ minutes or until lightly browned. Turn bread slices over.
5. BROIL 2 to 2½ minutes or until lightly browned.   6 Slices Toast

CREAM COFFEE CAKE

½ **cup butter or margarine**
¾ **cup sugar**
3 **eggs**
1 **teaspoon vanilla**
2 **cups unsifted all-purpose flour**
1 **teaspoon baking powder**
½ **teaspoon soda**
½ **cup milk**
½ **cup sour cream**

Streusel
1 **cup packed brown sugar**
1½ **teaspoons cinnamon**
¾ **cup chopped nuts**
¾ **cup flaked coconut**
¼ **cup butter or margarine**

1. MICROWAVE butter in small glass mixing bowl 1½ to 2 minutes or until softened.
2. Preheat oven to 350° F.
3. Add sugar to butter and beat together until light and fluffy; beat in eggs and vanilla. Stir in flour, baking powder, soda, milk and sour cream.
4. Spread half of batter in 2-quart (12x7) glass baking dish, greased on bottom only. Combine brown sugar, cinnamon, nuts and coconut in medium mixing bowl; cut in butter. Sprinkle half of Streusel mixture over batter. Top with remaining batter, then remaining Streusel mixture.
5. BAKE 15 minutes. ✿
6. MICROWAVE-BAKE 5 to 5½ minutes or until toothpick inserted in center comes out clean.
                      10 to 12 Servings

PUFFY PANCAKES

2 **tablespoons butter or margarine**
4 **eggs**
⅔ **cup unsifted all-purpose flour**
1 **tablespoon sugar**
½ **teaspoon salt**
⅔ **cup milk**

1. Preheat oven to 425° F.
2. Divide butter between two 8 or 9-inch round glass baking dishes; place in preheating oven to melt butter.
3. Beat eggs with rotary beater in medium mixing bowl. Add remaining ingredients and beat just until smooth.
4. Tilt baking dishes to coat with butter. Divide batter between pans.
5. BAKE 5 minutes. ✿
6. MICROWAVE-BAKE 6 to 7 minutes or until golden brown. (Pancakes may collapse slightly when removed from oven.) Cut into quarters and serve with powdered sugar, honey-butter or sweetened fruit.
                      2 Large Pancakes

A light, airy bread. Like a popover, but usually not hollow.

POP-UPS

1 **tablespoon butter or margarine**
2 **eggs**
1 **cup milk**
1 **cup unsifted all-purpose flour**
½ **teaspoon salt**

1. MICROWAVE butter in medium glass mixing bowl 1½ to 2 minutes or until melted.
2. Preheat oven to 450° F.
3. Add eggs to melted butter; beat with rotary beater until well blended. Add milk, flour and salt; beat just until smooth.
4. Pour into 8 well greased 5 or 6-oz. glass custard cups.
5. BAKE 15 minutes. ✿
6. MICROWAVE-BAKE 5 to 6 minutes or until golden brown.   8 Pop-Ups

Pictured: Puffy Pancake, this page.

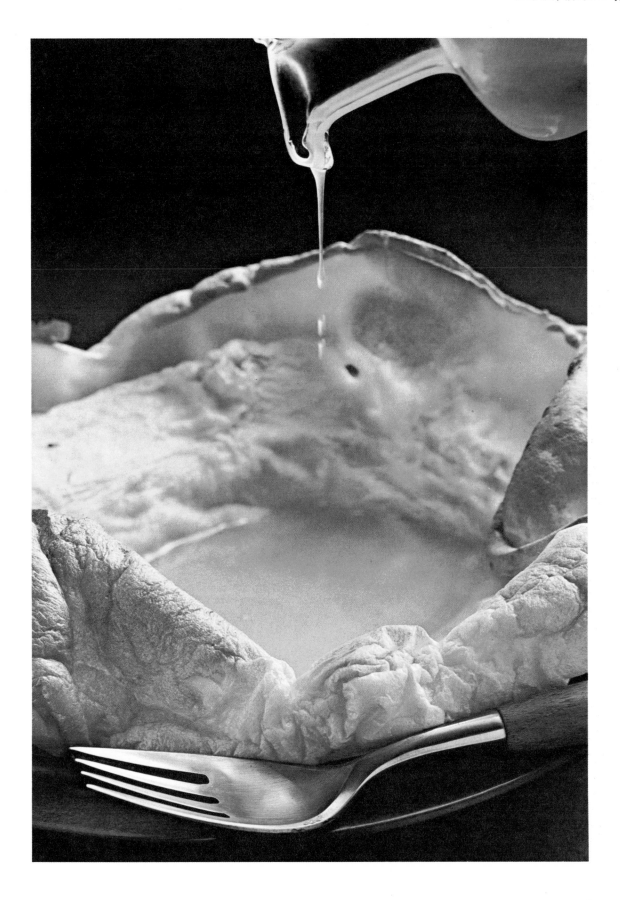

YEAST BREADS: An especially moist, spongy interior can be achieved by cooking yeast breads with combination cooking. As with quick breads, the temperature is similar to regular baking. After the bake temperature has started to brown the bread and allowed the bread to slowly rise, microwave cooking is added to quickly set and cook the interior. Be careful not to overcook in an effort to achieve conventional heat browning and crusting. It is normal for the baked bread to be a little lighter in color than usual and it may seem a little softer to handle. If you are uncertain of the doneness, use a toothpick to see if the interior is doughy. When additional cooking is necessary, use just the bake setting without microwave cooking. Overcooked yeast breads are chewy and dry.

When available, glass baking dishes are the best to use. However, since glass baking sheets are not available, we use metal. Time and technique are very similar to when breads are cooked in glass baking dishes.

A no-knead, easily made casserole bread.

NATURE CASSEROLE BREAD

2½ cups buttermilk or sour milk
⅓ cup butter or margarine
2 cups whole wheat flour
1 cup rolled oats
½ cup cornmeal
2 packages active dry yeast
1 tablespoon salt
½ cup molasses
3½ cups unsifted all-purpose flour

1. Combine buttermilk and butter in 4-cup glass measure.
2. MICROWAVE 4 to 4½ minutes or until very warm (120°-130°).
3. Combine whole wheat flour, rolled oats, cornmeal, dry yeast and salt. Stir in buttermilk mixture, molasses and 1 cup all-purpose flour. Beat at medium speed 4 minutes.
4. Stir in remaining 2½ cups flour. Cover; let rise in warm place until light and doubled in size, about 1 hour.
5. Stir down dough. Turn into well greased 2-quart glass casserole. Cover; let rise in warm place until doubled in size, about 45 minutes.
6. Preheat oven to 400° F.
7. BAKE 15 minutes. ✤
8. MICROWAVE-BAKE 7 to 8 minutes or until bread sounds hollow when tapped. Turn out of casserole; cool. 1 Loaf

This recipe is a good example of a loaf of bread baked on a metal baking sheet.

SWISS EGG BRAID

4½ to 5 cups unsifted all-purpose flour
1 package active dry yeast
2 tablespoons sugar
2 teaspoons salt
1¼ cups milk
½ cup butter or margarine
2 eggs (reserve 2 tablespoons)
1 tablespoon water

1. Combine 1½ cups flour, dry yeast, sugar and salt in large mixing bowl. Combine milk and butter in 4-cup glass measure.
2. MICROWAVE milk mixture about 3 minutes or until very warm (120°-130°). Add to flour mixture along with eggs. Beat at medium speed 3 minutes. Stir in remaining 3 to 3½ cups flour to form a stiff dough. Knead on floured surface until smooth and elastic, about 5 minutes.
3. Place in greased bowl, turning to grease top. Cover; let rise in warm place until light and doubled in size, 1½ to 2 hours.
4. Punch down dough; divide into 4 equal parts. Shape each part into a strip about 20 inches long. Place the 4 strips side by side on greased metal baking sheet. Pinch strips together at one end to seal. Braid by weaving far right strip over and under other strips to left; then weave next far right strip over and under other strips to left. Continue the weaving until loaf is braided; pinch ends together to seal. Cover; let rise in warm place until light and doubled in size, about 45 minutes.
5. Preheat oven to 400° F.
6. Combine reserved egg and 1 tablespoon water; brush over loaf.
7. BAKE 15 minutes. ✤
8. MICROWAVE-BAKE 4 to 4½ minutes or until loaf sounds hollow when tapped. (Do not overcook.) Remove from pan; cool.
1 Large Loaf

Bread cooked with combination cooking has a special moistness and lightness. Be careful not to overcook. It will be less crusty and lighter in color than traditionally baked bread.

WHITE BREAD

5½ to 6 cups unsifted all-purpose flour
2 packages active dry yeast
3 tablespoons sugar
2 teaspoons salt
2 cups milk
¼ cup butter or margarine

1. Combine 2 cups flour, dry yeast, sugar and salt in large mixing bowl. Combine milk and butter in 4-cup glass measure.

2. MICROWAVE milk mixture about 4 minutes or until very warm (120°-130°). Add to flour mixture; beat at medium speed until smooth. Add 1 cup flour. Beat at medium speed 3 minutes. Stir in remaining 2½ to 3 cups flour to form a stiff dough. Knead on floured surface until smooth and elastic, 5 to 7 minutes.

3. Place in greased bowl, turning to grease top. Cover; let rise in warm place until light and doubled in size, 1 to 1½ hours.

4. Punch down dough; divide in half. Shape each half into a loaf. Place in greased 1½ or 2-quart (8x4 or 9x5) glass loaf dish. Cover; let rise in warm place until light and doubled in size, about 45 minutes.

5. Preheat oven to 400° F.

6. BAKE 15 minutes. ✿

7. MICROWAVE-BAKE 5 to 5½ minutes or until bread sounds hollow when tapped. (Do not overcook.) Remove from pans; cool.

2 Loaves

TIP • For 1 loaf, bake 15 minutes, then microwave-bake 3 to 3½ minutes or until bread sounds hollow when tapped.

CINNAMON ROLLS

1 cup milk
3 tablespoons butter or margarine
3 to 3½ cups unsifted all-purpose flour
1 package active dry yeast
1 teaspoon salt
¼ cup sugar
1 egg

Filling
¼ cup butter or margarine
½ cup packed brown sugar
2 teaspoons cinnamon

1. MICROWAVE milk and 3 tablespoons butter in 2-cup glass measure about 3 minutes or until milk is very warm (120°-130°).

2. Combine 1½ cups flour, dry yeast, salt and sugar in large mixing bowl. Stir in milk mixture and egg. Beat at medium speed 2 minutes. Stir in remaining 1½ to 2 cups flour to form a stiff dough. Knead on floured surface until smooth and elastic, about 5 minutes.

3. Place in greased bowl, turning to grease top. Cover; let rise in warm place until light and doubled in size, 1 to 1½ hours.

4. Punch down dough. Roll out to form an 18x15-inch rectangle.

5. MICROWAVE ¼ cup butter in small glass bowl 2 to 2½ minutes or until melted.

6. Spread dough with butter. Sprinkle with brown sugar and cinnamon. Roll up, jelly-roll fashion, starting with 18-inch side. Cut into 12 slices. Place cut-side-down in greased 3-quart (13x9) glass baking dish.

7. Cover; let rise in warm place until light and doubled in size, about 45 minutes.

8. Preheat oven to 425° F.

9. BAKE 7 minutes. ✿

10. MICROWAVE-BAKE 3 to 3½ minutes or until no longer doughy in center. Turn out of pan; cool.

12 Cinnamon Rolls

DINNER ROLLS

1. Prepare dough for Cinnamon Rolls. After rising, punch down dough and divide into 15 pieces. Shape each into a round ball. Arrange in greased 2-quart (12x7) glass baking dish.

2. Cover; let rise in warm place until doubled in size. Continue as directed in steps 8, 9 and 10.

15 Dinner Rolls

Fruit Desserts

FRUIT SAUCES: Microwaves provide the only cooking necessary for simmering fresh fruits and preparing warm fruit sauces. Fresh fruits are cooked until tender and sauces are cooked until heated. Or, when there is a thickening such as cornstarch or flour, sauces are cooked until the mixture boils and the starch thickens.

RHUBARB SAUCE

4 cups sliced rhubarb (½-inch pieces)
2 tablespoons water
¾ to 1 cup sugar

1. Combine rhubarb and water in 3-quart glass casserole.
2. MICROWAVE, covered, 10 to 12 minutes or until rhubarb is tender. Stir in sugar.

About 3 Cups Sauce

PEACH MELBA

1 package (10 oz.) frozen raspberries
1 can (29 oz.) peach halves, undrained
2 tablespoons cornstarch
Dash salt
½ teaspoon almond extract
Red food coloring, if desired
Vanilla ice cream

1. MICROWAVE frozen raspberries 3 to 4 minutes or until thawed. Drain juice from raspberries into medium glass mixing bowl. Drain juice from can of peaches into same bowl. Set fruits aside. Stir cornstarch and salt into juices.
2. MICROWAVE 7 to 8 minutes or until mixture boils and thickens, stirring once during last half of cooking time. Stir in raspberries, almond extract and food coloring.
3. Arrange scoops of ice cream in individual dessert dishes; top with peach half and spoon raspberry sauce over all.   6 to 8 Servings

Pictured: Peach and Blueberry Fruit Cobbler, page 141 and Cherries Jubilee, this page.

APPLESAUCE

6 cups sliced cooking apples
½ cup water
½ to ¾ cup sugar
½ teaspoon nutmeg, if desired

1. Combine apples and water in 2-quart glass casserole.
2. MICROWAVE, covered, 12 to 15 minutes or until apples are tender. Stir in sugar and nutmeg.   About 3 Cups Sauce

CHERRIES JUBILEE

1 can (16 oz.) pitted Bing Cherries, undrained
¼ cup red currant jelly
1½ tablespoons cornstarch
¼ cup brandy or Cognac
Ice cream

1. Combine cherries, jelly and cornstarch in 4-cup glass or pottery serving dish; mix well.
2. MICROWAVE 10 to 12 minutes or until mixture boils and thickens, stirring once during last half of cooking time.
3. MICROWAVE brandy in 1-cup glass measure about ½ minute or until just warm. Flame and carefully pour over cherry sauce. Serve over ice cream.   6 to 8 Servings

TIP • This sauce is also delicious served with cheese cake.

Warm bananas served flaming in a brown sugar and butter sauce.

BANANAS FLAMBE

¼ cup orange juice
¼ cup butter or margarine
½ cup packed brown sugar
2 tablespoons light cream or milk
½ teaspoon cinnamon
4 firm bananas, peeled and halved
2 to 4 tablespoons orange liqueur or rum
Ice cream

1. Combine orange juice, butter, brown sugar, cream and cinnamon in 8 or 9-inch round glass baking dish.
2. MICROWAVE 4 minutes or until just bubbly. Stir in bananas, coating with sauce.
3. MICROWAVE 1½ to 2 minutes or until bananas are warm.
4. MICROWAVE liqueur in 1-cup glass measure about ½ minute or until just warm. Flame and carefully pour over bananas. Serve banana halves and sauce over scoops of ice cream in individual serving dishes.

About 8 Servings

FRUIT FONDUE

¼ **cup sugar**
¼ **cup lemon juice**
½ **cup orange marmalade**
½ **cup orange juice**
¾ **cup water**
2½ **tablespoons cornstarch**
Dash salt
**Apple slices, strawberries, banana slices,
    cherries or pineapple chunks**

1. Combine all ingredients except fruit in 4-cup glass or pottery fondue pot; mix well.
2. MICROWAVE 7 to 8 minutes or until bubbly and thickened, stirring once during last half of cooking time. Keep warm over fondue burner while serving. Dip fruits into sauce.

                                    2 Cups Sauce

TIP • Substitute for marmalade: red currant jelly. Add a few drops red food coloring, if desired.

BAKED APPLES

4 **medium baking apples**
4 **tablespoons brown sugar**
2 **tablespoons butter or margarine**
Cinnamon

1. Wash and core apples; place in 8-inch square or round baking dish.
2. Place 1 tablespoon brown sugar and ½ tablespoon butter in center of each apple. Sprinkle with cinnamon.
3. MICROWAVE, covered, 10 to 12 minutes or until apples are tender.   4 Apples

TIPS • If desired, add with the brown sugar ½ tablespoon raisins, chopped nuts or mincemeat.

   • For 6 apples, microwave 16 to 18 minutes.

FRUIT CRISPS AND COBBLERS: Combination cooking is used when the fruit dessert includes a topping. The conventional baking browns and crisps the topping while microwaves quickly cook the fruit. With most of these desserts, the two types of cooking are used simultaneously. One exception is when the fruit is wrapped in a crust. Here conventional heat is used until the crust sets, then microwave cooking is added. If the crust is not set before the microwave cooking begins, steam from the fruit may cause the crust to slide off the fruit.

DUTCH APPLE TORTE

Crust
1½ **cups unsifted all-purpose flour**
⅓ **cup sugar**
1 **teaspoon grated lemon peel**
¼ **teaspoon salt**
¼ **teaspoon baking powder**
½ **cup butter or margarine**
1 **egg**

Filling
1 **cup sour cream**
¾ **cup sugar**
1 **egg**
2 **tablespoons all-purpose flour**
¼ **teaspoon nutmeg or cinnamon**
¼ **teaspoon salt**
5 **cups peeled sliced apples**
1 **can (16 oz.) sliced peaches, drained**

Topping
¼ **cup unsifted all-purpose flour**
¼ **cup packed brown sugar**
½ **teaspoon nutmeg or cinnamon**
¼ **cup butter or margarine**

1. Preheat oven to 425° F.
2. Combine flour, sugar, lemon peel, salt and baking powder for Crust in medium mixing bowl. Cut in butter until mixture is crumbly. Stir in egg. Press evenly over bottom and halfway up sides of 2-quart (12x7) glass baking dish.
3. Combine Filling ingredients in medium mixing bowl; spread over crust.
4. Combine flour, brown sugar, and nutmeg for Topping in small mixing bowl. Cut in butter until mixture is crumbly. Sprinkle over fruit filling.
5. MICROWAVE-BAKE 14 to 16 minutes or until apples are tender.   12 to 15 Servings

APPLE CRISP

    **6 cups (6 med.) peeled, sliced cooking
      apples
    1 tablespoon water
    1 tablespoon lemon juice**

Topping
    **¾ cup packed brown sugar
    ½ cup unsifted all-purpose flour
    ½ cup rolled oats
    1 teaspoon cinnamon
    ½ cup butter or margarine**

1. Preheat oven to 400° F.
2. Place apples in 8-inch square glass baking dish. Sprinkle with water and lemon juice.
3. Combine brown sugar, flour, rolled oats and cinnamon in medium mixing bowl. Cut in butter until crumbly. Sprinkle over apples.
4. MICROWAVE-BAKE 12 to 15 minutes or until apples are tender.   5 to 6 Servings

CHERRY-RHUBARB COBBLER

    **1 cup unsifted all-purpose flour
    ¼ cup sugar
    ½ teaspoon salt
    ⅛ teaspoon baking powder
    ⅓ cup butter or margarine**

Cherry-Rhubarb Filling
    **1 can (21 oz.) prepared cherry pie filling
    3 cups thinly sliced fresh rhubarb
    ¼ cup sugar
    1 tablespoon cornstarch
    1 teaspoon cinnamon**

Sour Cream Topping
    **1½ cups sour cream
    2 tablespoons packed brown sugar
    1 teaspoon vanilla**

1. Preheat oven to 400° F.
2. Combine flour, sugar, salt and baking powder in medium mixing bowl; cut in butter until mixture is crumbly. Press into 2-quart (12x7) glass baking dish.
3. Combine filling ingredients in medium mixing bowl; pour over crust.
4. MICROWAVE-BAKE 6 to 8 minutes or until rhubarb is tender.
5. Mix together sour cream, brown sugar and vanilla in small mixing bowl. Drop spoonfuls on hot fruit filling.
6. MICROWAVE-BAKE 1 to 1½ minutes or until topping is set.   10 to 12 Servings

    TIP • Sour Cream Topping may be omitted and dessert served with ice cream or whipped cream.

APPLE DUMPLINGS

    **1 package (11 oz.) pie crust mix
    6 medium apples, peeled and cored
    ⅓ cup packed brown sugar
    ¾ teaspoon cinnamon
    ½ teaspoon nutmeg
    ½ teaspoon allspice, if desired
    2 tablespoons butter or margarine
    2 cups water
    1 cup packed brown sugar**

1. Preheat oven to 450° F.
2. Prepare pastry as directed on package; roll out to an 18x12-inch rectangle. Cut into 6 squares.
3. Place an apple on center of each pastry square. Fill apples with mixture of ⅓ cup brown sugar and the spices. Dot each with 1 teaspoon butter. Moisten edges of pastry. Bring up corners to top of apple; pinch edges together to seal. Place in 2-quart (12x7) glass baking dish. Combine water and 1 cup brown sugar; mix well and pour over dumplings.
4. BAKE 12 minutes. ✿
5. MICROWAVE-BAKE 8 to 10 minutes or until apples are tender. Spoon sauce over dumplings before serving.   6 Dumplings

A simple-to-make version of apple dumplings.

APPLE WRAP-UPS IN ORANGE SAUCE

    **2 tablespoons butter or margarine
    2 large or 4 medium apples, peeled and
      cored
    1 can (8 oz.) refrigerated crescent rolls
    ½ cup sugar
    1 teaspoon cinnamon
    ½ cup orange juice**

1. MICROWAVE butter in 8-inch square glass baking dish about 2 minutes or until melted; set aside.
2. Preheat oven to 425° F.
3. Cut large apples into eighths or medium apples into quarters. Separate crescent dough into 8 crescents; halve each lengthwise to make 16. Place an apple wedge at wide end of each piece of dough; roll up toward narrow end.
4. Arrange in baking dish, turning each piece to coat with butter. Combine sugar and cinnamon; sprinkle over rolls. Pour orange juice over rolls.
5. BAKE 10 minutes. ✿
6. MICROWAVE-BAKE 7 to 8 minutes or until golden brown and apples are tender.
    5 to 6 Servings

    TIP • Substitute for apples: fresh peaches.

FRUIT COBBLER

    4 cups fresh blueberries or sliced peaches
    ½ cup sugar
    1 tablespoon cornstarch
    1 teaspoon lemon juice

Topping
    1 cup unsifted all-purpose flour
    2 tablespoons sugar
    1 teaspoon baking powder
    ½ teaspoon salt
    ¼ cup butter or margarine
    ½ cup milk

1. Preheat oven to 425° F.
2. Combine fruit, sugar, cornstarch and lemon juice in 8-inch square glass baking dish; set aside.
3. Combine flour, sugar, baking powder and salt for Topping in large mixing bowl. Cut in butter until crumbly. Stir in milk just until moistened. Drop spoonfuls on fruit mixture.
4. MICROWAVE-BAKE 10 to 12 minutes or until bubbly in center.   8 to 9 Servings

CHERRY CRUNCH DESSERT

    ½ cup butter or margarine
    1 can (21 oz.) prepared cherry pie filling
    1 can (8 oz.) sliced peaches or crushed pineapple, undrained
    1 package (9 oz.) yellow cake mix (1-layer size)
    ½ cup chopped nuts

1. MICROWAVE butter in glass dish 2½ to 3 minutes or until melted.
2. Preheat oven to 375° F.
3. Combine pie filling and peaches in 8-inch square glass baking dish. Sprinkle cake mix over fruit filling; top with nuts. Drizzle melted butter over top.
4. MICROWAVE-BAKE 15 to 17 minutes or until golden brown and no longer doughy.
                              8 to 10 Servings

FRUIT 'N CRUNCH MIX

1. Preheat oven to 375° F.
2. Prepare 1 package (18 oz.) favorite flavor fruit 'n crunch mix as directed on package, using an 8-inch square glass baking dish.
3. MICROWAVE-BAKE 8 to 10 minutes or until golden brown and no longer doughy.
                              6 to 8 Servings

Pictured: Apple Wrap-Ups in Orange Sauce and Apple Dumplings, page 139.

CAKE-TYPE FRUIT DESSERTS: With these heavy, moist cake-like desserts, the cake technique is used. This method begins with a baking temperature to brown the cake and start the leavening process. Then microwave cooking is added to finish cooking the interior.

FRUIT COCKTAIL DESSERT

    1 can (16 oz.) fruit cocktail
    3 tablespoons butter or margarine, softened
    ½ cup sugar
    1 egg
    1 cup unsifted all-purpose flour
    1 teaspoon salt
    ¼ teaspoon soda
    ¼ teaspoon baking powder
    ⅓ cup packed brown sugar
    ¼ cup chopped nuts

1. Preheat oven to 350° F.
2. Drain fruit cocktail, reserving ⅓ cup liquid. Beat together butter, sugar and egg. Stir in drained fruit cocktail, the reserved liquid and remaining ingredients except brown sugar and nuts.
3. Pour into greased 8-inch square glass baking dish. Sprinkle with mixture of brown sugar and nuts.
4. BAKE 18 minutes. ✿
5. MICROWAVE-BAKE 6 to 7 minutes or until toothpick inserted in center comes out clean.
                              About 9 Servings

APPLE-DATE PUDDING CAKE

    1 cup unsifted all-purpose flour
    ⅔ cup packed brown sugar
    ½ teaspoon soda
    ½ teaspoon salt
    ½ teaspoon cinnamon
    ¼ teaspoon nutmeg
    ½ cup cooking oil
    1 egg
    2 cups shredded apple
    1 cup chopped dates

1. Preheat oven to 375° F.
2. Combine all ingredients in large mixing bowl; stir until dry ingredients are moistened.
3. Spread in 8-inch glass baking dish, greased on bottom only.
4. BAKE 18 minutes. ✿
5. MICROWAVE-BAKE 3 to 5 minutes or until toothpick inserted in center comes out clean. Serve with favorite dessert sauce or whipped cream.   About 9 Servings

TIP • Substitute for dates: 1 cup raisins or ½ cup each dates and nuts.

Pudding Desserts

PUDDINGS: Microwave cooking heats the pudding from all sides, eliminating any chance of scorching.

The 4-cup glass measure is convenient for puddings — either homemade or mix. You can measure the liquid and cook in the same container.

Stirring once or twice during the last half of the cooking time is important. The starches tend to settle in the uncooked pudding and, if they are not dispersed throughout during the cooking, they cook in a firm mass on the bottom. Then when stirred after cooking, the firm mass breaks into lumps.

PUDDING AND PIE FILLING MIX

1. Combine in 4-cup glass measure, 1 package pudding and pie filling mix with amount of milk specified on package.
2. MICROWAVE 9 to 10 minutes for 4-serving size and 15 to 16 minutes for 6-serving size or until mixture boils. Stir occasionally during last half of cooking time.

4 to 6 Servings

TAPIOCA PUDDING

  2 cups milk
¼ cup sugar
  3 tablespoons quick-cooking tapioca
¼ teaspoon salt
  2 eggs, separated
  2 tablespoons sugar
  1 teaspoon vanilla

1. Combine milk, ¼ cup sugar, tapioca, salt and egg yolks in 4-cup glass measure; mix well.
2. MICROWAVE 8 to 10 minutes or until mixture boils, stirring once during last half of cooking.
3. Beat egg whites until frothy. Gradually add 2 tablespoons sugar, beating until mixture forms soft peaks. Beat in vanilla. Fold in pudding. Serve warm or cold. 4 to 6 Servings

TIP • If desired, fold 1 to 2 cups sliced or chopped drained fresh or canned fruit into cooked pudding.

VANILLA CREAM PUDDING

½ cup sugar
  2 tablespoons cornstarch
¼ teaspoon salt
2½ cups milk
  1 egg
  1 teaspoon vanilla

1. Combine all ingredients except vanilla in 4-cup glass measure. Beat until smooth.
2. MICROWAVE 10 to 12 minutes or until mixture boils, stirring once during last half of cooking time. Stir in vanilla. Serve warm or cold. 5 to 6 Servings

CHOCOLATE CREAM PUDDING

Prepare vanilla pudding as directed above except add 1 envelope (1 oz.) premelted unsweetened chocolate to cooked pudding.

Start with a pudding mix — add rice, fruit and whipped cream to make it special.

EASY RICE PUDDING SUPREME

2½ cups milk
  1 package (4-serving size) vanilla pudding and pie filling mix
½ cup quick-cooking rice
½ cup raisins
½ cup whipping cream, whipped, or 1 cup frozen whipped topping, thawed
  1 can (17 oz.) fruits for salad, drained

1. Combine milk, pudding mix, rice and raisins in 4-cup glass measure.
2. MICROWAVE 11 to 13 minutes or until mixture boils, stirring once during last half of cooking time. Cool.
3. Fold pudding, whipped cream and fruit together in large mixing bowl. Refrigerate until served. 6 to 8 Servings

TIP • Substitute for fruits for salad: fruit cocktail, sliced peaches or other favorite canned fruit.

Pictured, top to bottom: Easy Rice Pudding Supreme, this page, Ice Cream Grasshopper, page 145, Cheese Cake garnished with Kiwi fruit, page 150 and Chocolate Angel Pie, page 149.

BAKED CUSTARDS: Combination cooking is used to cook custards. Usually the custard dish or cups are set in water during cooking. This slows the cooking and prevents overcooking, the cause of curdling and separation. The amount and depth of the water affects the cooking time.

With individual custards, some may be cooked before others. These should be removed from the oven so they will not overcook.

Some custards cook a little better using the defrost feature. The ''Tips'' include directions for ovens not having the defrost feature.

To test custards for doneness, insert a knife about halfway between the edge and the center. If the custard mixture does not cling to the knife, it is done. The center may still be soft, but will finish cooking as the custard cools.

Apples and raisins add a tart flavor to this bread pudding.

APPLE 'n RAISIN BREAD PUDDING

    ¼ cup butter or margarine
    4 cups fresh bread cubes
    2½ cups peeled, sliced apples
    ¼ cup raisins
    ¼ cup sugar
    1½ teaspoons grated lemon peel
    3 tablespoons lemon juice
    3 eggs, separated
    ⅔ cup milk
    ½ cup sugar

1. MICROWAVE butter in 1½-quart glass casserole about 2½ minutes or until melted.
2. Preheat oven to 400° F.
3. Add bread, apples, raisins, ¼ cup sugar, the lemon peel and juice, egg yolks and milk to melted butter; mix well. Beat egg whites in medium mixing bowl until frothy; gradually beat in ½ cup sugar until soft peaks form. Fold into bread mixture.
4. Set casserole in 8-inch square glass baking dish. Add 1½ cups cold tap water to baking dish.
5. MICROWAVE-BAKE 16 to 17 minutes or until knife inserted near center comes out clean (center will still be soft). If desired, serve with Lemon Sauce, page 119.

                                5 to 6 Servings

BAKED CUSTARD

    1¾ cups milk
    ¼ cup sugar
    3 eggs
    ¼ teaspoon salt
    ¼ teaspoon nutmeg
    ½ teaspoon vanilla

1. Preheat oven to 375° F.
2. Combine all ingredients in 1-quart glass casserole. Beat with rotary beater until smooth. Set casserole in 8 or 9-inch round or square glass baking dish. Add 1½ cups cold tap water to baking dish.
3. DEFROST-BAKE 17 to 20 minutes or until knife inserted near center comes out clean.
                                4 to 5 Servings

TIP • If your oven does not have a defrost feature, microwave-bake 9 to 10 minutes or until knife inserted near center comes out clean.

INDIVIDUAL CUSTARDS

1. Prepare mixture for Baked Custard above. Pour into 4 or 5 (6 oz.) glass custard cups. Set in 8-inch square glass baking dish. Add 1½ cups cold tap water to the baking dish.
2. MICROWAVE-BAKE at 375° for 8 to 12 minutes or until knife inserted in center comes out clean. (Some custards may cook faster than others; remove the ones that are done and continue cooking the others a little longer.)

TIP • CARAMEL FLAN: Microwave ½ cup packed brown sugar, 1½ tablespoons butter or margarine and ¼ teaspoon water in 2-cup glass measure 3 minutes or until bubbly. Pour into 5 (6 oz.) glass custard cups. Add mixture for Baked Custard and bake as directed for individual custards. Cool and turn upside down onto serving plate.

SOFT CUSTARDS: These have ingredients similar to custard but are occasionally stirred during cooking so they are sauce-like in consistency.

Microwave cooking is used for this type of dessert. It quickly heats the mixture causing the eggs to thicken as they become hot. Most custards of this type should cook until just about boiling. If they boil very much, the eggs overcook causing the sauce to curdle. Stirring occasionally helps the mixture heat and thicken evenly and smoothly.

RICE PUDDING WITH RAISINS

3 eggs
½ cup sugar
1 tablespoon cornstarch
1 teaspoon vanilla
¾ teaspoon salt
½ teaspoon nutmeg
1½ cups cooked rice
2½ cups milk
½ cup raisins

1. Preheat oven to 400° F.
2. Combine all ingredients in 1½-quart glass casserole; mix well. Set casserole in 8-inch square glass baking dish. Add 1½ cups cold tap water to baking dish.
3. DEFROST-BAKE 24 to 26 minutes or until knife inserted near center comes out clean. Stir after 15 minutes of cooking to mix rice evenly throughout custard.   6 to 8 Servings

TIP • If your oven does not have a defrost feature, microwave-bake 14 to 15 minutes, stirring after 8 minutes.

A rich chocolate custard. Serve in small dishes lavishly topped with whipped cream.

POTS de CREME

1 cup (6-oz. pkg.) semi-sweet chocolate pieces
1 cup light cream
2 eggs
1½ tablespoons rum or brandy, if desired
½ teaspoon vanilla
Dash salt
Sweetened whipped cream
Chocolate curls or chopped nuts

1. MICROWAVE chocolate in 4-cup glass measure 5 to 6 minutes or until melted.
2. Preheat oven to 375° F.
3. Stir cream gradually into melted chocolate with rotary beater; beat in remaining ingredients, except whipped cream and chocolate curls.
4. Pour into six 6-oz. glass custard cups or oven-proof demitasse cups. Place in 2-quart (12 x 7) glass baking dish. Add 1½ cups cold tap water to baking dish.
5. MICROWAVE-BAKE 4 to 6 minutes or until almost set; remove individual dishes as they are done so as not to overcook. Chill; serve topped with whipped cream and chocolate curls.   6 Servings

TIP • To make chocolate curls, peel thin layers from a bar of sweetened milk chocolate, using a vegetable peeler. Use a toothpick to transfer curls to the whipped cream.

ICE CREAM BRANDY ALEXANDERS

1 pint vanilla ice cream
3 tablespoons brandy
3 tablespoons dark crème de cocoa

1. MICROWAVE ice cream in carton (set in another dish) ½ to 1 minute or until slightly soft.
2. Fold brandy and crème de cocoa into ice cream. Pour into chilled stemmed glasses. Serve at once or place in freezer for several hours.   4 to 6 Servings

TIP • For a coffee flavor, substitute coffee-flavored liqueur (kahlúa) for crème de cocoa.

ICE CREAM GRASSHOPPERS

Follow recipe for Ice Cream Brandy Alexanders except substitute crème de menthe for the brandy and use white crème de cocoa.

Prepare the custard ahead, then have a neighborhood gathering with old fashioned homemade ice cream.

VANILLA CUSTARD ICE CREAM

2 cups milk
2 eggs
¾ cup sugar
⅛ teaspoon salt
1 tablespoon vanilla
2 cups light cream or whipping cream

1. Combine milk, eggs, sugar and salt in 4-cup glass measure. Beat with rotary beater.
2. MICROWAVE 8 to 9 minutes or until mixture begins to bubble, stirring occasionally during last half of cooking time. Cool completely.
3. Prepare ice cream freezer according to manufacturer's directions. Pour prepared custard into freezer can along with vanilla and cream. Freeze as directed by manufacturer.   2 Quarts

CHOCOLATE CUSTARD ICE CREAM

Prepare Vanilla Custard Ice Cream (above) except increase sugar to 1 cup and before cooking, add 2 squares (1 oz. each) unsweetened chocolate, melted, or 2 envelopes premelted chocolate. Before adding cream, beat until smooth with rotary beater.

STRAWBERRY ICE CREAM

Prepare Vanilla Custard Ice Cream (above) except increase sugar to 1 cup and add 2 cups crushed fresh strawberries with cream; omit vanilla.

GELATIN DESSERTS: Microwave cooking is used to heat the liquid and dissolve the gelatin. When egg yolks are added, the mixture is sometimes heated so the yolks will thicken. It should not be allowed to boil hard or the mixture will curdle.

A light, special occasion pudding. Serve spooned into dishes or make in your favorite shaped mold. Unmold to serve.

MOCHA MOUSSE

    1 envelope unflavored gelatin
    ¼ cup water
    1 square (1 oz.) unsweetened chocolate
    ⅓ cup sugar
    ½ tablespoon instant coffee
    1 cup milk
    3 eggs, separated
    1 teaspoon vanilla
    ⅛ teaspoon salt
    ⅓ cup sugar
    1 cup whipping cream, whipped
    2 tablespoons brandy, if desired

1. Soften gelatin in water in large glass mixing bowl; add chocolate, ⅓ cup sugar, the coffee and milk.

2. MICROWAVE 6 to 7 minutes or until chocolate is completely melted and mixture is smooth, stirring once. Beat egg yolks; slowly blend into hot chocolate mixture. Stir in vanilla and salt. Cool until slightly thickened.

3. Beat egg whites at high speed until frothy. Gradually add ⅓ cup sugar, beating until stiff peaks form. Fold into chocolate mixture along with whipped cream and brandy. Refrigerate at least 4 hours.   6 to 8 Servings

TIP • The milk-chocolate mixture must be heated enough to melt the chocolate flecks. If not, the finished mousse will maintain a flecked appearance.

FROSTY LIME SOUFFLE

    2 envelopes unflavored gelatin
    1 cup water
    ½ teaspoon salt
    2 cans (6 ozs. each) frozen limeade
    6 eggs, separated
    ¼ cup light rum
    Green food coloring
    ⅔ cup sugar
    2 cups whipping cream, whipped

1. Combine gelatin and water in 4-cup glass measure. Let stand 5 minutes.

2. Prepare a 4-cup soufflé dish by forming a collar of wax paper around the outside of the top of the dish so that it extends about 3 inches above the dish. Secure with string or tape.

3. Stir the salt and limeade into gelatin mixture.

4. MICROWAVE 6 to 8 minutes or until gelatin is dissolved. Beat the egg yolks slightly. Slowly blend them into the hot mixture. Stir in rum and food coloring. Cool until slightly thickened.

5. Beat egg whites until frothy. Gradually beat in sugar, beating until mixture forms stiff peaks. Fold into gelatin mixture along with whipped cream. Pour into prepared dish. Chill 6 hours before removing paper collar and serving. If desired, garnish with twist of sliced fresh lime or chopped hazelnuts.   8 to 10 Servings

CUSTARD BAVARIAN CREAM

    1 envelope unflavored gelatin
    ⅔ cup sugar
    ⅛ teaspoon salt
    2 cups milk
    4 eggs
    2 cups whipping cream
    2 teaspoons vanilla

1. Combine gelatin, sugar, salt, milk and eggs in 4-cup glass measure; beat well.

2. MICROWAVE 12 to 14 minutes or until mixture just starts to bubble, stirring occasionally during last half of cooking time. Cool.

3. Beat cream until thickened. Fold in vanilla and gelatin mixture. Pour into 2-quart mold. Chill at least 4 hours or until firm. Unmold. If desired, serve with fresh fruits or favorite dessert sauce.   6 to 8 Servings

TIPS • Substitute for vanilla: ¼ cup favorite orange-flavored liqueur.

• Substitute for whipping cream: 10-oz. carton frozen whipped topping, thawed.

Pictured: Cream Puff, page 148.

MERINGUES AND CREAM PUFFS: Both meringues and cream puffs are cooked primarily with conventional baking. However, the addition of microwave cooking quickly cooks the interior, shortening the cooking time about ⅓.

With cream puffs, it is best to use the traditional metal baking pan. The cooking is not affected by the metal baking pan.

Meringues are normally cooked on paper. If a double layer of paper is used, it is firm enough so that no baking pan is needed. When the meringue is used for Angel Pie, a glass pie plate is used.

Both cream puffs and meringues cook quickly when microwave cooking is added. If overcooked, they will scorch.

Serve this dessert like a sweet roll with a cup of coffee or top with sweetened strawberries or peaches.

SWEDISH KRINGLA

  1 cup water
  ½ cup butter or margarine
  1 cup unsifted all-purpose flour
  3 eggs

Crust

  1 cup unsifted all-purpose flour
  ½ cup butter or margarine
  2 tablespoons water

Glaze

  1 cup powdered sugar
  1 teaspoon almond extract
  1 to 2 tablespoons milk or cream

1. MICROWAVE water and butter in large glass mixing bowl 5 to 6 minutes or until mixture boils hard. Immediately add flour and stir until mixture leaves sides of dish and forms a ball. Add eggs, one at a time, beating vigorously after each. Set aside.

2. Preheat oven to 425° F.

3. Cut butter into flour for Crust in small mixing bowl. Stir in water until crumbly. Press mixture evenly over bottom of 3-quart (13 x 9) glass baking dish. Spread reserved cream puff mixture over crust.

4. BAKE 14 minutes. ✿

5. MICROWAVE-BAKE 8 to 10 minutes or until golden brown.

6. Combine Glaze ingredients, adding milk until mixture drizzles. Spoon over baked kringla. Serve warm or cold.

About 24 Squares

CREAM PUFFS

  ½ cup butter or margarine
  1 cup water
  1 cup unsifted all-purpose flour
  ½ teaspoon salt
  4 eggs

1. MICROWAVE butter and water in large glass mixing bowl 5 to 7 minutes or until mixture boils hard.

2. Preheat oven to 425° F.

3. Immediately add flour and salt to water mixture; stir until mixture leaves sides of dish and forms a ball. Add eggs, one at a time, beating vigorously after each.

4. Spoon dough by tablespoonfuls onto ungreased metal baking pan.

5. BAKE 20 minutes. ✿

6. MICROWAVE-BAKE 10 to 12 minutes or until puffs hold their shape. Remove from pan and cool. Split and remove excess webbing from interior. Fill with Cream Puff Filling and fresh fruit, or with ice cream and favorite ice cream sauce.   12 Cream Puffs

CREAM PUFF FILLING

  ½ cup sugar
  2 tablespoons cornstarch
  ⅛ teaspoon salt
1⅔ cups milk
  1 egg, beaten
  1 teaspoon vanilla
  ¾ cup whipping cream, whipped

1. Combine sugar, cornstarch and salt in 4-cup glass measure. Stir in milk.

2. MICROWAVE 7 to 8 minutes or until mixture boils, stirring once during last half of cooking time. Stir in egg and vanilla. Cool. Fold into whipped cream. Spoon into cooled cream puffs. If desired, top with sweetened fresh fruit.   3 Cups Filling

Lightly browned islands of meringue float on soft custard. Serve over fresh strawberries, peaches or other fresh fruit.

FLOATING ISLAND DESSERT

2 cups milk
2 eggs
¼ teaspoon cream of tartar
½ cup sugar
½ teaspoon vanilla
1 egg
¼ cup sugar
⅛ teaspoon salt
1 teaspoon vanilla
2 cups (1 pint) fresh fruit

1. MICROWAVE milk in 2-quart shallow uncovered glass casserole 8 to 9 minutes or until hot.
2. Separate 2 eggs placing whites in small mixing bowl and setting aside yolks. Beat egg whites and cream of tartar at high speed until frothy. Gradually add ½ cup sugar, beating until mixture forms stiff peaks. Beat in ½ teaspoon vanilla.
3. Spoon meringue onto hot milk forming about 6 mounds.
4. MICROWAVE-BROIL 3 to 4 minutes or until meringues are set and lightly browned. Remove meringues from milk using slotted spoon; place on plate and set aside.
5. Combine 2 egg yolks, 1 egg, ¼ cup sugar and the salt. Beat into milk used for cooking meringues.
6. MICROWAVE, uncovered, 3 to 4 minutes or until mixture just starts to bubble, stirring occasionally during last half of cooking time. Stir in 1 teaspoon vanilla. Place meringues on soft custard. Cool. Serve over fresh fruit. About 6 Servings

Microwave cooking is used in this recipe to speed the drying of the meringue crust. The meringue must first be set before the microwave cooking is used. Once the microwave cooking is used, the meringue should be watched carefully as it will toast very quickly.

CHOCOLATE ANGEL PIE

Meringue Crust
2 egg whites
¼ teaspoon salt
⅛ teaspoon cream of tartar
⅔ cup sugar
½ teaspoon vanilla
½ cup chopped nuts

Chocolate Filling
1 cup (6-oz. pkg.) semi-sweet chocolate pieces
¼ cup water
2 egg yolks
3 tablespoons sugar
2 tablespoons brandy or rum
1 cup whipping cream

1. Preheat oven to 275° F.
2. Beat egg whites, salt and cream of tartar at high speed until frothy. Gradually add sugar, beating until stiff peaks form. Fold in vanilla and nuts.
3. Spread over bottom and sides of greased 9-inch glass pie plate.
4. BAKE 35 minutes. ✻
5. MICROWAVE-BAKE 2 to 2½ minutes or just until meringue starts to brown. Cool.
6. Combine chocolate pieces and water in 2-cup glass measure.
7. MICROWAVE 2½ to 3 minutes or until water is bubbly. Stir to melt chocolate. Blend in egg yolks, sugar and brandy. Cool until mixture thickens. Beat whipping cream until thickened. Fold in chocolate mixture. Pour into cooled meringue crust. Refrigerate at least 2 hours before serving. If desired, serve with whipped cream. 6 to 8 Servings

TIP • Substitute for brandy: 1 teaspoon vanilla.

MERINGUE SHELLS

Prepare Meringue Crust as directed above, omitting nuts. Spoon meringue mixture into 6 mounds on heavy folded paper bag. Make a well in the center of each mound, spreading the shell to 4 inches in diameter. Bake as directed in steps 4 and 5. Cool. Remove from paper. Top with ice cream and sweetened fruit or favorite ice cream sauce.

PUDDING CAKES AND CHEESE CAKES:
The method for preparing these types of
desserts is similar to that used for cakes. First,
conventional heat forms the crust and starts
the cooking. Then combination heat is used to
finish the browning and cook the interior.

*Serve this traditional cheese cake plain or
with sweetened fresh fruit.*

CHEESE CAKE

  ½ cup unsifted all-purpose flour
   1 tablespoon sugar
  ¼ teaspoon baking powder
  ⅛ teaspoon salt
   3 tablespoons butter or margarine
 1½ tablespoons milk

Filling
   2 packages (8 ozs. each) cream cheese
   1 cup sugar
 1½ tablespoons flour
  ½ tablespoon grated lemon peel
  ½ teaspoon vanilla
   4 eggs
   3 tablespoons cream or milk

1. Combine flour, sugar, baking powder and
   salt in medium mixing bowl. Cut in butter;
   sprinkle with milk. Stir until moistened.
   Press evenly over bottom of 8 or 9-inch
   round glass baking dish. Set aside.
2. MICROWAVE cream cheese in medium
   glass mixing bowl about 2½ minutes or
   until softened.
3. Preheat oven to 400° F.
4. Beat cream cheese until light and fluffy.
   Gradually beat in sugar, flour, lemon peel
   and vanilla. Add eggs, one at a time, beating
   well after each. Blend in cream. Pour into
   pastry-lined baking dish.
5. BAKE 15 minutes.✿
6. MICROWAVE-BAKE 9 to 10 minutes or
   until knife inserted near center comes out
   clean.   8 to 10 Servings

PUMPKIN DESSERT CAKE

  ½ cup butter or margarine
   4 eggs
   1 cup sugar
   1 cup packed brown sugar
 1½ cups unsifted all-purpose flour
   1 teaspoon baking powder
  ½ teaspoon soda
   1 teaspoon cinnamon
  ½ teaspoon cloves
  ¼ teaspoon salt
   2 teaspoons vanilla
   1 can (15 oz.) pumpkin
  ½ cup raisins

1. MICROWAVE butter in large glass mixing
   bowl about 1½ minutes or until softened.
2. Preheat oven to 350° F.
3. Add remaining ingredients to softened butter.
   Beat at medium speed 2 minutes. Pour into
   2-quart (12 x 7) glass baking dish, greased
   on bottom only.
4. BAKE 15 minutes. ✿
5. MICROWAVE-BAKE 8 to 10 minutes or until
   toothpick inserted in center comes out clean.
   Serve with whipped cream. 10 to 12 Servings

*Serve as a bar, or top with a fruit sauce for a
delicious dessert.*

LEMON CRUNCH DESSERT SQUARES

  ½ cup butter or margarine
  ½ cup packed brown sugar
   1 cup unsifted all-purpose flour
 1½ cups granola cereal
  ½ teaspoon salt
  ½ teaspoon cinnamon
   1 can (14 oz.) sweetened condensed milk
   2 eggs
   1 tablespoon grated lemon peel
  ¼ cup lemon juice

1. MICROWAVE butter in medium glass mixing
   bowl 1½ to 2 minutes or until softened.
2. Preheat oven to 400° F.
3. Add brown sugar, flour, cereal, salt and
   cinnamon to softened butter; mix until
   crumbly. Press half of mixture into 8-inch
   square glass baking dish.
4. Combine sweetened condensed milk (do not
   confuse with evaporated milk), eggs, lemon
   peel and juice. Pour over crumb mixture.
   Sprinkle remaining crumbs over top.
5. MICROWAVE-BAKE 8 to 10 minutes or until
   filling is set. Cool and cut into squares.
           24 Bars or 9 Dessert Squares

Spicy squares of gingerbread topped with a pretty peach and mincemeat sauce.

SPICY GINGERBREAD DESSERT

    1 package (14 oz.) gingerbread mix
¾ cup water
½ cup prepared mincemeat

Peachy Sauce
    1 can (16 oz.) sliced peaches
¼ cup sugar
    1 tablespoon cornstarch
¼ teaspoon salt
    2 tablespoons butter or margarine
½ cup prepared mincemeat
    1 tablespoon lemon juice

1. Preheat oven to 350° F.
2. Blend together gingerbread mix, water and prepared mincemeat in small mixing bowl; beat 2 minutes at medium speed. Pour into greased 8-inch square glass baking dish.
3. BAKE 15 minutes. ✿
4. MICROWAVE-BAKE 3 to 3½ minutes or until toothpick inserted in center comes out clean.
5. Drain syrup from peaches into 4-cup glass measure; add water to make 1 cup liquid. Stir in sugar, cornstarch, salt and butter.
6. MICROWAVE 6 to 7 minutes or until bubbly, stirring once during last half of cooking time. Stir in peaches, mincemeat and lemon juice. Cut gingerbread into squares and top with Peachy Sauce.

HOT FUDGE PUDDING CAKE

    1 cup unsifted all-purpose flour
¾ cup sugar
    2 tablespoons unsweetened cocoa
    1 teaspoon baking powder
¼ teaspoon salt
½ cup milk
    2 tablespoons cooking oil
    1 cup chopped nuts
    1 cup packed brown sugar
¼ cup unsweetened cocoa
1¾ cups hot water

1. Preheat oven to 350° F.
2. Combine flour, sugar, 2 tablespoons cocoa, the baking powder and salt in 2-quart glass casserole. Blend in milk and oil; stir in nuts. Spread batter evenly in dish.
3. Combine brown sugar and ¼ cup cocoa in small bowl. Sprinkle over batter; pour hot water over sugar mixture.

4. BAKE 12 minutes. ✿
5. MICROWAVE-BAKE 8 to 9 minutes or until cake portion is no longer doughy. Serve warm or cold with cream or ice cream.
6 to 8 Servings

STEAMED PUDDINGS: Steamed puddings are often served during the holidays. They are usually set in a large container that fills with steam as the water boils. With microwave cooking, the same effect can be achieved by covering the casserole dish. No conventional heat is used since the pudding needs the moistness of steam to develop the characteristic texture.

Microwave cooking can also be used to reheat already steamed pudding and to make a hot buttery sauce to serve over the pudding.

A covered casserole and microwave cooking simplify the preparation of a steamed pudding.

CRANBERRY STEAMED PUDDING

    ¾ cup butter or margarine
2½ cups raw cranberries
1½ cups fine vanilla wafer crumbs
1½ cups unsifted all-purpose flour
1½ cups water
    ½ cup chopped nuts
    2 teaspoons baking powder
    1 teaspoon cinnamon
¾ teaspoon salt
½ teaspoon cloves
¼ teaspoon ginger
    3 eggs
¾ cup milk

1. MICROWAVE butter in large glass mixing bowl 2½ to 3 minutes or until melted. Stir in remaining ingredients; beat well. Pour into greased 2-quart casserole.
2. MICROWAVE, covered, 22 to 25 minutes or until toothpick inserted in center comes out clean. Loosen with spatula and turn out onto serving plate. Serve warm wedges with Hot Butter Sauce, page 119.
10 to 12 Servings

Cakes

CAKES: Cakes are cooked using a technique similar to the method for cooking breads and other leavened products. They are baked first to form the crust and start the browning. Then microwaves are added to cook the interior.

Glass cake dishes need to be greased for easy pan removal. When the cake is to be removed from the pan, the dish should be greased and floured on bottom and sides. When the cake will be cut into pieces and served from the pan, the baking dish is greased on the bottom only. Greasing the sides of cake dishes without also flouring is not recommended because the cake slips on the greased sides as it tries to rise. Also the volume of the baked cake is lower and the top is not properly rounded.

Most cakes, mix or other types, cook very nicely in the combination oven. Two exceptions are the 2-step angel food cake mix and the streusel cake mixes. Both bake in metal tube pans and with these mixes the metal pan distorts the cooking of the cake. The one-step angel food cake mix, chiffon cake mixes and bundt-type cake mixes cook nicely in the metal pans and we have included directions for these cakes.

Cupcakes are the easiest to cook in the metal muffin pans. The shallowness of the metal pan does not affect the cooking.

1. Preheat oven to 375° F.
2. Prepare favorite 2-layer shortening cake recipe. Pour batter into two greased and floured 8-inch round glass baking dishes or one 13x9-inch glass baking dish.
3. BAKE 15 minutes. ✤
4. MICROWAVE-BAKE 3 to 3½ minutes or until toothpick inserted in center comes out clean. Cool 10 minutes before removing layers from pans.   2-layer or 13x9-inch Cake

TIP • For a 1-layer cake, preheat oven to 350° F., bake 12 minutes, then microwave-bake 3 to 3½ minutes.

CAKE MIX

1. Preheat oven to 375° F. (350° F. for white cake mix).
2. Prepare favorite 2-layer cake mix as directed on package. Pour batter into two greased and floured 8-inch round or square glass baking dishes or one 13x9-inch glass baking dish.
3. BAKE 12 minutes (15 minutes for 13x9). ✤
4. MICROWAVE-BAKE 3 to 3½ minutes or until toothpick inserted in center comes out clean. Cool 10 minutes before removing layers from pans.   2-layer or 13x9-inch Cake

TIP • For a 1-layer cake, bake 10 minutes, then microwave-bake 3 to 4 minutes.

CUPCAKES

1. Preheat oven to 400° F.
2. Fill 12 paper-lined or greased metal muffin cups ⅔ full with cake batter.
3. BAKE 5 minutes. ✤
4. MICROWAVE-BAKE 2 to 2½ minutes or until toothpick inserted in center comes out clean.   12 Cupcakes

CAKE CONES

1. Fill 6 flat-bottom ice cream cones about half full with cake batter. Place in glass pie plate.
2. MICROWAVE 5 to 6 minutes or until toothpick inserted in center comes out clean. Cool. Frost with a fluffy-type frosting or top each with a scoop of ice cream.   6 Cake Cones

TIP • If the oven is already hot, microwave-bake at 375° F. for 3½ to 4 minutes.

BUNDT-TYPE CAKE MIX

1. Preheat oven to 350° F.
2. Prepare a bundt-type cake mix as directed on package, using greased and floured metal bundt cake pan.
3. BAKE 15 minutes. ✤
4. MICROWAVE-BAKE 3 to 4 minutes or until toothpick inserted in center comes out clean.
                                                1 Cake

Pictured, top to bottom: Lemon Cream Cake, page 155, Holiday Fruitcake, page 159 and Easy Butter-Sponge Cake, page 157.

The addition of microwave cooking for angel food cakes speeds the cooking and reduces the chances of over-browning the top crust.

ANGEL FOOD CAKE MIX

1. Place oven rack in lowest position. Preheat oven to 375° F.
2. Prepare a one-step angel food cake mix as directed on package, using ungreased metal tube pan.
3. BAKE 20 minutes. ✿
4. MICROWAVE-BAKE 4 to 4½ minutes or until cake springs back when lightly touched.
5. Invert cake pan on bottle; cool completely. Loosen cake with spatula; remove from pan.

1 Cake

TIP • If using a two-step angel food cake mix, bake conventionally as directed on package.

CHIFFON CAKE MIX

Prepare chiffon cake mix as directed on package. Pour into ungreased metal tube pan. Bake and microwave-bake as directed above for Angel Food Cake.

PINEAPPLE UPSIDE-DOWN CAKE

    ¼ cup butter or margarine
    ½ cup packed brown sugar
    1 can (8 oz.) sliced or crushed pineapple, drained
    8 Maraschino cherries
    1 package (9 oz.) yellow cake mix (1-layer size)

1. MICROWAVE butter in 8-inch round or square glass baking dish 1½ to 2 minutes or until melted.
2. Preheat oven to 375° F.
3. Stir brown sugar into butter. Top with pineapple and cherries; set aside.
4. Prepare cake mix as directed on package; pour over pineapple mixture.
5. BAKE 12 minutes. ✿
6. MICROWAVE-BAKE 4 to 5 minutes or until toothpick inserted in center comes out clean. Loosen edges with spatula; invert onto serving plate.   8-inch Round or Square Cake

TIP • A pineapple cake mix may also be used. Prepare topping and cake as directed on package. Cook as directed in steps 5 and 6.

UPSIDE-DOWN GERMAN CHOCOLATE CAKE

    ¼ cup butter or margarine
    ½ cup packed brown sugar
    ½ cup chopped pecans
    ½ cup shredded coconut
    ¼ cup milk
    3 squares or envelopes (1 oz. each) unsweetened chocolate
    ¼ cup butter or margarine
  1¼ cups unsifted all-purpose flour
  1¼ cups sugar
    ¼ teaspoon soda
    ½ teaspoon baking powder
    ½ teaspoon salt
    1 teaspoon vanilla
    2 eggs
    ¾ cup buttermilk or sour milk

1. MICROWAVE ¼ cup butter and the brown sugar in 8-inch square glass baking dish 2 to 2½ minutes or until melted; mix well. Sprinkle pecans, coconut and milk over butter mixture; set aside.
2. MICROWAVE chocolate and ¼ cup butter in small glass mixing bowl 2 to 3 minutes or until chocolate and butter are melted.
3. Preheat oven to 350° F.
4. Stir remaining ingredients into chocolate mixture; beat at medium speed 2 minutes. Spoon over nut mixture in pan, spreading to cover.
5. BAKE 15 minutes. ✿
6. MICROWAVE-BAKE 6 to 7 minutes or until toothpick inserted in center comes out clean. Cool 5 minutes; invert onto serving plate.

8-inch Square Cake

LEMON CREAM CAKE

    8-oz. package cream cheese
½ **cup butter or margarine**
1¼ **cups sugar**
    3 eggs
    1 tablespoon grated lemon peel
2¼ **cups unsifted all-purpose flour**
    3 teaspoons baking powder
    1 teaspoon salt
    1 cup milk

Glaze
¼ **cup lemon juice**
⅓ **cup sugar**

1. MICROWAVE cream cheese and butter in large mixing bowl 2 to 3 minutes or until softened.
2. Preheat oven to 375° F.
3. Add sugar to butter mixture; beat well. Beat in eggs and lemon peel. Add flour, baking powder, salt and milk; mix at low speed just until combined. Spoon into greased and floured 9 or 10-inch bundt pan.
4. BAKE 15 minutes. ✿
5. MICROWAVE-BAKE 8 to 10 minutes or until toothpick inserted in center comes out clean. Turn off oven.
6. MICROWAVE lemon juice and sugar for Glaze in 1-cup glass measure 1 to 2 minutes or until sugar is dissolved. Prick cake with toothpick or long tined fork; pour Glaze evenly over cake. Cool 30 minutes; remove from pan. If desired, sprinkle with powdered sugar.   1 Cake

POUND CAKE MIX

1. Preheat oven to 350° F.
2. Prepare a pound cake mix as directed on package, using greased and floured 1½-quart (8x4) glass loaf dish.
3. BAKE 20 minutes. ✿
4. MICROWAVE-BAKE 5 to 6 minutes or until toothpick inserted in center comes out clean.   1 Loaf Cake

RUM POUND CAKE

½ **cup butter or margarine**
1½ **cups unsifted all-purpose flour**
    1 cup sugar
½ **teaspoon salt**
¼ **teaspoon baking powder**
⅛ **teaspoon soda**
    2 teaspoons grated lemon peel
    1 teaspoon vanilla
½ **cup sour cream**
    2 eggs

Rum Sauce
⅓ **cup sugar**
    2 tablespoons water
¼ **cup butter or margarine**
    1 tablespoon rum

1. MICROWAVE butter in large glass mixing bowl 1½ to 2 minutes or until softened.
2. Preheat oven to 350° F.
3. Stir remaining ingredients, except Rum Sauce, into butter; beat at medium speed 2 minutes. Pour into 2-quart (9x5) glass loaf dish, greased on bottom only.
4. BAKE 20 minutes. ✿
5. MICROWAVE-BAKE 5 to 6 minutes or until toothpick inserted in center comes out clean. Turn oven off; leave cake in pan. Combine ingredients for Rum Sauce, except rum, in 2-cup glass measure.
6. MICROWAVE 2½ to 3 minutes or until bubbly. Stir in rum. Prick cake with toothpick or long tined fork; pour hot sauce evenly over cake. Cool 10 minutes; remove from pan.   1 Loaf Cake

TIP • Substitute for rum: 1 teaspoon rum flavoring.

A quick cake for family or company. Serve with the suggested broiled topping or, omit the topping and serve with sweetened strawberries and whipped cream.

EASY BUTTER-SPONGE CAKE

¼ cup milk
¼ cup butter or margarine
¼ teaspoon almond extract
2 eggs
¾ cup sugar
¾ cup unsifted all-purpose flour
½ teaspoon baking powder
½ teaspoon salt

Topping
¼ cup sugar
1 tablespoon milk
1 tablespoon all-purpose flour
¼ cup butter or margarine
⅓ cup slivered almonds or flaked coconut

1. MICROWAVE milk and butter in 1-cup glass measure 2 to 2½ minutes or until butter is melted. Add almond extract; set aside.

2. Preheat oven to 350° F.

3. Beat eggs at high speed in medium mixing bowl until light colored. Gradually add sugar, beating until thickened. Blend in flour, baking powder, salt and milk mixture just until combined. Pour into 8-inch square glass baking dish, greased on bottom only.

4. BAKE 12 minutes. ❖

5. MICROWAVE-BAKE 3 to 4 minutes or until toothpick inserted in center comes out clean.

6. Combine Topping ingredients in 2-cup glass measure.

7. MICROWAVE Topping 3 to 4 minutes or until mixture bubbles. Spoon over cake, spreading to cover.

8. BROIL 2 to 2½ minutes or until bubbly and golden brown.   8-inch Cake

BLUEBERRY STREUSEL CAKE

2 cups unsifted all-purpose flour
½ cup sugar
2 teaspoons baking powder
1 teaspoon salt
¼ cup cooking oil
1 cup milk
1 egg
1 teaspoon vanilla
2 cups fresh or frozen blueberries

Streusel Topping
½ cup unsifted all-purpose flour
½ cup rolled oats
½ cup packed brown sugar
½ teaspoon cinnamon
¼ cup butter or margarine

1. Preheat oven to 375° F.

2. Combine flour, sugar, baking powder, salt, oil, milk, egg and vanilla. Blend just until smooth. Spread in 2-quart (12x7) glass baking dish, greased on bottom only. Sprinkle with blueberries.

3. Combine ingredients for topping, cutting in butter until crumbly. Sprinkle over blueberries.

4. BAKE 15 minutes. ❖

5. MICROWAVE-BAKE 5 to 7 minutes or until toothpick inserted in center comes out clean.
                                    12x7-inch Cake

TIP • Substitute for blueberries: sliced fresh peaches or pears.

Pictured: Carrot Cake, page 159 with Whipped Frosting, page 161.

CHOCOLATE CHIP CAKE

¾ cup shortening
1 cup sugar
2 eggs
1 teaspoon vanilla
1¾ cups unsifted all-purpose flour
1 tablespoon unsweetened cocoa
1 teaspoon salt
½ teaspoon soda
1 cup water
1 cup chopped dates
1 cup chopped nuts
1 cup (6-oz. pkg.) semi-sweet chocolate pieces

1. Preheat oven to 350° F.
2. Combine shortening, sugar, eggs and vanilla in large mixing bowl. Beat at medium speed until blended. Stir in flour, cocoa, salt, soda and water. Fold in dates, ½ cup nuts and ½ cup chocolate pieces.
3. Pour batter into 2-quart (12x7) glass baking dish, greased on bottom only. Sprinkle top with remaining nuts and chocolate pieces.
4. BAKE 15 minutes. ✿
5. MICROWAVE-BAKE 6 to 7 minutes or until toothpick inserted in center comes out clean.
12x7-inch Cake

SOUR CREAM FUDGE CAKE

3 squares or envelopes (1 oz. each) unsweetened chocolate
½ cup water
1½ cups sugar
2 eggs
1¾ cups unsifted all-purpose flour
1 teaspoon soda
1 teaspoon salt
½ cup shortening
1 cup sour cream
1 teaspoon vanilla

1. MICROWAVE chocolate in large mixing bowl 2 to 3 minutes or until melted.
2. Preheat oven to 375° F.
3. Add water, sugar and eggs to chocolate; beat well. Add remaining ingredients; beat 2 minutes at medium speed. Spread in 2-quart (12x7) glass baking dish, greased on bottom only.
4. BAKE 15 minutes. ✿
5. MICROWAVE-BAKE 5 to 6 minutes or until toothpick inserted in center comes out clean. Cool. If desired, frost with Quick Fudge Frosting, page 161.
12x7-inch Cake

OATMEAL CAKE

1¼ cups water
1 cup rolled oats
½ cup butter or margarine
1 cup sugar
1 cup packed brown sugar
1½ cups unsifted all-purpose flour
½ teaspoon baking powder
½ teaspoon soda
½ teaspoon salt
1 teaspoon cinnamon
1 teaspoon vanilla
2 eggs

Topping
⅔ cup packed brown sugar
¼ cup butter or margarine, softened
½ cup light cream or evaporated milk
1 cup flaked coconut
½ cup chopped nuts

1. MICROWAVE water and rolled oats in large glass mixing bowl 6 to 8 minutes or until oats are softened.
2. Preheat oven to 350° F.
3. Stir butter and remaining ingredients except Topping, into oat mixture. Beat at medium speed 2 minutes. Pour into 2-quart (12x7) glass baking dish, greased on bottom only.
4. BAKE 15 minutes. ✿
5. MICROWAVE-BAKE 5½ to 6 minutes or until toothpick inserted in center comes out clean.
6. Mix together Topping ingredients in small mixing bowl; spread over warm cake.
7. BROIL 2½ to 3 minutes or until Topping is golden brown. 12x7-inch Cake

SPICY APPLE CAKE

  ¼ **cup butter or margarine**
   1 **cup unsifted all-purpose flour**
  ¾ **cup packed brown sugar**
  ½ **teaspoon baking powder**
  ½ **teaspoon salt**
  ½ **teaspoon nutmeg**
  ½ **teaspoon cinnamon**
  ¼ **teaspoon soda**
  ¼ **teaspoon vanilla**
   2 **eggs**
   2 **cups (2 med.) shredded apple**
  ½ **cup chopped nuts**

1. MICROWAVE butter in large glass mixing bowl 1 to 1½ minutes or until softened.
2. Preheat oven to 350° F.
3. Stir remaining ingredients into butter until well blended. Spread in 8-inch square glass baking dish, greased on bottom only.
4. BAKE 15 minutes. ✤
5. MICROWAVE-BAKE 3 to 3½ minutes or until toothpick inserted in center comes out clean. Serve with whipped cream or ice cream.

                  8-inch Square Cake

CARROT CAKE

   3 **cups unsifted all-purpose flour**
   2 **cups sugar**
 1½ **teaspoons baking powder**
  ½ **teaspoon soda**
   1 **teaspoon salt**
   2 **teaspoons cinnamon**
   1 **teaspoon vanilla**
   4 **eggs**
 1⅓ **cups cooking oil**
   1 **can (13½ oz.) crushed pineapple, undrained**
   2 **cups (2 large) shredded carrot**

1. Preheat oven to 350° F.
2. Combine all ingredients in large mixing bowl. Beat at medium speed 2 minutes.
3. Pour into 3-quart (13x9) glass baking dish, greased on bottom only.
4. BAKE 15 minutes. ✤
5. MICROWAVE-BAKE 8 to 10 minutes or until toothpick inserted in center comes out clean.

                  13x9-inch Cake

BANANA CAKE

 2¼ **cups unsifted all-purpose flour**
 1¼ **cups packed brown sugar**
 1½ **teaspoons baking powder**
  ½ **teaspoon soda**
  ½ **teaspoon salt**
  ½ **cup shortening**
   2 **eggs**
  ¾ **cup buttermilk or sour milk**
   1 **cup (2 med.) mashed banana**
   1 **teaspoon vanilla**

1. Preheat oven to 350° F.
2. Combine all ingredients in large mixing bowl. Beat 2 minutes at medium speed. Pour into 2-quart (12x7) glass baking dish, greased on bottom only.
3. BAKE 15 minutes. ✤
4. MICROWAVE-BAKE 5½ to 6 minutes or until toothpick inserted in center comes out clean. Cool. If desired, frost with Coconut Pecan Frosting, page 161.   12x7-inch Cake

HOLIDAY FRUITCAKE

   2 **eggs**
  ¾ **cup packed brown sugar**
  ½ **cup orange juice or brandy**
   2 **tablespoons dark molasses**
  ⅓ **cup cooking oil**
 1½ **cups unsifted all-purpose flour**
   1 **teaspoon baking powder**
  ½ **teaspoon salt**
   1 **teaspoon cinnamon**
  ¼ **teaspoon allspice**
  ¼ **teaspoon nutmeg**
  ¼ **teaspoon ground cloves**
   8 **ozs. mixed candied fruits**
   8 **ozs. candied cherries**
   8 **ozs. pitted dates, chopped**
   1 **cup raisins**
   1 **cup chopped nuts**

1. Preheat oven to 325° F.
2. Beat eggs in medium mixing bowl; blend in brown sugar, orange juice, molasses and oil. Stir in remaining ingredients, mixing well.
3. Grease 2-quart (9x5) glass loaf dish; line bottom and sides with brown or wax paper. Pour cake mixture into dish.
4. BAKE 15 minutes. ✤
5. MICROWAVE-BAKE 10 to 12 minutes or until toothpick inserted in center comes out clean. Cool. Turn out of dish; remove paper. Wrap cake in cheesecloth, then foil. Let stand several weeks before slicing.   1 Loaf Cake

Frostings

FROSTINGS: Frostings that require heating or cooking can be prepared in the combination oven using microwave cooking.

When a frosting is broiled or baked on a cooked cake, only the broil or bake heat is used. If microwaves are added, the cake might overcook before the frosting is done.

FLUFFY MERINGUE FROSTING

    1 cup sugar
    ⅓ cup water
    ¼ teaspoon cream of tartar
    Dash salt
    2 egg whites
    1 teaspoon vanilla

1. MICROWAVE sugar, water, cream of tartar and salt in 2-cup glass measure 5½ to 6 minutes or until mixture boils.
2. Beat egg whites at high speed in small mixing bowl until soft peaks form. Gradually pour in hot syrup, beating until mixture is thick and fluffy, about 5 minutes; blend in vanilla.
                Frosts 13x9-inch or 2-layer Cake

FLUFFY JELLY FROSTING

    ½ cup jelly
    1 egg white
    Dash salt

1. MICROWAVE jelly in 1-cup glass measure 2½ to 3 minutes or until boiling.
2. Beat egg white and salt in small mixing bowl at high speed until frothy; gradually beat in hot jelly. Beat until light and fluffy.
            Frosts 1-layer Cake or 12 Cupcakes

TIP • The color of the frosting will vary according to flavor of jelly used.

CHERRY CREAM FROSTING

1. MICROWAVE 1 package (3 oz.) cream cheese and ¼ cup butter or margarine in small glass mixing bowl 1½ to 2 minutes or until softened.
2. Beat in 2 cups powdered sugar and 2 to 3 tablespoons Maraschino cherry juice or until mixture spreads easily. Spread over cooled bars.   Frosts 8-inch Pan of Bars or Cake

Pictured: Quick Fudge Frosting, this page.

A not-so-sweet creamy frosting.

WHIPPED FROSTING

    ¾ cup sugar
    ¼ cup all-purpose flour
    ¾ cup milk
    ½ cup butter or margarine
    1 teaspoon vanilla

1. Combine sugar, flour and milk in small glass mixing bowl.
2. MICROWAVE 6 to 7 minutes or until mixture boils and thickens, stirring once during last half of cooking time. Stir well. Add butter and chill several hours or until cold.
3. Add vanilla; beat at high speed until light and fluffy.   Frosts 13x9-inch Cake

TIP • On very warm days, the frosting may separate during the beating in step 3 unless thoroughly chilled.

Traditional topping for German chocolate cake. Also delicious with spice, banana and yellow cakes.

COCONUT-PECAN FROSTING

    1 cup sugar
    1 cup evaporated milk
    3 eggs
    ½ cup butter or margarine
    1 teaspoon vanilla
    1⅓ cups flaked or shredded coconut
    1 cup chopped pecans

1. Combine sugar, milk and eggs in 4-cup glass measure. Beat until smooth. Add butter.
2. MICROWAVE 10 to 11 minutes or until mixture boils, stirring once during last half of cooking time. Stir in vanilla, coconut and pecans. Cool.
                Frosts 13x9-inch or 2-layer Cake

QUICK FUDGE FROSTING

    ½ cup butter or margarine
    2 cups sugar
    ½ cup milk
    3 squares or envelopes (1 oz. each)
      unsweetened chocolate
    ¼ teaspoon salt
    1½ teaspoons vanilla

1. Combine all ingredients except vanilla in medium glass mixing bowl.
2. MICROWAVE 11 to 12 minutes or until mixture boils, stirring once during last half of cooking time. Stir in vanilla.
3. Place bowl in ice water and beat until smooth. Let stand in ice water until thickened to spreading consistency, stirring occasionally.
                Frosts 13x9-inch or 2-layer Cake

Cookies

COOKIES: The use of combination bake and microwave cooking for cookies reduces the cooking time by about one-half. The method, technique and finished product are similar to conventionally baked cookies.

Since there is no good glass substitute for a metal baking sheet and because the cookies cook very well on the metal, we have used metal baking sheets for all the cookie recipes. If the baking sheet is especially small or less than half-full, the cooking time may be about one minute less.

Most cookies cook very nicely using the combination method. The only exception we found in our testing was the commercially refrigerated cookie dough. Most flavors of this type cookie spread more than normal with the combination cooking.

SPRITZ

  1 cup butter or margarine
  ⅔ cup sugar
  1 egg
  ½ teaspoon almond extract
  2⅓ cups unsifted all-purpose flour

1. MICROWAVE butter in large mixing bowl 2 to 2½ minutes or until softened. Beat in sugar, egg and extract. Blend in flour.

2. Preheat oven to 400° F.

3. Form cookies by pressing through cookie press onto ungreased metal baking sheets. If desired, sprinkle with colored sugars.

4. MICROWAVE-BAKE, one pan at a time, 4½ to 5 minutes or until cookies are set. Cool slightly; remove from pan.
                              About 6 Dozen Cookies

SCOTTISH SHORTBREAD

  1 cup butter or margarine
  ¾ cup sugar
  1 egg yolk
  2¼ cups unsifted all-purpose flour

1. MICROWAVE butter in medium glass mixing bowl about 2 minutes or until softened.

2. Preheat oven to 375° F.

3. Beat sugar and egg yolk into butter. Blend in flour; divide dough into 2 portions.

4. Roll out 1 portion on metal baking sheet to a 13x9-inch rectangle. Cut through dough to form 24 squares; prick each with fork.

5. MICROWAVE-BAKE 7 to 8 minutes or until golden brown. Cool slightly; remove from pan.

6. Repeat from step 4 with remaining dough.
                              48 Bars

Pictured: Crunchy Toffee Bars, page 167, Chocolate Chip Cookies, page 164 and Cherry Thumbprint Cookies, page 164.

Now you can bake the all-time favorite cookie in just 4 minutes.

PEANUT BUTTER COOKIES

  ½ cup butter or margarine
  ½ cup peanut butter
  ½ cup sugar
  ½ cup packed brown sugar
  1 egg
  ½ teaspoon vanilla
  1¼ cups unsifted all-purpose flour
  ¼ teaspoon soda
  ¼ teaspoon salt

1. MICROWAVE butter in medium glass mixing bowl about 1½ minutes or until softened.

2. Preheat oven to 425° F.

3. Beat peanut butter and sugars into butter. Blend in egg and vanilla. Stir in remaining ingredients. Shape into 1-inch balls. Place 2 inches apart on ungreased metal baking sheets. Flatten with fork.

4. MICROWAVE-BAKE, one pan at a time, 4 to 4½ minutes or until lightly browned. Cool slightly; remove from pan.
                              About 4 Dozen Cookies

An easy-to-handle sugar cookie dough.

SUGAR COOKIES

  3 cups unsifted all-purpose flour
  1 teaspoon salt
  ½ teaspoon soda
  1 teaspoon cream of tartar
  1 cup shortening
  2 eggs
  1 cup sugar
  1 teaspoon vanilla

1. Preheat oven to 425° F.

2. Combine flour, salt, soda and cream of tartar in large mixing bowl. Cut in shortening until mixture is like fine meal. Stir in eggs, sugar and vanilla; mix well using hands to form a dough.

3. Roll out dough to ⅛-inch thickness on floured, cloth-covered surface. Cut with cookie cutter. Place 1 inch apart on ungreased metal baking sheets.

4. MICROWAVE-BAKE, one pan at a time, 4 to 4½ minutes or until edges are golden brown. Remove from baking sheet; cool.
                              3 to 4 Dozen Cookies

TIP • Instead of rolling out dough, try shaping into 1-inch balls. Then flatten with bottom of glass dipped in sugar. Microwave-bake 4½ to 5 minutes.

SOUR CREAM-BUTTERSCOTCH COOKIES

½ cup shortening
1 cup packed brown sugar
¾ cup sour cream
2 eggs
1 teaspoon vanilla
2½ cups unsifted all-purpose flour
¼ teaspoon baking powder
¼ teaspoon soda
½ teaspoon salt
1 cup (6-oz. pkg.) butterscotch pieces
¾ cup chopped nuts

1. Preheat oven to 425° F.
2. Beat together shortening, brown sugar, sour cream, eggs and vanilla in medium mixing bowl. Stir in remaining ingredients. Drop by teaspoonfuls, 2 inches apart, onto ungreased metal baking sheets.
3. MICROWAVE-BAKE, one pan at a time, 4 to 4½ minutes or until lightly browned. Cool slightly; remove from pan. Frost with Browned Butter Frosting.   About 4 Dozen Cookies

CHOCOLATE CHIP COOKIES

¾ cup butter or margarine
1 cup packed brown sugar
¼ cup sugar
1 egg
1½ teaspoons vanilla
2 cups unsifted all-purpose flour
½ teaspoon soda
½ teaspoon salt
1 cup (6-oz. pkg.) semi-sweet chocolate pieces
1 cup chopped nuts

1. MICROWAVE butter in large glass mixing bowl 1½ to 2 minutes or until softened.
2. Preheat oven to 425° F.
3. Beat the sugars, egg and vanilla into butter. Stir in remaining ingredients. Drop by teaspoonfuls, 2 inches apart, onto ungreased metal baking sheets.
4. MICROWAVE-BAKE, one pan at a time, 4 to 4½ minutes or until lightly browned. Cool slightly; remove from pan.
                    4 to 5 Dozen Cookies

Since the oven is already hot from baking the cookies, a microwave-bake method is used for browning the butter. If the oven is cool, just use microwave cooking and increase time a minute or two.

BROWNED BUTTER FROSTING

¼ cup butter or margarine
1 cup powdered sugar
½ teaspoon vanilla
2 to 3 tablespoons hot tap water

1. MICROWAVE-BAKE butter in 1-quart glass casserole at 425° F. for 7 to 8 minutes or until lightly browned.
2. Beat in remaining ingredients, adding water just until mixture spreads easily.
                    Frosts 3 to 4 Dozen Cookies

Christmas brings visions of these dainty cookies. Try the different versions, too.

CHERRY THUMBPRINT COOKIES

½ cup butter or margarine
¼ cup sugar
1 egg, separated
½ teaspoon vanilla
1½ teaspoons grated lemon peel
1 tablespoon lemon juice
1 cup unsifted all-purpose flour
¾ cup finely chopped nuts
12 red Maraschino cherries, halved and drained

1. MICROWAVE butter in medium glass mixing bowl about 1½ minutes or until softened.
2. Preheat oven to 400° F.
3. Beat sugar into butter. Add egg yolk, vanilla, lemon peel and juice; mix well. Blend in flour. If necessary, chill dough for easier handling. Shape into 1-inch balls. Beat egg white slightly. Dip each ball into egg white; roll in nuts. Place 2 inches apart on ungreased metal baking sheets. Press cherry half into center of each ball.
4. MICROWAVE-BAKE, one pan at a time, 4 to 4½ minutes or until lightly browned. Cool slightly; remove from pan.
                    About 24 Cookies

TIPS • Thumbprint cookies: Omit Maraschino cherries; press thumb deeply into center of each cookie to make depression. Bake as directed. Fill depressions with jam or jelly.

• If desired, roll cookies in crushed cornflake crumbs or flaked coconut instead of nuts.

ALMOND CRISPS

1 cup butter or margarine
1 cup sugar
1 cup packed brown sugar
1 egg
1 teaspoon almond extract
2¼ cups unsifted all-purpose flour
½ teaspoon salt
¼ teaspoon soda
1 cup chopped almonds or other nuts

1. MICROWAVE butter in large glass mixing bowl about 2 minutes or until softened.
2. Beat sugars, egg and almond extract into butter. Stir in remaining ingredients. Divide dough into 3 equal portions. Shape dough into rolls 2-inches in diameter; wrap in wax paper and refrigerate at least 4 hours.
3. Preheat oven to 425° F.
4. Slice chilled cookie roll into ¼-inch thick slices. Place 2 inches apart on ungreased metal baking sheet.
5. MICROWAVE-BAKE 4 to 4½ minutes or until edges are lightly browned. Cool slightly; remove from baking sheet.

About 6 Dozen Cookies

TIP • Substitute for nuts: 1 cup raisins or chopped maraschino cherries.

TEACAKES

1 cup butter or margarine
½ cup powdered sugar
1 egg
1 teaspoon vanilla
2⅓ cups unsifted all-purpose flour
1 cup chopped nuts
Powdered sugar

1. MICROWAVE butter in medium glass mixing bowl 2 minutes or until softened.
2. Preheat oven to 400° F.
3. Beat powdered sugar, egg and vanilla into butter. Stir in flour and nuts. Shape into 1-inch balls; place 1 inch apart on ungreased metal baking sheets.
4. MICROWAVE-BAKE, one pan at a time, 4 to 4½ minutes or until no longer doughy. Cool slightly; remove from pan and roll in powdered sugar.   About 4 Dozen Cookies

TIP • Mint-flavored chocolate pieces or chopped Maraschino cherries may be substituted for part of the nuts.

Pictured: Spritz, page 163 and Teacakes, this page.

BARS: These are cooked using a method similar to preparing cakes. Bake is used to start the leavening process, then microwave cooking is added to set the center.

Glass baking dishes are used for all the bar cookie recipes included in this section.

Both mixes and favorite recipe bar cookies cook very well using the combination oven. Use the recipes here as guides for cooking other favorite bar cookies recipes.

Cooking time is about the same for regular and family-size mixes.

BROWNIE MIX

1. Preheat oven to 350° F.
2. Prepare 1 package (15½ oz. or 22½ oz.) brownie mix as directed on package, spreading in 8-inch square or 3-quart (13x9) glass baking dish, greased on bottom only.
3. BAKE 10 minutes. ❖
4. MICROWAVE-BAKE 4 to 4½ minutes or until toothpick inserted in center comes out clean.
   3 to 4 Dozen Brownies

CHOCOLATE BROWNIES

   2 squares or envelopes (1 oz. each) unsweetened chocolate
   ⅓ cup butter or margarine
   1 cup sugar
   2 eggs
   1 cup unsifted all-purpose flour
   ¼ teaspoon baking powder
   ¼ teaspoon salt
   ½ teaspoon vanilla
   ½ cup chopped nuts

1. MICROWAVE chocolate and butter in large glass mixing bowl 2 to 3 minutes or until chocolate and butter are melted.
2. Preheat oven to 350° F.
3. Add sugar to chocolate mixture; beat in eggs. Stir in remaining ingredients. Spread in greased 8-inch square glass baking dish.
4. BAKE 5 minutes. ❖
5. MICROWAVE-BAKE 3 to 3½ minutes or until toothpick inserted in center comes out clean. Cool; cut into bars.   16 to 24 Bars

DREAM BAR MIX

1. Preheat oven to 325° F.
2. Prepare 1 package (12½ oz.) dream bar mix as directed on package, pressing crust into 8-inch square glass baking dish.
3. MICROWAVE-BAKE 3 minutes. Spread topping over crust.
4. BAKE 5 minutes. ❖
5. MICROWAVE-BAKE 2½ to 3 minutes or until golden brown.   About 16 Bars

DREAM BARS

   ½ cup butter or margarine
   ½ cup packed brown sugar
   1 cup unsifted all-purpose flour
Topping
   2 eggs
   1 cup packed brown sugar
   1 tablespoon all-purpose flour
   1 teaspoon vanilla
   ½ teaspoon baking powder
   ¼ teaspoon salt
   1 cup shredded or flaked coconut
   ½ cup chopped nuts

1. MICROWAVE butter in medium glass mixing bowl 1½ to 2 minutes or until softened; blend in brown sugar and flour.
2. Preheat oven to 325° F.
3. Spread dough over bottom of 3-quart (13x9) glass baking dish.
4. MICROWAVE-BAKE 3½ minutes or until partially cooked.
5. Combine Topping ingredients in medium mixing bowl; mix well. Spread over crust.
6. BAKE 5 minutes. ❖
7. MICROWAVE-BAKE 4 to 5 minutes or until golden brown.   About 24 Bars

DATE BAR MIX

1. Preheat oven to 375° F.
2. Prepare 1 package (14 oz.) date bar mix as directed on package, placing in 8-inch square glass baking dish.
3. BAKE 12 minutes. ❖
4. MICROWAVE-BAKE 3 to 3½ minutes or until light golden brown.   About 16 Bars

LEMON SQUARES

Crust
1 cup unsifted all-purpose flour
¼ cup powdered sugar
Dash salt
½ cup butter or margarine

Filling
2 eggs
1 cup sugar
2 tablespoons all-purpose flour
½ teaspoon baking powder
1 tablespoon grated lemon peel
2 tablespoons lemon juice

Frosting
¼ cup butter or margarine
1 cup powdered sugar
2 to 3 tablespoons milk or cream

1. Preheat oven to 325° F.
2. Combine flour, powdered sugar and salt in medium mixing bowl. Cut in butter until crumbly. Press evenly over bottom of 8-inch square glass baking dish.
3. MICROWAVE-BAKE 4 to 5 minutes or until just set.
4. Mix together Filling ingredients in medium mixing bowl; pour over Crust.
5. MICROWAVE-BAKE 6 to 6½ minutes or until bubbly. Cool.
6. MICROWAVE butter in small glass mixing bowl about 1 minute or until softened. Beat in remaining Frosting ingredients, adding milk just until mixture spreads easily. Spread over cooled bars.   About 24 Bars

A very moist, rich date bar.

GRAHAM DATE SQUARES

3 eggs
1 cup sugar
1 teaspoon vanilla
1 cup chopped dates
1 cup chopped walnuts
2⅓ cups graham cracker crumbs (about 28 squares)
1 teaspoon baking powder
¼ teaspoon salt

1. Preheat oven to 350° F.
2. Beat eggs, sugar and vanilla in medium mixing bowl. Stir in dates and walnuts; blend in remaining ingredients. Spread in greased 2-quart (12x7) glass baking dish.
3. BAKE 10 minutes. ✿
4. MICROWAVE-BAKE 4 to 5 minutes or until toothpick inserted in center comes out clean. Cool; cut into bars.   About 32 Bars

These bars are pretty as a picture on any cookie tray.

FESTIVE DATE-NUT CHEWS

2 eggs
⅔ cup sugar
½ teaspoon vanilla
⅔ cup unsifted all-purpose flour
½ teaspoon salt
½ teaspoon baking powder
½ cup chopped nuts
1 cup chopped dates
¾ cup halved Maraschino cherries, drained

1. Preheat oven to 350° F.
2. Beat eggs, sugar and vanilla in medium mixing bowl. Stir in remaining ingredients. Spread in greased 8-inch square glass baking dish.
3. BAKE 12 minutes. ✿
4. MICROWAVE-BAKE 3 to 4 minutes or until toothpick inserted in center comes out clean. Cool; if desired, frost with Cherry Cream Frosting, page 161. Cut into bars.
          About 24 Bars

These taste like a candy bar, but have added nutrition from rolled oats, granola and peanut butter.

CRUNCHY TOFFEE BARS

⅔ cup butter or margarine
1 cup packed brown sugar
⅓ cup light corn syrup
1 teaspoon salt
1 teaspoon vanilla
3 cups quick-cooking rolled oats
2 cups granola cereal
½ cup peanut butter
1 cup (6-oz. pkg.) semi-sweet chocolate pieces

1. MICROWAVE butter in large glass mixing bowl 2½ to 3 minutes or until melted.
2. Preheat oven to 350° F.
3. Add brown sugar, corn syrup, salt and vanilla to butter; mix well. Stir in rolled oats and granola. Pat evenly into greased 2-quart (12x7) glass baking dish.
4. MICROWAVE-BAKE 6½ to 7½ minutes or until bubbly throughout. Cool 5 minutes; spoon peanut butter over top, spreading evenly. Sprinkle with chocolate pieces.
5. MICROWAVE-BAKE ½ to 1 minute or until chocolate pieces are softened. Spread evenly over bars. Refrigerate to set frosting. Cut into bars.   About 36 Bars

Candies

CANDIES: Microwave cooking heats the candy ingredients to the desired temperature. Since the cooking comes from all sides, there is little chance of scorching.

Some candies have one or two ingredients that are heated until they melt. Then these are blended with other ingredients or used to coat and bind other ingredients together. Other candies require cooking a sugar mixture until it reaches a specified temperature.

The usual candy thermometer should not be used in the oven when microwave cooking is required. When the sugar mixture has cooked the minimum time, remove it from the oven and test with a candy thermometer. If the thermometer does not register the specified temperature, remove the thermometer and return the mixture to the oven for a minute or two more or until the thermometer registers the specified temperature when placed in the mixture.

CHOCOLATE CLUSTERS

    2 cups (12-oz. pkg.) semi-sweet
        chocolate pieces
 1½ cups salted Spanish peanuts
 1½ cups chow mein noodles

1. MICROWAVE chocolate pieces in medium glass mixing bowl 2 to 2½ minutes or until melted. Stir in peanuts and noodles.
2. Drop by teaspoonfuls onto wax paper. Chill until chocolate is set.   About 24 Clusters

CARAMELED APPLES

 1 bag (14 oz.) caramels
 2 tablespoons water
 5 apples, washed and dried
 5 wooden sticks

1. Combine unwrapped caramels with water in 4-cup glass measure.
2. MICROWAVE 6 to 7 minutes or until caramels are melted, stirring occasionally during last half of cooking time. Insert a stick into stem end of each apple.
3. Dip each apple into hot caramel mixture, turning to coat. Remove excess mixture from bottom of apples by scraping on edge of dish. Place apples on greased wax paper. Chill until set.

TIP • If wax paper is not greased, it will stick to the caramel mixture.

Pictured: Carameled Apples, Chocolate Clusters and Pecan Pralines, this page.

These popcorn bars will become the children's favorite.

PEANUTTY POPCORN BARS

 ½ cup butter or margarine
 1 cup (6-oz. pkg.) butterscotch pieces
 4 cups miniature marshmallows
 2 quarts unsalted popped corn
 1 cup salted Spanish peanuts

1. MICROWAVE butter and butterscotch pieces in large glass mixing bowl 2 minutes. Stir in marshmallows.
2. MICROWAVE 2 to 2½ minutes or until melted. Stir in remaining ingredients. Press into buttered 3-quart (13x9) baking dish. Chill; cut into bars.   About 32 Bars

PEANUT BUTTER FUDGE

 ½ cup butter or margarine
 ⅓ cup milk
 1¾ cups sugar
 ¼ teaspoon salt
 ⅛ teaspoon cream of tartar
 2½ cups miniature marshmallows
 ½ cup butterscotch pieces
 ½ cup peanut butter
 1 teaspoon vanilla

1. Butter a 2-quart glass casserole. Add butter, milk, sugar, salt and cream of tartar. Stir to combine.
2. MICROWAVE, covered, 5 minutes. Remove cover and stir.
3. MICROWAVE, uncovered, 4 to 5 minutes or until candy thermometer placed in mixture registers 232° F. Stir in remaining ingredients until consistency is smooth. Pour into buttered 8-inch square baking dish. Cool; cut into squares.   About 24 Squares

PECAN PRALINES

 2 cups sugar
 1 teaspoon soda
 1 cup buttermilk
 ¾ cup butter or margarine
 1 teaspoon vanilla
 2 cups pecan halves

1. Butter a 3-quart glass casserole. Add sugar, soda, buttermilk and butter. Stir to combine.
2. MICROWAVE, covered, 10 minutes. Remove cover and stir.
3. MICROWAVE, uncovered, 14 to 18 minutes or until candy thermometer placed in mixture registers 236° F. Beat with electric mixer on medium speed about 5 minutes or until slightly thickened. Stir in vanilla and pecans. Pour into buttered 2-quart (12x7) baking dish. Chill; cut into squares.   About 36 Squares

Pies

PASTRY SHELLS: Pastry shells can be cooked with just microwave cooking. They become flakey and crisp; however, there is little browning. This method is especially convenient when you don't wish to turn on conventional heat for the short time necessary to cook a crust.

When a browned crust is preferred, it is best to cook it conventionally.

Cookie-crumb crusts use microwaves to melt the butter and then heat the crumb mixture to make it set and hold its shape.

For an easy finish, substitute this Streusel Topping for a traditional top pastry crust on fruit pie.

STREUSEL TOPPING

¾ cup unsifted all-purpose flour
½ cup packed brown sugar
½ teaspoon cinnamon
½ cup butter or margarine
¼ cup chopped nuts, if desired

1. Preheat oven to 450° F.
2. Combine flour, brown sugar and cinnamon in small mixing bowl. Cut in butter until crumbly; stir in nuts. Sprinkle over an unbaked 1-crust fruit pie in a glass pie plate.
3. MICROWAVE-BAKE 12 to 14 minutes or until fruit is cooked and topping golden brown.

PASTRY FOR 2-CRUST PIE

2 cups unsifted all-purpose flour
1 teaspoon salt
⅔ cup shortening
5 to 7 tablespoons cold water

1. Combine flour and salt in large mixing bowl; cut in shortening until mixture is in fine pieces. Sprinkle water over mixture, a tablespoonful at a time, while stirring lightly with fork. Add just enough water until dough holds together.
2. Roll out as directed in pie recipe.

2-crust Pastry

Tip • For 1-crust pastry, halve each ingredient amount.

For a regular baked pie shell, use conventional heat. When you do not wish oven heat, try cooking it with this method using only microwaves.

BAKED PASTRY SHELL

1. Prepare favorite pastry for 1-crust pie. Line 8, 9 or 10-inch glass pie plate. Trim and flute edge; prick bottom and sides with fork.
2. MICROWAVE 8 to 10 minutes or until pastry has a dry, flakey appearance.   1 Pastry Shell

GRAHAM CRACKER CRUST

¼ cup butter or margarine
1¼ cups graham cracker crumbs
¼ cup sugar

1. MICROWAVE butter in 9 or 10-inch glass pie plate about 2 minutes or until melted. Stir in crumbs and sugar. Press mixture over bottom and up sides of pie plate.
2. MICROWAVE 2½ to 3 minutes or until set. Cool.   9 or 10-inch Crust

CHOCOLATE WAFER CRUST

3 tablespoons butter or margarine
1 cup chocolate wafer crumbs (about 16)

1. MICROWAVE butter in 9-inch glass pie plate about 2 minutes or until melted. Stir in crumbs. Press mixture over bottom and up sides of pie plate.
2. MICROWAVE 1½ to 2 minutes or until set. Cool.   9-inch Crust

A crunchy, no-bake crust for your favorite chilled or frozen pie filling.

GRANOLA PIE CRUST

3 tablespoons butter or margarine
¼ cup packed brown sugar
1½ cups granola cereal

1. MICROWAVE butter and brown sugar in medium glass bowl 5 to 6 minutes or until bubbly. Stir in granola. Press mixture over bottom and up sides of 9 or 10-inch pie plate; chill.   9 or 10-inch Crust

Pictured, top to bottom: Peachy Pear Pie, page 172, Pecan Pie, page 174 and Banana Cream Pie, page 176.

TWO-CRUST PIES: These pies require combination cooking — microwave cooking to quickly cook the filling and conventional heat to brown and crisp the crust. Combination cooking makes a nice finished pie because it is fast and the filling cooks quickly before the crust becomes soggy. For baking frozen pies, see the Freezer Chapter.

Use this recipe as a guide for cooking other 2-crust fresh fruit pies.

OLD-FASHIONED APPLE PIE

Pastry for 2-crust pie
6 cups (6 med.) peeled, sliced cooking apples
¾ to 1 cup sugar
1 tablespoon flour
1 teaspoon cinnamon
¼ teaspoon nutmeg
1 tablespoon lemon juice
2 tablespoons butter or margarine

1. Preheat oven to 450° F.
2. Roll out half of pastry to fit a 9-inch glass pie plate. Line pie plate with pastry, trimming crust even with edge of pan. Set aside remaining pastry.
3. Combine apples, sugar, flour, cinnamon, nutmeg and lemon juice in large mixing bowl. Pile into pastry-lined pan; dot with butter.
4. Roll out remaining pastry to circle the size of pie pan. Cut slits in center for escape of steam. Moisten edge of bottom crust with water. Place top crust over filling. Fold edge of top crust under bottom crust; pinch together to seal edge.
5. **MICROWAVE-BAKE** 10 minutes.
6. **BAKE** 5 to 7 minutes or until golden brown and apples are tender.   9-inch Pie

TIP • See the freezer chapter for cooking frozen fruit pies.

The microwave cooking time for pies using prepared pie filling is slightly less than for fresh fruit pies.

PEACHY PEAR PIE

Pastry for 2-crust pie
1 can (21 oz.) prepared peach pie filling
1 can (8 oz.) sliced pears, drained
⅓ cup raisins
1 tablespoon lemon juice
½ teaspoon cinnamon

1. Preheat oven to 450° F.
2. Roll out half of pastry to fit a 9-inch glass pie plate. Line pie plate with pastry, trimming crust even with edge of pan. Set aside remaining pastry.
3. Combine remaining ingredients; spoon into pastry shell.
4. Roll out remaining pastry to circle the size of pie pan. Cut slits in center for escape of steam. Moisten edge of bottom crust. Place top crust over filling. Fold edge of top crust under bottom crust, pinch together to seal edge.
5. **MICROWAVE-BAKE** 8 minutes.
6. **BAKE** 5 to 7 minutes or until golden brown.
                                              9-inch Pie

DEEP DISH APPLE PIE

6 cups (6 med.) peeled, sliced cooking apples
¾ to 1 cup sugar
1 tablespoon all-purpose flour
1 tablespoon lemon juice
1 teaspoon cinnamon, if desired
Pastry for 1-crust pie
1 tablespoon milk
1 tablespoon sugar

1. Preheat oven to 450° F.
2. Combine apples, sugar, flour, lemon juice and cinnamon in 2-quart (12x7) glass baking dish.
3. Roll out pastry to a 13x8-inch rectangle. Top apple mixture with pastry; flute edges and slit top. Brush pastry with milk and sprinkle with 1 tablespoon sugar.
4. **MICROWAVE-BAKE** 10 to 12 minutes or until top is golden brown and apples are tender.   6 to 8 Servings

DEEP DISH CINNAMON-APPLE PIE

Microwave ¾ cup sugar, ¼ cup red cinnamon candies and ½ cup water in 2-quart (12x7) glass baking dish 5 to 5½ minutes or until candies are almost melted. Stir in apples and ¼ cup all-purpose flour. Continue with steps 3 and 4.

Pictured: Strawberry Bavarian Pie, page 177.

CUSTARD-TYPE PIES: Custard, pumpkin, pecan and other custard-type pies use microwave cooking to quickly cook the filling while conventional heat browns and crisps the single crust. Cooking is faster with this combination of heat and there is less chance of the crust becoming soggy.

CUSTARD PIE

  9-inch unbaked pastry shell
  4 eggs
  ⅔ cup sugar
  ½ teaspoon salt
  ¼ teaspoon nutmeg
  1 teaspoon vanilla
  2½ cups milk

1. Preheat oven to 450° F.
2. Prepare pastry shell in glass pie plate; set aside.
3. Beat together remaining ingredients in medium mixing bowl. Pour into pastry shell.
4. MICROWAVE-BAKE 7 minutes.
5. BAKE 12 to 13 minutes or until knife inserted near center comes out clean. Cool.

9-inch Pie

PUMPKIN PIE

  9-inch unbaked pastry shell
  3 eggs
  ½ cup whipping cream
  ½ cup milk
  ¾ cup packed brown sugar
  1 teaspoon cinnamon
  ½ teaspoon salt
  ½ teaspoon ground ginger
  ½ teaspoon nutmeg
  ⅛ teaspoon ground cloves
  1 can (15 oz.) pumpkin

1. Preheat oven to 450° F.
2. Prepare pastry shell in glass pie plate; set aside.
3. Beat together remaining ingredients in medium mixing bowl. Pour into pastry shell.
4. MICROWAVE-BAKE 9 minutes.
5. BAKE 7 to 9 minutes or until knife inserted near center comes out clean. Cool. If desired, serve with whipped cream.

9-inch Pie

TIP • Substitute for whipping cream and milk: 1 cup evaporated milk.

PECAN PIE

  9-inch unbaked pastry shell
  ¼ cup butter or margarine
  1½ cups dark corn syrup
  4 eggs
  ½ tablespoon flour
  2 tablespoons brandy, if desired
  1 teaspoon vanilla
  1½ cups pecan halves

1. Prepare pastry shell in glass pie plate; set aside.
2. MICROWAVE butter in medium glass mixing bowl 2 to 2½ minutes or until melted.
3. Preheat oven to 450° F.
4. Add remaining ingredients except pecans to butter; beat well with rotary beater. Stir in pecans. Pour into pastry shell.
5. MICROWAVE-BAKE 9 to 10 minutes or until knife inserted near center comes out clean. Cool.

9-inch Pie

RHUBARB CUSTARD PIE

  Pastry for 2-crust pie
  3 eggs, beaten
  1⅓ cups sugar
  2 tablespoons all-purpose flour
  ¼ teaspoon nutmeg
  ⅛ teaspoon salt
  4 cups sliced rhubarb
  2 tablespoons butter or margarine

1. Preheat oven to 450° F.
2. Roll out half of pastry to fit a 9-inch glass pie plate. Line pie plate with pastry, leaving ½ inch extending beyond edge of pan. Set aside remaining pastry.
3. Combine remaining ingredients except butter in large mixing bowl; mix well. Pour into pastry-lined pan; dot with butter.
4. Roll out remaining pastry. Cut into strips, ½ inch wide. Twist strips and lay across filling in parallel rows, about ½ inch apart. Twist more strips and lay at right angles to first rows, forming a crisscross pattern. Trim ends even with pastry. Fold extended pastry over ends of strips to form a rim; flute.
5. MICROWAVE-BAKE 10 minutes.
6. BAKE 9 to 11 minutes or until knife inserted near center comes out clean.   9-inch Pie

TIP • If you prefer a woven lattice, interweave strips on baking sheet. Freeze until firm. Slide frozen crust onto top of pie and continue as directed.

CREAM & MERINGUE PIES: A cream filling is cooked with microwaves using the same techniques used for puddings. The flour or cornstarch mixture should come to a boil to cook the starch and avoid a starchy or flour-like taste. Stirring during the last half of cooking prevents the starches, that settle to the bottom, from cooking into a mass and lumping when stirred.

Meringue toppings on cream pies are best cooked conventionally. The addition of microwaves causes the meringue to shrink and toughen. When you don't wish to turn on the conventional oven to cook the meringue, try folding it into the cream filling as in the Coconut Cream Pie recipe.

The meringue is folded into this cream filling. Cream cheese adds a special flavor.

COCONUT CREAM PIE

9-inch Baked Pastry Shell, page 171
½ cup sugar
¼ cup cornstarch
Dash salt
1¼ cups milk
2 eggs, separated
1 package (3 oz.) cream cheese
¼ cup sugar
1 cup flaked or shredded coconut
1 teaspoon vanilla

1. Prepare pastry shell; cool.
2. Combine ½ cup sugar, the cornstarch, salt and milk in 4-cup glass measure.
3. MICROWAVE 8 to 9 minutes or until mixture boils and thickens, stirring once during last half of cooking time. Gradually add some of hot mixture to beaten egg yolks; then blend into remaining milk mixture. Stir in cream cheese.
4. MICROWAVE 1 minute. Beat with fork to blend in cream cheese.
5. Beat egg whites in medium mixing bowl until frothy; gradually add ¼ cup sugar, beating until soft peaks form. Fold in cream cheese mixture, coconut and vanilla.
6. Spoon into baked pastry shell. Refrigerate until served. 9-inch Pie

TIP • VANILLA CREAM PIE: omit coconut and turn into 8-inch baked pastry shell.

Microwaves are used to cook the filling, but not the meringue topping.

LEMON MERINGUE PIE

9-inch baked Pastry Shell, page 171
1 cup sugar
¼ cup cornstarch
½ teaspoon salt
1½ cups water
3 eggs, separated
2 tablespoons butter or margarine
2 teaspoons grated lemon peel
⅓ cup lemon juice
¼ teaspoon cream of tartar
¼ cup sugar

1. Prepare pastry shell; cool.
2. Combine 1 cup sugar, the cornstarch, salt and water in 4-cup glass measure.
3. MICROWAVE 9 to 10 minutes or until mixture boils and thickens, stirring once. Gradually add some of hot mixture to beaten egg yolks; then blend into remaining mixture.
4. MICROWAVE 1 minute.
5. Stir in butter, lemon peel and lemon juice. Pour into baked pastry shell.
6. Preheat oven to 350° F.
7. Beat egg whites and cream of tartar in medium mixing bowl until frothy; gradually add ¼ cup sugar, beating until soft peaks form. Spoon over lemon filling, carefully spreading to seal meringue to edge and cover filling.
8. BAKE 10 to 12 minutes or until golden brown; cool. 9-inch Pie

BANANA CREAM PIE

> 9-inch Baked Pastry Shell, page 171
> ½ cup sugar
> ½ cup unsifted all-purpose flour
> ¼ teaspoon salt
> 1½ cups milk
> 1 egg, beaten
> 2 tablespoons butter or margarine
> 2 tablespoons rum, if desired
> ½ teaspoon vanilla
> 2 bananas, sliced
> Sweetened whipped cream

1. Prepare pastry shell; cool.
2. Combine sugar, flour, salt and milk in 4-cup glass measure.
3. MICROWAVE 7 to 7½ minutes or until mixture boils and thickens, stirring once during last half of cooking time. Gradually add some of the hot mixture to beaten egg; then blend into remaining milk mixture.
4. MICROWAVE 1 minute. Stir in butter, rum and vanilla.
5. Spread about one third of cream filling mixture over pastry shell. Top with one sliced banana; repeat, ending with cream filling. Decorate or serve with whipped cream. Refrigerate until served.   9-inch Pie

Pudding mix makes this pie easy.

EASY BLACK BOTTOM PIE

> 9-inch Baked Pastry Shell, page 171
> 2 cups milk
> 1 package (4 oz.) vanilla pudding and pie filling mix
> 1 envelope unflavored gelatin
> 1 square or envelope (1 oz.) unsweetened chocolate
> 1 cup whipping cream
> 2 tablespoons rum, if desired

1. Prepare pastry shell; cool.
2. Combine milk, pudding mix and gelatin in 4-cup glass measure.
3. MICROWAVE 10 to 11 minutes or until mixture boils, stirring once during last half of cooking time.
4. Divide mixture in half; stir chocolate into one half until melted. Pour into pastry shell, spreading evenly. Refrigerate. Let remaining half of pudding stand at room temperature until cool.
5. Beat cream until thickened. Fold in rum and pudding; spoon over chocolate layer. Refrigerate until served.   9-inch Pie

GRASSHOPPER PIE

> Chocolate Wafer Crust, page 171
> ½ cup milk
> 30 large marshmallows or 3 cups miniature marshmallows
> 2 to 3 tablespoons white crème de cocoa
> 2 to 3 tablespoons green crème de menthe
> 1 cup whipping cream, whipped, or 2 cups frozen whipped topping

1. Prepare chocolate wafer crust, reserving 1 tablespoon crumb mixture for topping; cool.
2. MICROWAVE milk and marshmallows in 4-cup glass measure 2½ to 3½ minutes or until marshmallows begin to puff. Stir until smooth. Blend in crème de cocoa and crème de menthe. Chill about 30 minutes or until consistency of unbeaten egg whites.
3. Fold in whipped cream. Spoon into crust. Sprinkle with reserved crumbs. Refrigerate at least 4 hours or until set.   9-inch Pie

Always a favorite.

FRESH STRAWBERRY PIE

> 9-inch baked Pastry Shell, page 171
> 1½ quarts strawberries, washed and hulled
> 1 cup sugar
> 3 tablespoons cornstarch
> ½ cup water
> 1 tablespoon lemon juice

1. Prepare pastry shell; cool.
2. Crush enough strawberries to make 1 cup. Combine crushed strawberries, sugar, cornstarch and water in large glass mixing bowl.
3. MICROWAVE 8 to 10 minutes or until mixture boils and thickens, stirring once. Stir in lemon juice. Cool.
4. Add whole strawberries to glaze mixture and coat well. Arrange in baked pastry shell. Chill. If desired, serve with whipped cream.
          9-inch Pie

TIP • The blender can be used to quickly crush strawberries.

A pumpkin pie that is cool and delightful any time of year.

PUMPKIN CHIFFON PIE

Granola Pie Crust, page 171
1 envelope unflavored gelatin
½ cup sugar
½ teaspoon salt
½ teaspoon ground ginger
½ teaspoon nutmeg
¾ teaspoon cinnamon
½ cup milk
3 eggs, separated
1 can (15 oz.) pumpkin
¼ cup sugar

1. Prepare crust and chill.
2. Combine gelatin, ½ cup sugar, the salt, ginger, nutmeg, cinnamon and milk in medium glass mixing bowl; mix well.
3. MICROWAVE 3½ to 4 minutes or until gelatin is dissolved and mixture hot. Stir in beaten egg yolks and pumpkin. Beat egg whites in medium mixing bowl until frothy. Gradually add ¼ cup sugar, beating until soft peaks form. Fold into pumpkin mixture.
4. Spoon into prepared crust. Refrigerate at least 2 hours or until set.   10-inch Pie

TIP • A baked pastry shell or graham cracker crust may be used with this pumpkin filling.

STRAWBERRY BAVARIAN PIE

9-inch Graham Cracker Crust, page 171
1 cup water
1 package (3 oz.) strawberry-flavored gelatin
1 package (10 oz.) frozen sliced strawberries
2 cups (4½ oz. carton) frozen whipped topping, thawed
Fresh strawberries for garnish, if desired

1. Prepare crust; cool.
2. MICROWAVE water in 4-cup glass measure 5 to 6 minutes or until hot.
3. Stir gelatin into hot water until dissolved. Add frozen strawberries. Let mixture set until berries are thawed and gelatin is slightly thickened. Fold into whipped topping. Spoon filling into crust. Refrigerate at least 2 hours or until set. If desired, garnish with additional whipped topping and fresh strawberries.
9-inch Pie

TIP • Substitute for frozen whipped topping: 1 cup whipping cream, whipped and sweetened.

This apple pie requires no oven heat, making it perfect for hot weather entertaining.

VERMONT APPLE PIE

9-inch baked Pastry Shell, page 171
¾ cup maple or maple-flavored syrup
¼ cup water
7 cups (7 med.) peeled, sliced cooking apples
¼ cup butter or margarine
3 tablespoons cornstarch
1 package (8 oz.) cream cheese
½ cup powdered sugar
1 teaspoon vanilla

1. Prepare pastry shell; cool.
2. MICROWAVE syrup, water and apples in covered 2-quart glass casserole 12 to 13 minutes or until apples are tender. Set aside.
3. MICROWAVE butter in 2-cup glass measure 2 to 2½ minutes or until butter is melted; stir in cornstarch and syrup mixture from cooked apples.
4. MICROWAVE 3 to 3½ minutes or until bubbly and thickened. Stir into apples, spoon into pastry shell; cool.
5. MICROWAVE cream cheese in small glass mixing bowl about 2 minutes or until softened. Beat until light and fluffy; beat in powdered sugar and vanilla. Spoon topping over filling, spreading to cover. Refrigerate until served. If desired, garnish with unpeeled apple slices dipped in lemon juice.
9-inch Pie

TIP • 1 can (16 oz.) prepared apple pie filling, may be substituted for the apple filling in this recipe.

Oven Meals

ABOUT THE CHAPTER: This chapter features the cooking of several foods in the oven at one time. Throughout the remainder of the book, the ideas are primarily for cooking one item at a time. Often, though, it is more convenient and energy saving to cook several foods together. Understanding this chapter will help you decide which foods to cook together for your own menu planning.

BASICS OF TIMINGS: With conventional baking or broiling, the addition of other items in the oven does not greatly affect the time necessary to cook the initial food. This is because the oven cavity is constantly filled with air at a certain temperature — plenty to surround and heat one or several food items. In contrast, with microwave cooking, the addition of other items increases the time necessary to heat or cook the initial food. This is because there are only a certain amount of microwaves available to penetrate the food. As additional foods are added, the concentration in any single food is diluted.

Thus, the more the food relies on microwave cooking for heating or cooking, the greater impact additional food items will have on the timing. And the more baking or broiling that is taking place when microwaves are being used, the less increase there is in cooking time.

BASICS OF COMBINATIONS: When deciding upon foods to combine, it is necessary to look at the cooking technique and time normally used. If both foods use the same technique and cook about equal time, combining the cooking is simple. If the techniques are different, then a compromise cooking technique must be used for the combination. When the times are different, you must decide which food can take the additional cooking. If that does not seem feasible, then one food will need to be removed before or added after the other.

This section features foods which cook together in one step. Some of the meals contain a vegetable and others do not. But, with any of the meals, a frozen vegetable can be added during the last 15 to 20 minutes of cooking. With the microwave-broil technique in ovens with two shelves, the vegetable can be placed on the shelf under the broiler pan, so it cooks primarily from the available microwaves.

Only one meal includes a dessert. If a dessert does not fit the timing being used, it can be cooked earlier or added for just a portion of the cooking.

Pictured: Meatloaf Dinner, this page.

MEATLOAF DINNER

Tangy Meatloaf, page 55
Oven-Browned Potatoes, page 112
Old-Fashioned Apple Pie, page 172

BASIS FOR SELECTION:
The meatloaf normally cooks with a microwave-bake technique at 350° for 22 to 25 minutes. The potatoes use the same technique, but need a slightly higher temperature for 20 to 22 minutes. And the pie cooks with microwave-bake at 450° for 10 minutes and then bakes 5 to 7 additional minutes.

In this meal a compromise temperature must be selected. The meatloaf can take a slightly higher temperature because the concentration of microwaves will be less with the additional foods. The pie can take a slightly lower temperature because it will be in the oven longer. Since here too, the microwave cooking is slowed by additional foods, the need to switch to just a bake setting is no longer valid. That technique was primarily to keep the pie from boiling over before it was browned enough. So, the 400° microwave-bake temperature is selected. With bake being used along with microwaves, there is only a slight increase in cooking time needed.

DIRECTIONS:
1. Prepare Tangy Meatloaf, page 55, through step 2.
2. Prepare Oven-Browned Potatoes, page 112, through step 1.
3. Prepare Old-Fashioned Apple Pie, page 172, through step 4.
4. Preheat oven to 400° F.
5. Place all items in the oven.
6. **MICROWAVE-BAKE** 25 to 30 minutes or until foods are done. Stir potatoes once during last half of cooking.   5 to 6 Servings

TIP • A frozen apple pie may be used, but be sure the edges are well sealed to keep the bubbling juices inside the pie. Increase cooking time for meal to 35 to 40 minutes.

ORIENTAL STEAK DINNER

Oriental Steak with Pea Pods, page 61
Fluffy White Rice, page 121

BASIS FOR SELECTION:

The steak with pea pods cooks with a microwave technique for 15 to 17 minutes and then 3 to 4 additional minutes after the thickening is added. Rice cooks with microwaves for 13 to 15 minutes. With the rice, the cooking time is dependent upon adequate time for the rice to rehydrate, so even a little slower cooking will not affect it.

Since both techniques were originally microwave, microwave cooking will be used for the combination. And since time is more a factor than speed of cooking, the time will not be greatly changed when going to two foods. Care needs to be taken with the rice that it does not overcook, so it is removed and allowed to stand while the thickenings are cooking in the casserole.

DIRECTIONS:

1. Prepare Oriental Steak with Pea Pods, page 61, through step 1.
2. Prepare Fluffy White Rice, page 121, through step 1. Cover both dishes and place in oven.
3. **MICROWAVE** 18 minutes.
4. Remove rice from oven and set aside. Stir remaining ingredients into steak dish.
5. **MICROWAVE** 3 to 4 minutes or until mixture boils and thickens. Fluff rice with fork and serve with the steak.   5 to 6 Servings

TIP • Two 2-quart casseroles are called for in the recipe, but the rice can be cooked in a 2½-quart or 3-quart casserole.

HAM AND SCALLOPED POTATO DINNER

Baked Ham, page 72
Scalloped Potatoes, page 112

BASIS FOR SELECTION:

The Baked Ham is cooked, covered, with microwave cooking for 20 minutes and then uncovered and cooked with a bake setting for the remainder of the time. Scalloped potatoes are cooked, partially covered, with microwave cooking until done, and then broiled for a few minutes to brown. Although different techniques, the end result and reason for each method of browning is somewhat similar. The potatoes would also brown with a longer bake setting whereas only one side of the ham would brown if it were finished with a broil setting. Thus, microwave cooking is used for the first part, and then the foods are completed with a bake setting. Since the potatoes have not started to boil hard by the time the cover is removed, the dish can be completely covered, rather than partially covered as in the original recipe.

DIRECTIONS:

1. Prepare Baked Ham, page 72, using a 3-lb. ham and preparing through step 1.
2. Prepare Scalloped Potatoes, page 112, through step 2. Cover both casseroles and place in oven.
3. **MICROWAVE** 20 minutes. Uncover both casseroles. Insert meat thermometer into thickest part of ham.
4. **BAKE** at 350° F. for about 30 minutes or until meat thermometer registers 115° F. and potatoes are tender.   5 to 6 Servings

BARBECUED RIBS DINNER

Oven-Barbecued Ribs, page 70
Baked Potatoes, page 111

BASIS FOR SELECTION:

The ribs normally cook with microwave-bake at 400° for 20 minutes, with rearranging and the addition of the sauce about half way through the cooking time. The potatoes cook with microwave-bake at 450° for 16 to 20 minutes. A higher oven temperature might scorch the sauce on the ribs, but a lower temperature for the potatoes would only lengthen the cooking time a little. Therefore the microwave-bake at 400° is the selected compromise cooking temperature. The time necessary for cooking is lengthened because both the potatoes and the ribs are dependent upon the microwaves for cooking the interior.

DIRECTIONS:

1. Prepare Oven-Barbecued Ribs, page 70, through step 1. Place ribs and 4 to 5 medium scrubbed potatoes in oven.
2. **MICROWAVE-BAKE** at 400° F. for 10 to 12 minutes or until ribs are no longer pink. Remove ribs from oven. Drain fat. Combine sauce ingredients from ribs recipe; spoon over ribs. Return ribs to oven where potatoes are cooking.
3. **MICROWAVE-BAKE** 15 to 18 minutes or until ribs and potatoes are done.   4 to 5 Servings

PORK CHOP DINNER

Broiled Pork Chops, page 68
Frozen French Fries
Broiled Tomatoes

BASIS FOR SELECTION:

Broiled Pork Chops use a microwave-broil technique cooking 4 minutes on one side and 4 to 5 minutes on the other. Herb-Butter Fries on page 112 gives the basic cooking for French fries which is a microwave-bake at 450° for 13 to 15 minutes. Because broil heat will best give the intense heat necessary for browning both chops and potatoes, microwave-broil is a good compromise technique. Since the heat comes from only one side though, the potatoes should be turned for even browning. Normally, tomatoes would just be broiled without the use of microwaves. However with the other foods on the broiler pan, the concentration of microwaves available will not affect the cooking and the tomatoes can be added for the last part of the cooking time.

DIRECTIONS:

1. Arrange 4 to 6 pork chops, cut ½ inch thick, on one end of metal broiler pan.
2. Arrange contents from 16-oz. package frozen French fries on other end of broiler pan.
3. Cut 2 to 3 tomatoes in half horizontally. Sprinkle cut sides with dry bread crumbs and dried parsley flakes; set aside.
4. Move oven rack to second position.
5. **MICROWAVE-BROIL** chops and potatoes 6 minutes. Turn chops over. Turn potatoes over and move toward center of broiler pan. Arrange tomato halves on end of broiler pan.
6. **MICROWAVE-BROIL** 5 to 6 minutes or until chops are done.   4 to 6 Servings

OVEN-BAKED CHICKEN DINNER

Oven-Baked Chicken, page 38
Dill 'n Chive Potatoes, page 112

BASIS FOR SELECTION:

The chicken normally cooks with microwave-bake at 400° for 20 to 25 minutes. The potatoes microwave in a covered casserole 10 to 11 minutes plus 2 to 3 minutes after adding seasonings. Since the chicken needs the bake heat to brown and become crispy and since the potatoes can still steam and cook even with the oven heat on, a microwave-bake technique is selected. When the chicken is added along with the potatoes, the cooking time will be longer for the potatoes. Yet, they will not overcook in the time necessary to cook the chicken. Thus, the 20 to 25 minute time for the chicken is used as a time guide. The seasonings for the potatoes are still added at the end of the cooking time.

DIRECTIONS:

1. Prepare Oven-Baked Chicken, page 38, through step 1.
2. Prepare Dill 'n Chive Potatoes, page 112, through step 1; cover. Place potatoes and chicken in oven.
3. **MICROWAVE-BAKE** at 400° F. for 20 minutes. Stir seasoning ingredients into potatoes; leave uncovered.
4. **MICROWAVE-BAKE** 3 to 4 minutes or until potatoes are tender and chicken is done.

4 to 5 Servings

ROAST CHICKEN DINNER

Roast Chicken, page 47
Onion-Filled Squash, page 114

BASIS FOR SELECTION:

Roast Chicken cooks with a microwave-bake setting at 400° for 24 to 26 minutes. The squash cooks with microwave-bake at 400° for 17 to 19 minutes. Then the filling is added and the squash cooks an additional 8 to 10 minutes. So, here the times and settings are very similar. The squash and chicken are started together. Then the squash is removed and filled with the onion filling while the chicken continues to cook on a bake setting. The squash is returned to the oven and the two dishes are completed with the microwave-bake setting. Since parts of the squash filling need just microwave cooking, these are completed before the actual cooking starts so that a cool oven can be used.

DIRECTIONS:

1. Prepare Roast Chicken, page 47, through step 2; set aside.
2. Prepare Onion-Filled Squash, page 114, steps 2 and 3; set aside.
3. Place chicken in oven along with 2 whole acorn squash.
4. **MICROWAVE-BAKE** at 400° F. for 20 to 25 minutes or until squash are done, turning squash over about halfway through cooking. Remove squash from oven. Continue baking chicken.
5. Prepare squash recipe, step 4. Return squash to oven.
6. **MICROWAVE-BAKE** 8 to 10 minutes or until chicken is done and squash are golden brown.

6 to 8 Servings

POLISH SAUSAGE AND BAKED BEAN DINNER

Southern Baked Beans, page 102
Polish Sausages, see Wieners page 74

BASIS FOR SELECTION:

The bean dish is cooked with microwave cooking 10 to 12 minutes in an uncovered casserole. The wieners cook in a covered casserole for 3 to 4 minutes. Although the techniques are the same, the difference in cooking time in these two foods is too great to just place them in the oven like individual dishes. The sausages will overheat causing them to burst and be dry or else the bean dish will not be hot enough. One alternative would be to add the sausages after about 5 minutes cooking time. Here though we have cooked all items together. In this case, the best way to accomplish this is to arrange the sausages on the top of the casserole. In this way, the sausages are the furthest distance from the source of the microwaves so will tend to cook a little slower. Also, the flavors of the sausage and beans will complement each other.

DIRECTIONS:

1. Prepare Southern Baked Beans, page 102, through step 1. Arrange 5 to 6 Polish sausages (about 1¼ lbs.) on top of onions.
2. **MICROWAVE** 15 to 16 minutes or until hot.
   5 to 6 Servings

FISH ROLL-UP DINNER

Asparagus Fish Roll-Ups, page 31
Fluffy White Rice, page 121

BASIS FOR SELECTION:

The fish dish is cooked using a microwave-bake technique at 375° for 12 to 15 minutes. The rice is normally cooked with just microwave cooking for 13 to 15 minutes. Since the fish has a sauce and cheese topping that needs the bake temperature to lightly brown, the microwave-bake technique is the best compromise with these two recipes. However, when rice is cooked with conventional heat as well as microwave cooking, the liquid will evaporate faster, so additional liquid is needed so that it will rehydrate properly.

DIRECTIONS:

1. Prepare Asparagus Fish Roll-Ups, page 31, through step 3.
2. Preheat oven to 375° F.
3. Prepare Fluffy White Rice, page 121, except increase water addition to 2¼ cups. Place fish in oven uncovered and rice in oven covered.
4. **MICROWAVE-BAKE** 15 to 18 minutes or until fish flakes easily and rice is just about tender. Let rice stand 5 minutes before fluffing with fork and serving.
   6 to 8 Servings

From the Freezer

ABOUT THE CHAPTER: This chapter specializes in ideas for recipes, from appetizers to desserts, that can go from freezer to combination oven. Microwave cooking combined with conventional baking or broiling speeds the thawing and heating of frozen foods. With many foods, the heating and cooking times are greatly reduced with this combination technique.

The first part of the chapter contains two ground beef freezer mixtures that you make up in quantity when time allows. This is followed by suggested ways to use the mixtures to make a variety of casseroles.

The remainder of the chapter is devoted to foods (self-prepared or commercially frozen) that are in the freezer, explaining how to prepare them from the frozen state. *WHEN THE IDEA REFERS TO A RECIPE IN ANOTHER PART OF THE BOOK, THE WORD "FREEZER" IS USED IN THE TITLE. OTHERWISE THE ITEM IS REFERRED TO AS "FROZEN".* Although the recipes call for a specific recipe or package size, the directions can be used interchangeably between home-prepared and commercially-prepared frozen foods. The heating techniques are similar, but slight time adjustments may be necessary where there are variances in quantity.

WRAPPING FOODS FOR THE FREEZER:
Foods should be wrapped in material that will retain the moisture and flavor, keeping air and the flavor of other foods out. Suitable materials include: aluminum foil (freezer foil or double thickness regular foil), heavy plastic bags or wrap, plastic freezer containers, straight-sided jars and freezer-to-oven casseroles and baking dishes.

With some foods, it may be most convenient to partially freeze before wrapping. A pie with a thin filling that can easily spill during wrapping, a cake with sticky frosting or meatballs that may freeze together are examples of such foods.

Sometimes you may want the frozen food to have the shape of a certain casserole for ease in reheating, but not have the casserole or baking dish in the freezer and out of use for 2 or 3 months. To avoid this, line the casserole or baking dish with foil, with the foil extending beyond the edge of the casserole. Arrange the mixture in the dish and freeze until just about firm. Then lift out the contents, using the extensions of foil as handles. Bring the foil around the contents, seal tightly and return to the freezer.

For the optimum preservation of food quality, wrap in a way that eliminates air pockets around the food and prevents air from entering the package.

GLASS BAKING DISHES: Since most frozen foods depend on microwaves to quickly thaw the interior, glass containers provide the best use of the microwaves. The exceptions where we have used metal include: a few quick-to-heat items such as sandwiches and cookies that are prepared on metal pans, TV dinners that will quickly heat in the shallow metal trays, and pot pies that need a certain shaped container, not available in glass, to hold the shape when thawing.

Care must be taken when freezing mixtures in glass baking dishes. Foods will freeze satisfactorily in glass provided there is an inch or two of room for expansion during the freezing process. However, only special freezer-to-oven dishes are designed to go from the temperature of a cold freezer to a hot preheated oven. When using dishes other than these, it is best to transfer the mixture out of the baking dish for freezing.

LABELING: Be sure to label all foods clearly. A complete label includes: what is being frozen, date of preparation, storage time and if applicable, cook book page reference when finishing the preparation. It may be convenient to keep a list of prepared foods that are in the freezer and when they should be used. This way you can avoid waste and lessening of quality.

STORING: A suggested storage time is given by foods that are home-prepared. This is the time the food can be frozen and still be assured of optimum quality. After this period, the food may show signs of drying or flavor change.

COOKING POUCHES: Foods packaged and sealed in heavy cooking pouches can be reheated in the same pouch. Microwave cooking without conventional heat is necessary since the conventional heat could melt the plastic. When the contents will become warm or hot, a small slit should be made on the top side of the pouch to allow escape of steam. Otherwise the steam will cause the bag to split or burst.

HEATING GUIDELINES: When heating a frozen item, look through this section and find a similar-type item. Use the directions as a guide, and also keep in mind these general guidelines that apply to heating frozen foods.

- Covering speeds heating, but hampers browning and crisping.
- Stirring speeds heating, but is not always possible.
- Browning a frozen food usually means a slightly lower oven temperature and slightly longer cooking time.
- Preheating of the oven is not necessary unless the cooking time is very short.

Beef 'n Seasonings

Brown a large quantity of ground beef at one time. Freeze and be ready for 5 quick meals as you need them.

FREEZER BEEF 'n SEASONINGS

    5 lbs. ground beef
    2 medium onions, chopped
    2 cloves garlic, finely chopped
    1 tablespoon salt
    ¾ teaspoon pepper

1. Crumble meat into 4-quart glass casserole or two 3-quart (13x9) glass baking dishes. Stir in onions and garlic.

2. MICROWAVE, uncovered, 23 to 25 minutes or until set. Stir to break meat into pieces; drain.

3. Stir in remaining ingredients; mix well. Cool quickly. Spread meat mixture on two ungreased baking sheets. Freeze for 1 hour. Crumble meat mixture into small pieces; place in heavy plastic bag or freezer containers. Seal securely and label. Freeze no longer than 3 months.   About 15 Cups

TIP • Each 3 cups Beef 'n Seasonings is the equivalent of: 1 lb. ground beef, ¼ cup chopped onion, 1 small clove garlic, ½ teaspoon salt and dash pepper.

Pictured, top to bottom: Shepherd's Beef Pie, Biscuit-Topped Pot Pies and Hamburger Chop Suey, page 187.

Add to a convenience dinner mix for a . . .

SUPER EASY DINNER MIX

**3 cups Freezer Beef 'n Seasonings
1 package (8 oz.) mix for cheeseburger
macaroni (or other favorite flavor)
dinner mix**

1. Place beef mixture in 2-quart casserole. Stir in noodles and sauce mix from dinner mix package. Add amount of water directed on package.
2. MICROWAVE, covered, 23 to 25 minutes or until macaroni is tender. Let stand 5 minutes before serving.   About 5 Servings

Add a vegetable and a potato topping for . . .

SHEPHERD'S BEEF PIE

**3 cups Freezer Beef 'n Seasonings
1 can (16 oz.) whole kernel corn, drained
1½ cups water
2 tablespoons butter or margarine
½ teaspoon salt
½ cup milk
1½ cups potato flakes
¼ cup catsup**

1. Combine beef mixture and corn in 1½-quart glass casserole; set aside.
2. MICROWAVE water, butter and salt in 4-cup glass measure 8 to 10 minutes or until hot. Stir in milk and potato flakes. Spoon over meat mixture; spreading to cover. Drizzle catsup over potatoes.
3. MICROWAVE-BROIL 15 to 17 minutes or until meat is hot and topping lightly browned.
          About 5 Servings

TIP • With the granular-type instant potatoes, use 1¾ cups.

Add Oriental vegetables and seasonings for . . .

HAMBURGER CHOP SUEY

**3 cups Freezer Beef 'n Seasonings
1 can (16 oz.) bean sprouts, drained
1 can (4 oz.) mushroom stems and pieces, undrained
1 can (6 oz.) water chestnuts, drained and sliced
2 tablespoons cornstarch
2 tablespoons soy sauce
1 tablespoon molasses
¼ teaspoon celery seed
Hot cooked rice**

1. Combine all ingredients except rice in 1½-quart glass casserole.
2. MICROWAVE, covered, 15 to 18 minutes or until mixture boils. Serve over rice.
          About 5 Servings

TIP • Substitute for water chestnuts: 6-oz. can bamboo shoots, drained.

Add potatoes and seasonings for . . .

BEEF HASH

**3 cups Freezer Beef 'n Seasonings
3 medium potatoes, peeled and cubed
½ cup water
1 teaspoon prepared horseradish
1 teaspoon Worcestershire sauce
¼ teaspoon salt**

1. Combine all ingredients in 1½-quart glass casserole.
2. MICROWAVE, covered, 20 to 22 minutes or until potatoes are tender, stirring once. If desired, serve with catsup. About 5 Servings

Add a vegetable and top with biscuits for . . .

BISCUIT-TOPPED POT PIES

**3 cups Freezer Beef 'n Seasonings
1 package (10 oz.) frozen peas
1 can (10¾ oz.) condensed cream of celery soup
1 can (8 oz.) refrigerated biscuits**

1. Preheat oven to 375° F.
2. Combine beef mixture, peas and soup in medium mixing bowl. Divide among five 10-oz. glass baking dishes. Divide roll of biscuits into 10 biscuits. Place 2 biscuits over meat mixture in each dish.
3. MICROWAVE-BAKE 10 to 12 minutes or until mixture is bubbly and biscuits are no longer doughy.   5 Servings

Beef 'n Tomato Sauce

Prepare this ground beef and tomato sauce recipe when time allows. Then enjoy 5 quick meals with a minimum of time and energy.

FREEZER BEEF 'n TOMATO SAUCE

> 5 lbs. ground beef
> 2 medium onions, chopped
> 1 green pepper, chopped
> 2 cans (15 ozs. each) tomato sauce
> 2 cans (6 ozs. each) tomato paste
> 1 tablespoon salt
> ¾ teaspoon pepper
> ¼ teaspoon garlic powder

1. Crumble meat into 4-quart glass casserole or two 3-quart (13x9) glass baking dishes. Stir in onions and green pepper.
2. **MICROWAVE,** uncovered, 18 to 20 minutes or until set. Stir to break meat into pieces; drain. Stir in remaining ingredients; mix well.
3. **MICROWAVE,** uncovered, 10 to 15 minutes or until flavors are well blended. Cool quickly. Divide mixture among five 1½-pint freezer containers. Cover, label and freeze no longer than 3 months.   Five 1½-pint Containers

TIP • Each container of Beef 'n Tomato Sauce mix is the equivalent of: 1 lb. ground beef, ¼ cup chopped onion, 2 tablespoons chopped green pepper, ¾ cup tomato sauce, ⅓ cup tomato paste, ½ teaspoon salt, ¼ teaspoon pepper and dash garlic powder.

Pictured, top to bottom: Freezer Sauce Sloppy Joes, Spanish Rice, Hearty Chili and Freezer Sauce Tacos, page 189.

Add bacon and rice for . . .

SPANISH RICE

    4 slices bacon, cut up
    1 container Freezer Beef 'n Tomato Sauce
    1 cup uncooked long-grain rice
    ½ teaspoon salt
2¼ cups water

1. Place bacon in 1½-quart glass casserole. Place casserole and frozen sauce in freezer container in oven.
2. MICROWAVE 7 to 8 minutes or until bacon is crisp. Drain bacon. Add freezer sauce to bacon casserole; break sauce into pieces. Stir in remaining ingredients.
3. MICROWAVE, covered, 23 to 25 minutes or until rice is tender, stirring once. Fluff with fork. Cover and let stand 5 minutes before serving.   **5 to 6 Servings**

Add seasonings and serve in taco shells for . . .

FREEZER SAUCE TACOS

    1 container frozen Freezer Beef 'n Tomato Sauce
½ teaspoon chili powder
Dash Tabasco sauce
12 taco shells
    1 cup shredded Cheddar cheese
    1 cup shredded lettuce
    1 tomato, chopped

1. MICROWAVE freezer sauce in freezer container 5 minutes. Place sauce in 1-quart glass casserole; break sauce into pieces. Stir in chili powder and Tabasco sauce.
2. MICROWAVE, uncovered, 15 to 18 minutes or until mixture is hot, stirring once.
3. Spoon meat mixture into taco shells. Top with cheese, lettuce and tomato.   **12 Tacos**

Add seasonings for . . .

FREEZER SAUCE SLOPPY JOES

    1 container Freezer Beef 'n Tomato Sauce
¼ cup water
    1 tablespoon Worcestershire sauce
Dash Tabasco sauce
5 hamburger buns, split and toasted

1. MICROWAVE frozen sauce in freezer container 5 minutes. Place sauce in 1-quart glass casserole; break sauce into pieces. Stir in remaining ingredients except buns.
2. MICROWAVE, covered, 15 to 18 minutes or until mixture is hot, stirring once. Serve over toasted buns.   **5 Servings**

Use just as it is for . . .

SPAGHETTI, MANICOTTI AND LASAGNA

Use defrosted Freezer Beef 'n Tomato Sauce to replace tomato meat sauce in favorite recipes. If the sauce recipe uses 1 lb. ground beef, use one container mix; if 2 lbs., use two containers. Defrost using directions below.

DEFROSTING FREEZER BEEF 'n TOMATO SAUCE

1. Place covered freezer container of frozen sauce in oven.
2. MICROWAVE 5 minutes or until mixture can be loosened from container; turn into glass casserole. Break into pieces.
3. MICROWAVE, covered, 5 minutes or until thawed.

TIP • Plastic freezer containers should not be placed in a hot oven. When oven is hot, dip the container into hot water to loosen mixture from container. Turn into casserole and defrost or heat as directed in step 3.

Add beans and chili seasonings for . . .

HEARTY CHILI

    1 container Freezer Beef 'n Tomato Sauce
    1 can (15½ oz.) kidney beans, undrained
    1 teaspoon chili powder
    ¼ teaspoon paprika
Dash cayenne pepper

1. MICROWAVE frozen sauce in freezer container 5 minutes. Place sauce in 1-quart glass casserole; break into pieces. Stir in remaining ingredients.
2. MICROWAVE, covered, 15 to 18 minutes or until mixture is hot, stirring once.
    4 to 5 Servings

Add macaroni for . . .

BEEF 'n MACARONI CASSEROLE

    1 container Freezer Beef 'n Tomato Sauce
    1 cup uncooked shell or elbow macaroni
    ½ teaspoon celery seed
1½ cups water

1. MICROWAVE frozen sauce in freezer container 5 minutes. Place sauce in 1½-quart glass casserole; break sauce into pieces. Stir in remaining ingredients.
2. MICROWAVE, covered, 18 to 20 minutes or until macaroni is tender, stirring once.
    4 to 5 Servings

DEFROSTING MEATS, FISH AND POULTRY:

With dense items such as meats, on-off microwave cooking is necessary to defrost the center without cooking the edges. The ideal defrost sequence keeps enough heat in the thawed portion to warm and defrost the interior, but not enough to cause the thawed portion to start cooking. This action happens automatically with use of the defrost feature, or it can be done manually by occasionally turning off the oven and letting the meat rest a few minutes (stand without microwave cooking being used).

Meats can be left in the plastic or paper wrappings, which help hold in the heat and speed the defrosting process. With individual pieces, it speeds defrosting to unwrap and separate the pieces as soon as they can be easily separated. Turning the frozen item over about half way through the defrost or microwave time also speeds and evens the defrosting, especially with large items.

When it is desirable to defrost only a portion of a package, wrap foil around the portion you wish to keep frozen. This way the microwaves will not reach this portion. Return the portion to the freezer as soon as it can be separated from the defrosted portion.

ABOUT THE DEFROSTING GUIDE:

If your oven has a defrost feature, use the Automatic Defrost Time column, or when in a hurry, use the 2-step Automatic Defrost Time column. The Manual Defrost Time column is the guide for defrosting in ovens without a defrost feature.

You will notice from the times in the chart that 7 to 8 minutes automatic defrost time are necessary for each pound of meat.

Since the automatic on-off cooking feature of the automatic defrost is not necessary until the edges begin to warm, the defrost time can be speeded by starting with microwave cooking and then turning on the defrost feature.

When converting these times to the manual defrost time, the microwave time is about half the automatic defrost time. The oven is turned off occasionally to let the meat rest. The microwave and rest periods are about equal to the weight of the meat.

These times should be used as guides. If the meat item appears to be getting too hot, increase the rest time. If meat is not thawed at the end of the time, allow the meat to rest a few minutes and then add a few extra minutes defrost time.

DEFROSTING GUIDE FOR MEAT, FISH AND POULTRY

Amount	Automatic Defrost Time	2-step Automatic Defrost Time	Manual Defrost Time
1 lb.	Defrost 7 to 8 minutes	Microwave 2 to 3 minutes Defrost 3½ to 4 minutes	Microwave 3½ to 4 minutes, resting every 1 to 2 minutes
2 lbs.	Defrost 14 to 16 minutes	Microwave 4 to 6 minutes Defrost 7 to 8 minutes	Microwave 7 to 8 minutes, resting every 2 minutes
3 lbs.	Defrost 21 to 24 minutes	Microwave 6 to 9 minutes Defrost 10 to 12 minutes	Microwave 10 to 12 minutes, resting every 3 minutes
4 lbs.	Defrost 28 to 32 minutes	Microwave 8 to 12 minutes Defrost 14 to 16 minutes	Microwave 14 to 16 minutes, resting every 4 minutes
5 lbs.	Defrost 35 to 40 minutes	Microwave 10 to 15 minutes Defrost 18 to 20 minutes	Microwave 18 to 20 minutes, resting every 5 minutes
6 lbs.	Defrost 42 to 48 minutes	Microwave about 15 minutes Defrost 21 to 24 minutes	Microwave 21 to 24 minutes, resting every 6 minutes
8 lbs.	Defrost 56 to 64 minutes	Microwave about 20 minutes Defrost 28 to 32 minutes	Microwave 28 to 32 minutes, resting every 8 minutes
10 lbs.	Defrost 70 to 80 minutes	Microwave about 20 minutes Defrost 40 to 45 minutes	Microwave 35 to 40 minutes, resting every 10 minutes
15 lbs.	Defrost 1¾ hours to 2 hours	Microwave about 20 minutes Defrost 45 to 60 minutes	Microwave 50 to 60 minutes, resting every 10 minutes
20 lbs.	Defrost 2½ hours to 2¾ hours	Microwave about 20 minutes Defrost 1½ to 1¾ hours	Microwave 1¼ to 1½ hours, resting every 10 minutes

Tip • Resting refers to turning off the oven and letting the meat item set or rest without microwave cooking being used.

APPETIZERS AND BEVERAGES: Use the combination range to thaw and heat homemade or commercially frozen appetizers and to thaw frozen juice concentrates.

FREEZER RUMAKI

1. Prepare Rumaki, page 21, through step 3, but do not place in baking dish. Wrap, label and freeze no longer than 2 months.
2. Unwrap appetizers; place in 2-quart (12x7) glass baking dish.
3. MICROWAVE-BAKE at 375° F. for 20 to 22 minutes or until bacon is crisp.

24 Appetizers

Appetizers in shells can be prepared ahead and frozen. When frozen, the microwave-broil time is increased and the shells placed further from the broiler.

FREEZER COQUILLES ST. JACQUES

1. Prepare Coquilles St. Jacques, page 25, through step 7. Wrap, label and freeze no longer than 2 months.
2. Unwrap appetizer shells; place on regular oven rack position.
3. MICROWAVE-BROIL 8 to 9 minutes or until mixture is bubbly and topping golden brown.

6 Servings

FREEZER TUNA-IN-A-SHELL

1. Prepare Tuna-In-A-Shell, page 25, through step 2. Wrap, label and freeze no longer than 2 months.
2. Unwrap appetizer shells.
3. MICROWAVE, uncovered, 12 to 14 minutes or until mixture is heated through and bubbly.

4 Servings

FROZEN EGG OR PIZZA ROLLS

1. Place egg or pizza rolls from 6-oz. package in 8-inch round or square glass baking dish.
2. MICROWAVE-BAKE at 375° F. for 4 to 5 minutes or until lightly browned and hot.

5 to 6 Servings

Use microwave cooking to quickly thaw orange and other frozen juices.

DEFROSTING FROZEN JUICES

1. Remove the lid from a 6 or 12-oz. can frozen juice.
2. MICROWAVE 1 to 2 minutes or until mixture is thawed.

MEATS: Meats can be partially prepared and frozen for quick last minute preparation. Or, you can start with a frozen roast, steak or chops and cook them to perfection with a combination of microwave and bake or broil cooking.

For frozen hamburger patties, bread crumbs and egg are added to the ground beef mixture. Without these additions the patties may be dry and tough.

FREEZER HAMBURGER PATTIES

1 lb. ground beef
½ cup dry bread crumbs
1 egg
1 small onion, chopped
1 teaspoon salt
Dash Tabasco sauce

1. Combine all ingredients in medium mixing bowl. Shape into 4 patties and stack, placing a double thickness wax paper between each. Wrap, label and freeze no longer than 3 months.
2. Unwrap; arrange frozen patties in 8-inch square glass baking dish.
3. MICROWAVE-BROIL 10 to 12 minutes or until meat is done.

4 Patties

FREEZER MINI MEAT LOAVES

1. Prepare Mini Meat Loaves, page 58, through step 2, but omit bacon and do not place in baking dish. Wrap, label and freeze no longer than 3 months.
2. Unwrap; place frozen loaves on rack in 2-quart (12x7) glass baking dish.
3. MICROWAVE-BAKE at 450° F. for 16 to 18 minutes or until meat is done.

6 Loaves

TIP • If wrapping loaves in bacon, microwave-bake 5 minutes. Place 1 slice bacon, halved, over each loaf. Continue with microwave-baking for 11 to 12 minutes.

Once meatballs are partially frozen they can be stacked or put together in a plastic bag without freezing together.

FREEZER MEATBALLS

1. Prepare Meatballs, page 54, through step 3, but do not place in baking dish. Wrap, label and freeze no longer than 3 months.
2. Unwrap; arrange frozen meatballs in 8-inch round or square glass baking dish.
3. MICROWAVE-BAKE at 375° F. for 8 to 10 minutes or until done; drain.

About 24 Meatballs

Frozen chops take just a few extra minutes when broiled using the microwave-broil technique.

FROZEN PORK CHOPS

1. Arrange 4 to 6 frozen pork chops, cut ½ inch thick, on metal broiler pan. Move oven rack to second position.
2. MICROWAVE-BROIL 6 minutes. Turn chops over.
3. MICROWAVE-BROIL 6 to 7 minutes or until meat is done.   4 to 6 Chops

TIP • Placing a double thickness wax paper between chops before freezing makes it easy to separate them.

FROZEN STEAK

1. Arrange 2 frozen T-bone or rib steaks, cut ½ inch thick (about 12 ozs. each), on metal broiler pan. Move oven rack to second position.
2. MICROWAVE-BROIL 6 minutes. Turn steaks over.
3. MICROWAVE-BROIL 5 to 6 minutes or until desired doneness.   2 Steaks

A pork roast goes from freezer to table in about 1¼ hours! The covered casserole and microwave cooking speed the thawing and cooking.

FREEZER PORK ROAST

1. Place a 2½ to 3-lb. frozen pork roast in 3 or 4-quart glass casserole or Dutch oven.
2. MICROWAVE-BAKE, covered, at 300° F. for 35 to 45 minutes (about 15 minutes per pound). Remove cover and insert meat thermometer.
3. BAKE 30 to 35 minutes or until meat thermometer registers 170° F.
                    About 8 Servings

FREEZER POT ROAST

Prepare Pot Roast, page 64, except use a frozen roast and increase baking time in step 3 to 2 to 2½ hours.

FROZEN CORN DOGS

1. Arrange 5 batter-dipped and fried hot dogs in 2-quart (12x7) glass baking dish.
2. MICROWAVE-BAKE at 400° F. for 6 to 8 minutes or until hot.   5 Corn Dogs

TIP • For one corn dog, microwave-bake 4 to 5 minutes.

Use these times for uncooked oven-baked chicken and the times for Frozen Fried Chicken when the chicken is cooked before freezing.

FREEZER OVEN-BAKED CHICKEN

1. Prepare Oven-Baked Chicken, page 39, through step 1, but do not arrange in baking dish. Wrap, label and freeze no longer than 3 months.
2. Unwrap chicken pieces; arrange in 2-quart (12x7) glass baking dish.
3. MICROWAVE-BAKE at 400° F. for 25 to 30 minutes or until done.   4 to 6 Servings

FROZEN FRIED CHICKEN

1. Arrange 2-lb. package frozen fried chicken in 3-quart (13x9) glass baking dish.
2. MICROWAVE-BROIL 12 to 14 minutes or until hot.   About 4 Servings

TIP • For 2 pieces chicken, place on plate and cover with wax paper. Microwave 4 to 5 minutes.

FROZEN WIENERS

1. Place frozen wieners in covered glass casserole.
2. MICROWAVE until wieners are hot, separating and rearranging wieners halfway through cooking time:

          2 wieners — 4 to 5 minutes
          4 wieners — 5 to 6 minutes
          6 wieners — 6 to 8 minutes
          8 wieners — 8 to 10 minutes
        10 wieners — 10 to 12 minutes

FREEZER CHEESY SALMON LOAF

1. Prepare Cheesy Salmon Loaf, page 37, through step 1. Wrap, label and freeze no longer than 3 months.
2. Unwrap loaf; return to 1½-quart (8x4) glass loaf dish if necessary.
3. MICROWAVE-BAKE at 325° F. for 20 minutes.
4. BAKE 5 to 6 minutes or until set in the center.
                    5 to 6 Servings

Pictured: Frozen Steak, page 192 with Batter-Fried Onion Rings, page 197, Freezer Stuffed Baked Potatoes, page 197, Freezer Apple Crisp, page 198 and Brown and Serve Rolls, page 197.

FREEZER CHICKEN BOURGUIGNON

1. Prepare Chicken Bourguignon, page 44, through step 1. Wrap, label and freeze no longer than 3 months.
2. Unwrap chicken. Melt 2 tablespoons butter in 10-inch freezer-to-range glass ceramic skillet over medium-high heat. Add chicken breasts and brown on both sides.
3. MICROWAVE 2 tablespoons cognac in 1-cup measure about ½ minute or until just warm. Flame and carefully pour over chicken. Remove chicken from pan and set aside. Add 2 tablespoons flour, 1 tablespoon beef bouillon and 1 tablespoon tomato paste to pan drippings; stir until smooth. Stir in ¾ cup water and ¼ cup wine; bring to boil. Return chicken pieces to skillet.
4. MICROWAVE-BAKE, uncovered, at 400° F. for 20 to 25 minutes or until well done, occasionally spooning sauce over chicken. Sprinkle with snipped parsley.

8 Chicken Breasts

CASSEROLES: When preparing your favorite casserole, make up an extra one and store in the freezer for later use. Combination cooking will quickly heat it in about 30 minutes. Sauces thickened with flour or cornstarch may separate after freezing, so it is best to add these thickening agents after freezing.

FREEZER QUICHE LORRAINE

1. Prepare Quiche Lorraine, page 88, through step 3. Wrap, label and freeze no longer than 2 months.
2. Unwrap pie; return to 9-inch glass pie plate if necessary.
3. MICROWAVE-BAKE at 375° F. for 15 minutes.
4. BAKE 20 to 25 minutes or until knife inserted near center comes out clean. Let stand 10 minutes before cutting.   About 6 Servings

FREEZER LASAGNA

1. Prepare Italian Lasagna, page 56, through step 3. Wrap, label and freeze no longer than 3 months.
2. Unwrap lasagna; return to 2 or 3-quart (12x7 or 13x9) glass baking dish if necessary.
3. MICROWAVE-BAKE at 375° F. for 30 to 35 minutes or until bubbly in center.

10 to 12 Servings

TIP • When cooking only one panful, cook minimum time.

With frozen Enchiladas, bake is added with the microwave cooking to speed the heating. Extra water is necessary because additional drying takes place.

FREEZER ENCHILADAS

1. Prepare Enchiladas, page 59, through step 4. Wrap, label and freeze no longer than 3 months.
2. Unwrap enchilada mixture; return to 3-quart (13x9) glass baking dish if necessary. Pour ⅓ cup water over enchilada mixture.
3. MICROWAVE-BAKE at 325° F. for 24 to 26 minutes or until hot and bubbly.

5 to 6 Servings

FREEZER TUNA-NOODLE BAKE

1. Prepare Tuna-Noodle Bake, page 34, through step 1. Wrap, label and freeze no longer than 3 months.
2. Unwrap casserole mixture; return to 1½-quart glass casserole if necessary.
3. MICROWAVE-BAKE, covered, at 300° F. for 30 to 35 minutes or until bubbly in center.

5 to 6 Servings

FREEZER PORK AND SAUERKRAUT DINNER

1. Prepare Pork and Sauerkraut Dinner, page 71, through step 2. Wrap, label and freeze no longer than 3 months.
2. Unwrap casserole mixture; return to 3 or 4-quart glass casserole if necessary.
3. MICROWAVE-BAKE, covered, at 325° F. for 30 to 35 minutes or until mixture is hot and pork is cooked, stirring once.

About 8 Servings

When frozen, these individual tuna pies need 25° lower oven temperature and 6 to 8 minutes longer baking.

FREEZER TUNA PASTIES

1. Prepare Tuna Pasties, page 98, through step 4, but do not place on baking sheet or prick tops. Wrap, label and freeze no longer than 2 months.
2. Preheat oven to 425° F. Unwrap pasties; place on metal baking sheet. Prick tops.
3. MICROWAVE-BAKE 18 to 20 minutes or until golden brown and filling is hot.

8 Pasties

DINNERS AND ENTREES: Individual casseroles or pieces of meat as well as completely assembled dinners — the kind you assemble yourself or purchase commercially prepared — are easily thawed and heated with microwave cooking.

FROZEN COOKED HAMBURGER PATTIES

1. Place ½-inch thick frozen cooked hamburger patties on glass plate. Cover with wax paper.
2. MICROWAVE until steaming hot:
   - 1 patty — 3 to 4 minutes
   - 4 patties — 7 to 8 minutes
   - 6 patties — 8 to 10 minutes

FROZEN COOKED MEATS

1. Place ¼-inch thick frozen meat slices on glass plate, overlapping if necessary. Cover with wax paper.
2. MICROWAVE until hot:
   - 1 slice — 2 to 3 minutes
   - 3 slices — 3 to 4 minutes
   - 6 slices — 6 to 7 minutes
   - 12 slices — 8 to 10 minutes

FROZEN COOKED CASSEROLES OR LEFTOVERS

1. Place frozen casserole mixture in covered glass dish or casserole.
2. MICROWAVE until hot, stirring once:
   - ½ cup — 7 to 8 minutes
   - 1 cup — 13 to 15 minutes
   - 2 cups — 18 to 20 minutes
   - 4 cups — 22 to 25 minutes

Use these times for 2-serving frozen casseroles such as cabbage rolls, stuffed green peppers and Salisbury steak.

FROZEN 2-SERVING CASSEROLES

1. Transfer the contents of a 14-oz. casserole from the foil pan to 1-quart glass casserole.
2. MICROWAVE, covered, 20 to 24 minutes or until hot.   2 Servings

FROZEN POT PIES

1. Remove five 8-oz. frozen pot pies from packages. Leave in foil pans.
2. MICROWAVE-BAKE at 425° F. for 15 minutes.
3. BAKE 10 to 13 minutes or until golden brown and filling is bubbly.   5 Pies

TIP • For one pie, reduce baking time in step 3 to 5 to 8 minutes.

Use these times for turkey, Salisbury steak or meatball dinners.

FROZEN TV DINNERS CONTAINING NON-FRIED FOODS

1. Remove dinner from package; remove foil cover. Return dinner (in foil tray) to package.
2. MICROWAVE 15 to 18 minutes or until hot.   1 Dinner

TIP • For 2 dinners, microwave 18 to 21 minutes.

Use these times for fried chicken dinners or when there is a bread or dessert that needs browning.

FROZEN TV DINNERS CONTAINING FRIED FOODS

1. Remove dinner from package; remove foil cover. Return dinner (in foil tray) to package.
2. MICROWAVE 10 minutes. Remove dinner from package.
3. MICROWAVE-BROIL 5 to 6 minutes or until golden brown and hot.   1 Dinner

TIP • For 2 dinners, increase microwave time in step 2 to 13 minutes.

To speed the heating of these dinners in deep-foil trays, the contents are removed from the foil. They take longer than regular TV dinners because the meat portion is often larger and uncooked and the trays have more depth.

FROZEN CALORIE CONTROLLED DINNERS

1. Remove foods for dinner from foil tray and arrange in glass pie plate or dinner plate. Cover with wax paper.
2. MICROWAVE 20 to 23 minutes or until meat is cooked.   1 Dinner

With the microwave-bake technique, preheating the oven can be eliminated.

FROZEN PIZZA

1. Remove one 13½-oz. frozen pizza from package; place on metal baking sheet.
2. MICROWAVE-BAKE at 450° F. for 8 to 10 minutes or until crust is brown and cheese is melted.   1 Pizza

You can make a batch of sandwiches and freeze up to 2 months. Then just broil and microwave when ready to serve. The time is slightly longer than for non-frozen sandwiches.

FROZEN GRILLED SANDWICHES

1. Place oven rack in second position. Place 1 to 4 frozen sandwiches on metal broiler pan.
2. BROIL 4 to 5 minutes or until toasted; turn over.
3. MICROWAVE-BROIL 2 to 2½ minutes or until golden brown and filling is hot.

                                    1 to 4 Sandwiches

FREEZER FRENCH TOAST

1. Prepare French Toast, page 132, through step 3, but do not melt butter or add bread slices to butter. Wrap, label and freeze no longer than 2 months.
2. MICROWAVE ¼ cup butter or margarine in metal 15x10x1-inch jelly roll pan 2 to 2½ minutes or until melted. Unwrap bread slices; place in butter.
3. MICROWAVE-BROIL 3 to 3½ minutes or until lightly browned. Turn bread slices over.
4. BROIL, with oven door slightly open, 2 to 3 minutes or until lightly browned.

                                    6 Slices Toast

FREEZER HAMBURGER ON A BUN

1. Prepare Hamburger On A Bun, page 97, through step 2, but do not arrange on broiler pan. Wrap, label and freeze no longer than 2 months.
2. Unwrap sandwiches; place meat-side-up on metal broiler pan.
3. MICROWAVE-BROIL 8 to 10 minutes or until meat is done.   6 Servings

FREEZER SOUPER BAKED SANDWICH

1. Prepare Souper Baked Sandwich, page 98, through step 4. Wrap, label and freeze no longer than 2 months.
2. Unwrap casserole; return to 8-inch square glass baking dish if necessary.
3. MICROWAVE-BAKE at 400° F. for 25 to 28 minutes or until knife inserted near center comes out clean.   6 to 8 Servings

HEATING FROZEN ROLLS

Place rolls directly on oven rack or place on napkin on oven rack. Microwave until rolls feel warm:

           1 Roll   — 1 to 1½ minutes
           4 Rolls — 2 to 3 minutes
           6 Rolls — 2½ to 3½ minutes
     Coffeecake — 2½ to 3½ minutes
French Bread — 2½ to 3½ minutes

THAWING FROZEN ROLLS

Place rolls directly on oven rack or place on napkin on oven rack. Microwave until rolls are no longer icy:

           1 Roll   — ½ to ¾ minute
           4 Rolls — 1 to 1½ minutes
           6 Rolls — 1½ to 2 minutes

DEFROSTING FROZEN BREAD

1. Place the loaf of frozen bread in a paper or plastic bag.
2. MICROWAVE 2 to 2½ minutes or until thawed.

Thaw and proof frozen bread dough in about 1½ hours. The water keeps the oven warm and helps prevent the dough from starting to cook during the short microwave cooking periods.

DEFROSTING AND COOKING FROZEN BREAD DOUGH

1. MICROWAVE 4 cups water in 4-cup glass measure 10 to 11 minutes or until hot.
2. Place loaf of frozen bread dough in greased 1½-quart (8x4) glass loaf dish. Place in oven with water.
3. MICROWAVE 1 minute. Let rest in oven 20 minutes. Repeat microwave and rest 3 times. Leave bread dough in oven until doubled in size, about 30 minutes. Remove bread and water from oven.
4. Preheat oven to 375° F.
5. BAKE 15 minutes. ✤
6. MICROWAVE-BAKE 3 to 3½ minutes or until bread sounds hollow when tapped.
                                    1 Loaf

TIPS • Covering is not necessary since the steam from the hot water keeps the bread moist.

• For 2 loaves, prepare as directed except increase time in step 6 to 5 to 5½ minutes.

Make up these rolls and keep in the freezer. Then just brown when ready to serve.

BROWN AND SERVE ROLLS

2 cups milk
6 tablespoons butter or margarine
6 to 6½ cups unsifted all-purpose flour
2 packages active dry yeast
2 teaspoons salt
½ cup sugar
2 eggs

1. MICROWAVE milk and butter in 4-cup glass measure about 3 minutes or until very warm (120°-130°).
2. Combine 3 cups flour, the dry yeast, salt and sugar in large mixing bowl. Add warm milk mixture and eggs. Beat at medium speed 2 minutes. Stir in remaining 3 to 3½ cups flour to form a stiff dough.
3. Cover; let rise in warm place until light and doubled in size, 1 to 1½ hours.
4. Turn dough onto floured surface. Toss to coat with flour; knead a few times until no longer sticky. Divide dough in half. Divide each half into 16 pieces; shape each piece into a ball. Place 16 balls in each of 2 greased 8-inch square glass baking dishes.
5. Cover; let rise in warm place until doubled in size, about 30 minutes.
6. MICROWAVE, both pans at once, 11 to 13 minutes or until rolls are set and no longer doughy. (Rolls will not brown.) Remove from pans. Cool completely. Wrap, label and freeze no longer than 3 months.
7. Preheat oven to 425° F.
8. Place frozen rolls (16 or 32 rolls) on ungreased metal baking sheet.
9. BAKE 12 to 14 minutes or until golden brown.
   32 Rolls

RICE AND VEGETABLES: Cooked rice can be easily frozen and then reheated using microwave cooking. Most vegetable recipes are found in the vegetable chapter, but we have included a few here that freeze especially well and are easily reheated using combination cooking.

FROZEN COOKED RICE

1. Place 3 cups frozen cooked rice in glass casserole.
2. MICROWAVE, covered, 13 to 15 minutes or until hot, stirring once. 3 Cups Rice

TIP • To thaw only, microwave rice, covered, 5 minutes. Stir to break apart. Cover and let stand 2 minutes.

FROZEN VEGETABLES

1. Place 1 package frozen vegetables in covered 1-quart glass casserole or remove 1 pouch frozen vegetables from carton and make a small slit in pouch.
2. MICROWAVE 10 to 12 minutes or until desired doneness. 3 or 4 Servings

TIPS • For 2 packages or pouches, increase microwave time to 14 to 16 minutes.

• For frozen corn on the cob, see page 108. See the Vegetable Chapter for recipes using frozen vegetables.

FROZEN BATTER-FRIED ONION RINGS

1. Arrange 7 ozs. frozen onion rings in 3-quart (13x9) glass baking dish.
2. MICROWAVE-BROIL 5 to 6 minutes or until hot, turning onion rings over during last half of cooking time. 4 to 5 Servings

In order to brown the crumb topping, this recipe is cooked uncovered.

FREEZER POTATOES AU GRATIN

1. Prepare Potatoes Au Gratin, page 110, through step 3. Wrap, label and freeze no longer than 3 months.
2. Unwrap potatoes; return to 1½-quart glass casserole if necessary.
3. MICROWAVE-BAKE, uncovered, at 300° F. for 30 to 35 minutes or until hot and bubbly.
   5 to 6 Servings

FREEZER STUFFED BAKED POTATOES

1. Prepare Stuffed Baked Potatoes, page 110, through step 3, but do not place in baking dish. Wrap, label and freeze no longer than 3 months.
2. Unwrap potatoes; place in 3-quart (13x9) glass baking dish.
3. MICROWAVE-BAKE at 400° F. for 18 to 20 minutes or until hot. 12 Stuffed Potatoes

With this delicate soufflé, the foil pan slows and enhances the cooking.

FROZEN SPINACH SOUFFLE

1. Remove cover from 12-oz. package frozen spinach soufflé. Leave in foil cooking pan.
2. MICROWAVE-BAKE at 350° F. for 25 to 30 minutes or until knife inserted near center comes out clean. 3 to 4 Servings

DESSERTS: This page shows a variety of desserts to partially prepare and then freeze. The frozen desserts are then freshly baked when ready to serve.

Now a frozen pie can be baked almost as quickly as a fresh pie. The microwaves help quickly thaw and cook the fruit filling.

FROZEN 2-CRUST FRUIT PIE

1. Preheat oven to 450° F.
2. Transfer a 9-inch frozen, unbaked, 2-crust fruit pie to 9-inch glass pie plate. Slit top crust, if necessary.
3. MICROWAVE-BAKE 14 to 16 minutes or until crust is golden brown and filling bubbly.
   9-inch Pie

Use this technique for commercially frozen pastry shells or for homemade. The frozen pastry increases the microwave time a few minutes.

FROZEN PASTRY SHELL

1. Place frozen pastry shell in glass pie plate.
2. MICROWAVE 12 to 14 minutes or until pastry has a dry, flaky appearance. 1 Pastry Shell

FREEZER PECAN PIE

1. Prepare Pecan Pie, page 174, through step 4. Wrap, label and freeze no longer than 3 months.
2. Unwrap pie; return to 9-inch glass pie plate if necessary.
3. MICROWAVE-BAKE at 375° F. for 15 minutes.
4. BAKE 12 to 15 minutes or until knife inserted near center comes out clean. Cool.
   9-inch Pie

Since a frozen pumpkin pie takes longer to cook, the bake temperature is reduced to avoid overbrowning.

FREEZER PUMPKIN PIE

1. Prepare Pumpkin Pie, page 174, through step 3. Wrap, label and freeze no longer than 3 months.
2. Unwrap pie; return to 9-inch glass pie plate if necessary.
3. MICROWAVE-BAKE at 375° F. for 25 minutes.
4. BAKE 15 to 17 minutes or until knife inserted near center comes out clean. Cool.
   9-inch Pie

FREEZER APPLE DUMPLINGS

1. Prepare Apple Dumplings, page 139, through step 3, but do not place in baking dish or add sugar mixture. Wrap, label and freeze no longer than 3 months.
2. Preheat oven to 400° F.
3. Unwrap dumplings; place in 2-quart (12x7) glass baking dish.
4. BAKE 20 minutes. Combine 1½ cups water and 1 cup packed brown sugar; mix well. Pour over dumplings.
5. MICROWAVE-BAKE 15 to 18 minutes or until apples are tender. Spoon sauce over dumplings before serving. 6 Dumplings

COMMERCIALLY FROZEN APPLE DUMPLINGS

1. Preheat oven to 400° F.
2. Arrange dumplings in 8-inch round or square glass baking dish.
3. BAKE 20 minutes; pour sauce over dumplings.
4. MICROWAVE-BAKE 15 to 18 minutes or until apples are tender. 4 Dumplings

FREEZER APPLE CRISP

1. Prepare Apple Crisp, page 139, through step 3. Wrap, label and freeze no longer than 3 months.
2. Unwrap dessert; return to 8-inch square glass baking dish if necessary.
3. MICROWAVE-BAKE at 375° F. for 20 to 22 minutes or until apples are tender.
   5 to 6 Servings

Refrigerated cookie dough can be frozen and fresh cookies baked as needed. The cooking time is not affected by the frozen dough when the microwave-bake technique is used.

FREEZER ALMOND CRISPS

1. Prepare dough for Almond Crisp Cookies, page 165, through step 2, except wrap in foil, label and freeze no longer than 3 months.
2. Preheat oven to 425° F.
3. Unwrap dough; slice into ¼-inch thick slices. Place 2 inches apart on ungreased metal baking sheets.
4. MICROWAVE-BAKE, one pan at a time, 4 to 4½ minutes or until edges are lightly browned. Cool slightly; remove from baking sheet. About 6 Dozen Cookies

DESSERTS: This page features a variety of desserts that are cooked and then frozen. Directions show how to quickly defrost and, if necessary, heat them for serving.

DEFROSTING FROZEN WHIPPED TOPPING

1. Place a 4½-oz. covered container frozen whipped topping in oven.
2. MICROWAVE 1 minute. Rest 3 minutes. Stir. If necessary microwave a few seconds longer.   2 Cups Whipped Topping

Cooked cheese cake freezes well and can be quickly thawed using the defrost feature. Start with the recipe on page 150, or with a commercially frozen cheese cake.

DEFROSTING FROZEN CHEESE CAKE

1. Place cheese cake on glass plate (unless it is already in a glass baking dish).
2. DEFROST 12 to 15 minutes. Let stand 5 minutes before serving.   8 to 10 Servings

TIP • If your oven does not have a defrost feature, microwave 2 minutes, rest 5 minutes, microwave 2 minutes and rest 5 minutes. If necessary, microwave 1 to 2 more minutes.

DEFROSTING FROZEN CREAM PIE

1. Remove a 14-oz. frozen cream pie from package. Leave in foil pan.
2. MICROWAVE 1 minute. Rest 5 minutes.
3. MICROWAVE ½ minute. Rest 2 minutes. Cut and serve.   1 Pie

DEFROSTING FROZEN BAKED FRUIT PIE

1. Transfer a frozen baked fruit pie to a glass pie plate.
2. MICROWAVE 10 minutes. Rest 5 minutes.
3. MICROWAVE 5 to 6 minutes or until thawed and slightly warm.   1 Pie

DEFROSTING FROZEN BAKED COOKIES

1. Place about 1 dozen frozen cookies on glass plate.
2. MICROWAVE 2 to 3 minutes or until thawed and slightly warm.   About 12 Cookies

This defrosting method is gradual enough for frosted brownies, too.

DEFROSTING FROZEN BROWNIES

1. Place an 8-inch square of frozen brownies on glass plate.
2. MICROWAVE 1 minute. Rest 2 minutes.
3. MICROWAVE 1 minute. Rest 2 minutes.
4. MICROWAVE ½ to 1 minute or until thawed and slightly warm.   8-inch Square Brownies

DEFROSTING FROZEN CAKE

1. Place a 1-layer frozen cake (frosted or unfrosted) on glass plate.
2. MICROWAVE 1 minute. Rest 3 minutes.
3. MICROWAVE 1 minute. Rest 3 minutes.
4. MICROWAVE ½ to 1 minute or until thawed and slightly warm.   1-layer Cake

DEFROSTING FROZEN FRUIT

1. MICROWAVE a 10-oz. package frozen fruit 3 minutes.
2. Transfer to a glass serving dish; break frozen chunk into pieces.
3. MICROWAVE about 1 minute or until just thawed.   1½ Cups Fruit

DEFROSTING FROZEN PUDDING

1. MICROWAVE a 17½-oz. covered container frozen pudding 4 minutes. Break frozen chunk into large pieces.
2. MICROWAVE, covered, 2 minutes. Stir well.
3. MICROWAVE, covered, 2 minutes or until just about thawed. Stir before serving.
4 Servings

Index

WEIGHTS AND MEASURES

3 teaspoons	=	1 tablespoon
16 tablespoons	=	1 cup or 8 fluid ounces
5⅓ tablespoons	=	⅓ cup
4 tablespoons	=	¼ cup
2 cups	=	1 pint
2 pints	=	1 quart
4 quarts	=	1 gallon
16 ounces	=	1 pound

1 gram	=	0.035 ounces
1 kilogram	=	2.21 pounds
1 ounce	=	28.35 grams
1 pound	=	453.59 grams
1 cup	=	236.6 milliliters
1 liter	=	1.06 quarts or 1,000 milliliters

EQUIVALENT AMOUNTS

1 pound apples	=	3 medium or 3 cups sliced
1 pound butter	=	2 cups
1 cup broth	=	1 teaspoon or cube instant bouillon + 1 cup water
4 ounces cheese	=	1 cup shredded
8 ounces cottage cheese	=	1 cup
6 ounces chocolate pieces	=	1 cup
4 ounces shredded coconut	=	about 1⅓ cups
½ pint whipping cream	=	1 cup, or 2 cups whipped
8 ounces sour cream	=	1 cup
1 medium lemon	=	1 tablespoon grated peel and 3 tablespoons juice
1 pound shelled nuts	=	about 4 cups
1 medium onion	=	½ to ¾ cup chopped
1 medium orange	=	2 tablespoons grated peel and ⅓ to ½ cup juice

EMERGENCY SUBSTITUTIONS

1 cup buttermilk	=	1 tablespoon vinegar or lemon juice plus milk to make 1 cup
1 tablespoon chopped chives	=	1 teaspoon freeze-dried chives
1 tablespoon cornstarch	=	2 tablespoons flour
1 clove garlic	=	⅛ teaspoon instant minced garlic or garlic powder or ½ teaspoon garlic salt
2 tablespoons green pepper	=	1 tablespoon dried pepper flakes
1 teaspoon dried leaf herbs	=	¼ teaspoon powdered herbs
1 teaspoon grated lemon peel	=	½ teaspoon dried lemon peel
1 teaspoon grated orange peel	=	½ teaspoon dried orange peel
1 small (¼ cup) onion	=	1 tablespoon instant minced onion or onion flakes, ¼ cup frozen chopped onion or 1 teaspoon onion powder
1 tablespoon snipped parsley	=	1 teaspoon dried parsley flakes
1 package active dry yeast	=	1 scant tablespoon dry or 1 cake compressed yeast